UNLEARNING TO FLY

Navigating the Turbulence and Bliss of Growing Up in the Sky

RUSS ROBERTS

Holt & Grooms Co. Ltd.

Unlearning to Fly:
Navigating the Turbulence and Bliss of Growing Up in the Sky

Russ Roberts

Published by Holt & Grooms Co. Ltd.
Carson City, Nevada

Holt & Grooms Co. Ltd.
Dept. 74888
PO Box 34628
Seattle, Washington 98124
E-mail: unlearningtofly@holtgrooms.com

Photographs, except where otherwise credited, are from the Roberts family collection

Limit of Liability/Disclaimer of Warranty:

PO/TA
Project Manager and Editorial Director: Helen Chang
Publishing Manager: Laurie Aranda

Library of Congress Control Number: 2020916072

ISBN: 978-1-7356413-2-4 -- hardback
978-1-7356413-0-0 -- paperback
978-1-7356413-1-7 -- ebook

Quantity sales. Special discounts are available on quantity purchases by corporations, associations, and others. For details, contact the publisher at the address above.

Printed in the United States of America

For my children

ACKNOWLEDGMENTS

Deleen Wills got me started on this project. A shorter version of the ferry flight story is included in her anthology, *Behind Colorful Doors.** But my tale in her book ended before we reached the trip's final destination. The story left her hanging. "What happened next? Did you live?" she asked. That chapter is the seed from which this memoir grew. In *Unlearning to Fly,* I have included major parts of "The Blue Cardinal" with Ms. Wills' permission.

Writing a good book takes a team. My thanks to literary professionals Helen Chang, Jane Constantineau, Laurie Aranda, Iris Sasing, Toni Weeks, and Matthew Caselli. Many thanks to my sister, Debs, and my daughter, Piper, for pulling together ancient family photos, a project akin to an archaeological dig. Thanks to my sisters, Jenny and Polly Ann, for recalling family memories. I appreciate the help of P. Clifford Burnette, Jr., and Ted Alman from the Virginia Department of Aviation, along with Elliott Dunn, Chet Burgess, Joanne Rideout, Ross Hunter, Dick Summer, Harry Lehman Jr., and John Ince. I also acknowledge the pilots from the old days at the Orange County Airport. Though not mentioned in the story, I value their contributions in building my life's foundation.

---

*   Roberts, R. D. (2016). The Blue Cardinal. In D. Wills (Ed.), *Behind Colorful Doors* (pp. 67-91). DFWills Publishing.

I'm grateful to my father and mother for giving me the raw material from which to craft a life and this story. I don't say they did the best they could, but they made interesting choices from what was possible.

AUTHOR'S NOTE

I have barely touched on the lives of my siblings. It is up to them to tell of their experiences in the Roberts family. My parents are both dead. They have no chance for rebuttal or to insist upon revisions. I have not tried to analyze or make judgments on their parenting. This is reportage, and that is all: who, what, when, where, and how. I left out the last *w*. I agreed with Gordon Lightfoot when he sang about the impossibility of knowing the why of many things.

Jonah Lehrer writes, in *Proust Was a Neuroscientist*, that memories change each time we remember them. So I fear my favorite memories —the ones I recall often— are the most inaccurate. Aware of this fallibility, I redoubled efforts for reliability. Take comfort that this book is not the result of only unreliable neural firings. Even though I'm sure I mixed up the chronology a few times —my mind realigning the timeline to make the puzzle pieces fit— my memory was assisted by some good hard evidence. My mother's Alaska journal (which provides our story's best dialog), the audiotaped recollections of my father's Alaska flying days, family photos, my logbooks, and my elder sister's unfailing memory of our family (which I take as gospel) give me confidence in the tale's accuracy. A few names were changed on purpose.

The story is true, as a good homemade soup is true.

—Russ Roberts, Panama, 2020

PROLOGUE

We pass nine thousand feet and get a jolt of turbulence. *Bam!* It surprises me. We've enjoyed a smooth flight over the ocean until now. Another bump comes. *Blam!* And then more, even stronger, jolts. *Blam, slam, bam!* Before I even have time for a breath, I'm tossed and thrown in my seat by violent turbulence.

My legs slam up against the bottom of the instrument panel of the single-engine Cessna Cardinal. The seatbelt gouges my stomach as my head hits the ceiling. I'm thrown back and forth between the fuel tank and the cabin door. I reach, with a somewhat out-of-control hand, to disengage the wing leveler. I now hand-fly the airplane, continuing to descend, hoping to get out of the icing conditions that threaten the airplane —threaten us.

We —the airplane and I— groan under the stress. The metal cables holding the fuel tanks in place twang under pressure, sounding like discordant strings from a fiend's guitar. The fuel sloshes. Another crashing judder dislodges dirt and dust from the crevices of the cabin. I breathe it in and cough. One bump sends several nuts and washers flying to the cabin ceiling. Where did *they* come from?

Gripping the control yoke, I strain to read the blurry instrument panel, which shakes in the violence. The instrument needles waver, and my eyes can't make out the numbers on the altimeter or airspeed indicator. The numbers on the gauges are a blur. Is the panel shaking, or is it my eyes that shake? Hard to say. But with the jittering, I can't tell with precision how fast I'm descending or how high I am now. The airplane is in a terrier's mouth. Back and forth, up and down, *blam, bam, blam!* How can it not rip to pieces?

In my windshield-mounted compass, the card is bouncing in the liquid, making an accurate reading very difficult. But with the next crash of rough air, the card falls off its pin and wedges itself at a macabre angle inside the compass case. I can't believe what I'm seeing. Magnetic compasses do not fail.

The compass had been the only reliable direction indicator in the airplane today. I really wish my compass hadn't broken. Flying over the trackless ocean, it would have been a good thing to know what direction I'm heading.

Blam! The floor drops out from under me. My feet lurch up from the rudder pedals and then slam back down. *Thud!* Have my heels left dents in the aluminum? No longer robotic, no longer a part of the machine, my body now tenses; I swallow hard, my human frailty undeniable.

My dry, raw throat reminds me I've forgotten to drink since leaving the Canadian coastline hours earlier. But in this turbulence, there is no way to drink.

For a moment, I forget scanning the instruments and fixate on the dead compass and its distorted shape. It's like I've left the thrashing airplane and am standing in a museum looking at a Picasso.

No, it's not a Picasso. It's a Dalí. It's like those clocks that drip and flow in his famous painting. Detached, I study the surreal art in front of me. And then —*slam, bam, blam!*— an invisible fist punches me back into the cockpit, high over the arctic sea.

A wave of emotion surges past the dike in my middle to reach my neck. I swallow hard again, ignoring the rawness, fighting back the flood.

The wings, loaded with ice, claw to hang on to flight. The turbulence is nonstop and threatens the airframe. I've lost my compass, and my directional gyro is unreliable, so I don't know for sure what direction I'm heading.

It seems likely that destruction will come soon from a structural failure or loss of lift. The airplane and I may soon float dead in the cold ocean below. With a strange time dilation and the actual duration of the problem, I contemplate my situation. It's the first time in my twenty-five years I've had this long to stew in my mortality.

My father, from a thousand miles away, speaks. Close to my ear, he says, "Well now, this is pretty dangerous. What are you going to do? Can we work out a plan?" He's using his deep, smooth flight instructor voice. He wants to hear my plan before he offers his own. In his mind, as always, his plan is the only plan.

Well, guess what? I know we're in danger, and you, Dad, are not here. You can do nothing to change my course now. This is my fix, my life. It's up to me alone to make the choices for my salvation or destruction.

"But I am here," he says, now bellicose like he's been hitting the bottle. "You've gotten yourself in a fine fix by not listening to me. *Now you're headed for a fall.*"

For years, this man, my father, kept me safe, warm, and fed, even though the family-burning flames of alcohol often sacrificed security. No doubt he gave me a great store of knowledge. Appropriate knowledge that I can always pull up and use. There is no denying that.

But today, I must push away much of what he taught. Many of his words don't fit anymore. Many of his ideas are outrageous. Today, I must unlearn... to fly. Now is the time for my own critical thinking. Flying now —living now— I must unlearn many of the things he and others taught me by word and example. Things that for a long time I believed were true. Skills and ideas believed to keep me safe and alive.

PART ONE

CHAPTER ONE

Russ Roberts at Washington-National Airport (1958)
dreaming about his future.

I stretch over the front seat of the car, listening to Mama talk about her day. She always talks about her day, recounting all that happened, what people said, and who did what. But tonight she looks forward to the party, talks about who might be there and what may happen. The yellow and red of the Virginia autumn countryside speed by, and I await my turn to wedge in some words.

My big sister, Debs, sits in the back seat by the window, fixing her doll's clothes and hair. She's two years older than me, and sometimes she treats me like her doll. She needn't fix me up tonight, though. I'm already dolled up for the party, my shirt tucked into my corduroys and hair combed with water. The neat line of a part plows my wheat-colored mop like a row in the fallow fields out the window.

Mama stops talking for a second. I jump in, "When can we eat at the Dixie Pig?" My mouth waters as we drive past the best barbecue restaurant in the world.

"Soon," she says.

"Who will be at the party tonight?"

She names several people, both men and women.

"What airplanes do they fly?" By "they," I mean the pilots she named. Nobody else matters.

My parents don't ignore me, but they give quick answers to my questions. I can tell by their voices and fancy clothes they're in pleasant moods. They're ready to party and not interested in quenching my nonstop curiosity.

From other trips out to Bob's house in Pohick, I know the territory well. We pass Beacon Field, a little airport in Alexandria built on the site of the old Groveton air mail beacon. Daddy learned to fly there, and I took my first airplane ride from that airport. It's where my father met the group of pilots we'll be with at Bob's party tonight. Beacon Field is the center of my universe. Lucky is the person who, like me, recognizes the magic that radiates from Beacon Field.

Beacon Field, Alexandria, Virginia
(Photo credit: Friends of Beacon Field)

The sun is gone as we drive by the airport. I lean farther forward, my eyes searching for airplanes under the airport lights. Spotting a twin-engine machine is the most exciting, and tonight I find a Bamboo Bomber. That's the best. A fabric-covered veteran of World War II, the Bamboo Bomber makes my heart thump like crazy. It's the airplane type Sky King flies on our twelve-inch television screen.

"How fast does it go, Daddy? Where do you think it's headed? Where do the bombs come out?" I pull my almost-five-year-old self halfway over the seat to get a better look.

My chin touches his soft sports jacket, and I smell the soap from his shiny black hair. My father doesn't use shampoo. "Soap is soap," he often says before payday. "Shampoo is just expensive soap. A waste."

My father looks a lot like Clark Gable; a neat mustache, black hair combed straight back. Daddy stands six feet tall and might be described as wiry. Like Gable, my father's voice changes when he talks to women.

Tonight, Daddy sighs. He makes a guess about the airplane's speed and says he doesn't know where it's going. "It's a UC-78, not really a bomber, Son. They call it a Bamboo Bomber to be funny, because it's made out of wood and cloth. They used them for training during the war."

I already know it's a wooden airplane. I've heard that rot is a concern among the pilots who fly the fifteen-year-old twin-engine Cessnas. I don't care. I like the way it looks with its stubby nose and two low-slung radial engines.

Mama says, "Mary Lewis told me that Bill Sellers brought the Bamboo Bomber in. Did you know Bill got engaged last week?"

Mary Lewis Lehman is the airport operator's wife, and Sellers is a very tall airline pilot who keeps his private airplane at Beacon Field. My mother always knows a lot about people. I can't figure out why Mama likes people more than airplanes.

She's twenty-six, about five feet five inches, with light brown
hair and hazel eyes.

A few minutes later, minutes that seem like hours, we turn
into the long driveway of Bob's house. Tall oak trees stand on
both sides of us, and my stomach gets tight. We're here. I flop
down into the back seat, pressing my face against the window
to get a closer look at the cars in the driveway. I see several
okay-looking cars —and then Bob's pickup truck. Wow. Bob's
truck is the coolest, because it's Bob's truck. But our white
Studebaker Flight Hawk, my family's nicest thing, is the fanci-
est car here.

Debs and I push the front seats forward and jump out, our
leather shoes crunching on the leaves. Daddy walks around to the
trunk and takes out his brown rifle case, and we climb the worn
wooden stairs to Bob's porch.

The wooden house looks old. The white paint is dirty, and
crooked green shutters hang by the windows. Compared to our
own house, though, it's a mansion. We step around some tools
on the porch. "Come on in, everybody!" Bob calls through the
screen door. He's looking at my parents. I don't think he's seen
Debs or me. He's in a sports coat with a tie. He talks with a cigarette in his mouth. His hands are full, the door pushed open in
one and a cocktail glass in the other. Smoke hangs on the kitchen
ceiling like a low overcast.

After letting us in, Bob walks back to the kitchen. I like the
sound of Bob's voice. I like everything about Bob. He's an airline
pilot. Airline pilots have the best jobs in the world. He is more
than human as he walks behind the kitchen counter to pour

drinks. His wife, Pat, comes over. She is a stewardess. Everybody at the party comes from the airlines. That's why the get-together is so exciting. It's a gathering of royalty.

The long, narrow living room seems to go for miles, kind of like an indoor runway. They've pushed the furniture against the walls, and a couple of light-brown rugs cover the old wood floor. But, old or not, it's wood, not beat up linoleum like the floor at our house. Bob's floor looks rich.

I lean into the puffy skirt of Mama's red-and-white dress. We walk over to Bob and the others in the kitchen. The kitchen counter serves as a bar. It's full of bottles, beer with no labels and lots of whiskeys, many glasses, and an ice bucket. The grownups shake hands and say friendly things to each other. Pat comes over and gives Debs and me hugs. I squirm. Pat smells like a flower.

A few of the pilots see Pat bending over, and then —when they notice us— call out to Debs and me. "Oh, hi kids."

"Hey, kids! Hello!" says Bob. "Want a drink?" People laugh.

It's past my normal dinner time, and my excitement does not mask that I'm starving. Pat sets a phone book on a chair for me at the round table in the kitchen. She gives Debs and me some Ritz crackers with ham and cheese, and juice glasses filled with ginger ale. We grin at each other. Snacks and soda before dinner! I know the word is *hors d'oeuvres*. It's a fancy word, and tonight, with my water-combed hair and a glass of ginger ale, I feel fancy.

The men at the kitchen counter talk about airplanes. They are all airline pilots except for my father. Daddy knows how to fly small airplanes, and he has a pilot's license, but he works as a mechanic for Capital Airlines. Me? I'm already an airline pilot with a few details remaining. All I need is somebody to give me a job, an airliner, and a schedule. Except for that —and little things like growing up and learning to fly— I'm already there.

Sharing my dream, Daddy wants to be a commercial pilot one day too. Who wouldn't? After flying my toy airplanes around the world every day, I can assure him it's a great life.

I eavesdrop while I chew on the crackers.

The men talk.

"They've been doing repaving in Buffalo. They're using the short runway this month. That's five and two-three."

"Lunken is closed because of that flood on the Ohio. It's a good thing they have the new airport across the river in Kentucky, or Cincinnati's folks would have to take a train."

"We landed in South Bend the other day because of cruddy weather at Midway. It dropped to zero-zero in less than an hour, even though the forecast was for VFR. Good thing we had extra fuel."

I don't miss a word of it. I'm a pilot too. I already have my own uniform and flight bag at home, both in scale for a three-foot-tall captain.

Pat comes over with two bowls of chili from a big, beat-up metal pot on the stove. The grownups stand in groups, talking, eating a little, and drinking a lot. Debbie and I sit quietly and eat, me listening to the men and Debs to the women. I see Bob wipe some spilled whiskey from his lapel. Pat straightens his tie. "Volare" plays on the Hi-Fi in the background. *"Nel blu, dipinto di blu."*

When finished, we clear our dishes, and Mama says we have a little while to play. We're always the only kids at Pohick. The grownups treat us kindly but mostly ignore us. We're told to play nice and quiet, like we always do, and stay out of the way.

I go into the living room and dig in my pockets, my fingers sorting through marbles, rocks, and string. Oh. And a car. I feel the hard wheels of a Matchbox MG Midget. Using the rug pattern as roads, I drive my sports car from my house to the airport. My ears keep listening. I like the talk and the sounds of frogs and birds from "Quiet Village" now playing on the record player. The men talk about guns.

"Feel this action. Nice and smooth, isn't it?" Captain Al says to Daddy. He shows him the design on his rifle stock. Checkering, Captain Al calls it. They talk about how some guns have tight patterns, but some scatter out. A tight group is a good thing. All the men brought at least one rifle and their own ammunition to the party tonight. That's how it goes at Pohick.

A montage of Pohick Party pictures of Bob and Pat.

Too soon, Mama says it's time for bed. She leads us to the guest room, at the opposite end of the living room from the kitchen. The grownups call out, "Goodnight!" They sound louder and happier than before. They're laughing and sometimes shouting over each other.

The beds look huge and tall. My sister and I change into our pajamas, climb up onto the beds, and crawl under the quilts. No story tonight. Mama wants to get back to the party. A kiss, and out she goes.

The lights from the living room shine through the tiny gaps around the door. I hear laughing, loud talking, clinking glasses. The party is really going now.

I fall asleep. But loud noises in rapid succession wake me up. *Ker-bam! Crack! Ping!* It's the sound of a rifle shooting, and the bullet hitting the target. I hear the men's laughter, deep voices, the tinkling of ice. A quiet pause. Then *bang!* Another shot. The sound is so loud, the shooting so exciting. I need to see for myself.

Debs looks like she's sleeping. How can she be sleeping with this much excitement, this much good action going on? I roll onto my belly and slide off the side of my bed. I reach up for the loose brown door-knob and turn it with care. I don't want to alert the adults. I pull the door open toward me. I squint my eyes in the bright lights. I see the women standing beside the far kitchen wall, glasses in their hands. Cigarettes in some, smoke rising in romantic curls.

I smell burned gunpowder, and now I see the men by the kitchen counter. Some of them hold rifles. More guns lie on the counter. Bob is taking a bead on the fireplace. Despite my wish to remain invisible, they see me, and Bob points his rifle down. Everyone talks in low voices so I can't hear.

"I need a glass of water," I say when Mama looks over.

"Okay, come on," Mama says, shaking her head and smiling at the other people.

I walk in my bare feet down the long firing range into the kitchen. The grownups start talking again. I hear the men say "cartridges" and "rounds" and they talk about types of gunpowder grains. Daddy taught me a lot about guns and I'd be talking too, if I was taller. But little children, especially ones out of bed without leave, should be seen and not heard.

Holding a bullet, Captain Al asks, "Is this from the box of light ammunition?"

"We've got to the use the right rounds," Daddy laughs. "We don't want to blow out the back of your fireplace, Bob." Daddy tips back a bottle of home-brewed beer.

Be careful, Daddy, I think. *That home-brew might be more dangerous than the bullets.*

The ammo they make never explodes, but the beer bottles do. "Buying brewers' yeast has been illegal since Prohibition," Daddy told me once while we capped bottles at home. "You can buy good gunpowder, but not safe yeast."

Daddy claims baking yeast is volatile, like old nitro. I know our home brew is dangerous, whether it's from bad yeast, microbes, or too much sugar. Every week or two, I hear a bottle explode in the basement. Daddy says that holding a capped and loaded home-brew bottle is like handling a glass hand grenade.

Since the beer Daddy is drinking is uncapped, I guess it's safe. But I look at all the uncapped bottles left on the countertop.

Tonight, nothing blows up, and no one shoots while I stand in the kitchen drinking my water, but I hope if I drink slowly enough, they might.

No luck. I finish the water, and Mama and Pat lead me back to my room. I notice paper targets, full of holes, hung by clothespins in the fireplace. With a quick pat on my bottom, Mama says, "Climb back into bed." I see Pat, smiling and weaving a little at the bedroom door. Mama closes the door with a firm click.

Pat had been the first naked woman I'd ever seen. Recently, Pat and Bob had spent the night at our place after a boozy house party. My father has always told us that, even when he's loaded, he's a safer driver than most people are sober. That's because of his superior reflexes, eyesight, and all. I guess Bob doesn't share my father's safe-drunk-driving gift. That's why he couldn't drive home that night.

The night they'd stayed over, I awoke to yelling. Bob and Pat were having a tremendous, loud, drunk argument. Concerned, my parents went to Bob and Pat's bedroom to check on them. I did too. The door was open. Bob was yelling and waving his hands around, making great smoke signals with his cigarette. Pat, without a stitch on, kneeled on the bed, crying and yelling back at Bob. To my eyes, Pat was a good-looking stewardess, even though she was as old as Mama. I noticed her nice parts. But at four years old, I found Bob's smoke rings more compelling.

With me back in bed and out of the way tonight at Pohick, gunshots start again. I'm happy now that I can picture the scene. It's my own version of *Gunsmoke* happening right outside the bedroom door. In my imagination, with Pat playing the role, Miss Kitty stands by swinging bar doors, with gunfire, carnage, and mayhem in the street. I smile. I am Matt Dillon in bed at the Long Branch. I'm so tired, and it's a good dream to ride to sleep.

It's still dark when my parents come in and scoop us out of bed. Daddy wraps me in a coat and carries me like a sack of dog food through the living room, which is quiet now.

Through half-open eyes, I see empty bottles and glasses all over the room. I recognize the gunpowder smell and other sweeter, acrid smells. Did a home-brew bottle blow up? I hear Bob and Pat call good night, and the cold air hits my face as Daddy carries me down the porch steps.

In the Studebaker, Daddy plops me behind his seat, leaning me up against the window. Mama puts Debs on the other side. They flip their seats back up and climb in, and our tires crunch down the gravel driveway.

"What time is it?" I mumble.

"It's midnight," Mama says. "You can go back to sleep in the car."

Midnight. I can't believe I'm awake at midnight! That's neat. I'll bet I'm the only boy in the world awake at midnight.

CHAPTER TWO

Back at our small, rented house the next evening in Alexandria, I play with model airliners on the kitchen floor. My folks rehash last night's party. I half-listen, but hear nothing new. Outside, birds chatter on a wire.

I fly my models not as toys, but as if they are real airliners. It feels like my job rather than play. My airplanes and I fly all over the world —engines aflame, thunder booming, and passengers in all states of health, good and ill. It's great fun. I never fly freighters. Flying boxes is not for me. I have passengers back there in my one-foot-long plastic fuselages. But my passengers show no concern. I'm a great pilot, and my well-dressed and well-hatted stewardess takes good care of them.

My stewardess looks like a uniformed Pat combined with the shape of my sister's new Barbie doll. Very attractive. I'm happy with my image too. A handsome four-year-old captain with "straight teeth and a crooked smile," I keep everyone safe in the dangerous world of 1950s make-believe aviation.

We are awash in airplanes in our family, as my father flies —with hope and GI Bill financing— toward an airline career. But we are also a gun family. Both airplanes and firearms are passions tied to money. Airlines will one day put money in the bank. Guns will save money by keeping the freezer full. Discussions at our house are always about money. There's no talk of passion or excitement. In their conversation, my parents rationalize, temper, and disguise everything in a suit of money.

But even though he doesn't talk about passion or excitement, I know my father loves flying as much as I do. I can tell he loves guns too.

Daddy keeps a rifle rack in the bedroom. At night, while Mama reads her hospital novels beside him, he often reaches overhead for a rifle to give it a good cleaning. He doesn't waste time in bed reading novels. I've never seen him read anything other than technical manuals. He's a practical man. In bed, after cleaning a rifle, he often "sights them in" and pretends to fire.

Tonight he chooses a .22 caliber scattershot gun, cleans it, wipes off the oil, and points it over the bedroom door. My mother doesn't care. Business as usual. And tonight, on paper, Max Brand's Dr. Kildare is riveting.

Daddy chambers a cartridge, puts his eye to the iron sight, and pulls the trigger. *Pow!*

That gets her attention. "Wow! What d'you do that for?" she asks, putting down her book.

"There was a spider over the door. Gone now."

She gets up to check on us. When she turns on the light, she finds me sitting up with my eyebrows arched. I expect news of a dead burglar or a commie invasion.

"There was a spider over the door," she says. "Daddy shot it."

Makes sense, I think, and go back to sleep.

*   *   *

For two years, my father's been sending applications to the airlines. He has the required pilot licenses, commercial and instrument. But so far, he hasn't gotten a single interview. Daddy thinks he needs more flight hours to flesh out his resume.

"Alaska's the place to be," says Daddy.

Mama nods. "Mm," she says.

There's been so much talk from my parents lately about Alaska, that tonight she understands the voluminous context of the topic with only Daddy's simple statement, "Alaska's the place to be." Alaska sounds far away and exotic. Many of my parents' discussions about Alaska include talk of guns and the allure of big-game hunting. Alaska, according to my father who offers no evidence, also promises good flying opportunities with good pay.

"Be good to shake this up a little bit," he says. "See new things."

But I suspect more than adventure at play. I've overheard uncomfortable one-sided conversations on the telephone. My mother yelling at her mother. And polite but nervous talk with strangers. "Yes, we'll be able to put a check in the mail next week."

Alaska is at the very end of North America's highway system. The brand-new state is as far you can go in the US from the East Coast without crossing water. In 1959, it's possible to run away without leaving the country.

My parents have no money. I know that from all the talk. Even though I have no money and no need for any, I know that having money is important to grownups. And more is better.

Flying, big game . . . and more money. From all my parents' talk, Alaska promises all three.

In Virginia, we have no cash. But thanks to Daddy's job at Capital Airlines, we have airline passes. One morning in the fall, Debs and I are awakened early.

"Wake up, kids! We're going to Alaska today!" Mama says.

"Today?"

"Yep. Get up and put these clothes on," she says and points to a set of nice clothes laid out on the foot of my bed. "We're flying for free to Alaska to check it out. Right now. Let's get going."

Later that whirlwind morning, we're off to Seattle aboard a Northwest Orient Airlines Boeing Stratocruiser. What an airplane. Based on the B-29 bomber, the Stratocruiser is big, loud, and luxurious. The airplane's interior carries the sophisticated and well-traveled aroma of stale nicotine, well-cured into the upholstery and headliner.

Knowing we're airline people, the crew invites the four of us down a spiral staircase behind the wing to the Fujiyama Lounge. We sit at a table bolted to the floor. They serve drinks and snacks. My sister and I drink Shirley Temples as the big radial engines thrum outside the three lower deck windows. The drinks come with two cherries speared on a tiny umbrella. My sister and I grin at each other. It's fun to work the umbrella up and down.

Back on the main deck, before we land, the stewardesses put a hat on Debbie and send her down the aisle to hand out Chiclets from a basket. "The chewing gum helps people's ears pop," says a hostess.

I visit the cockpit and get a certificate signed by the captain. Maybe I could put this flight time in my pilot logbook. After all, I don't get to fly a big four-engine Stratocruiser every day. Nobody has to know I never touched the controls or my legs were too short to reach the rudder pedals.

In Seattle, we get bumped from two flights that go out full with paying passengers. We are very tired after more than a full day of travel, but it's nighttime again before we continue on to Anchorage on an Alaska Airlines DC-6. Onboard, we find another saloon, movies, and a piano. I can't imagine life ever getting better. Even with the fanciness, I fall asleep right away to the throbbing drone of the Pratt & Whitney engines out on the wings.

Daddy wakes me up in the middle of the night.

"Look, Son. See the propeller?" He points through the cabin window. "They feathered it. That means they turned off the engine and stopped the prop."

"That's neat," I say. It's cool to see stuff like that. I don't worry about an engine failure. Why worry? The airplane has four engines. I smile at seeing all three blades on the feathered propeller stopped in midair and go back to sleep.

Arriving in Anchorage, we make a deal with Avis to ferry a rental car to Fairbanks. We only have to pay for gas. That's it. It's a good deal, and by driving we see a lot of the state.

Right off the bat, my parents like what they find in Alaska. The snow-clad Chugach Mountains punch tall into the clouds, and tendrils of fog spin into the valleys. Beautiful scenery, along with the promise of good flying, wild game, wide-open spaces, big paychecks, and no relatives, builds Alaska's appeal.

"I can probably shoot a moose every year," says Daddy. "Just one would really fill a freezer. Think about it." He's never eaten one but says, "Moose is good eating."

We drive up the Glenn Highway to Meekin's Lodge, a log building ripped from the pages of a Jack London version of *House Beautiful* magazine.

"Look at that!" says Debs. "They've got more cabins out back. And a restaurant with picture windows!"

Our car crunches into Meekin's gravel lot, and we get out. The Matanuska Glacier snakes down the valley below. I breathe in the crisp glacial air. Stupendous. Magic, even. Then I remember that if I exhale, I can take in yet another breath of this delicious air. So I breathe in, breathe out, over and over again. Breath after breath. I twirl around to see it all. Right behind the lodge, Sheep Mountain —gray, rocky, with many patches of snow, and the cotton dots of faraway wild Dall sheep— rises straight up and tilts my universe.

"Are we staying here?" I ask, hoping.

"No, no," says Mama, looking at Daddy. "Way too expensive. We'll just have lunch here." She digs into a cheap cooler we bought in Anchorage. "Here, unwrap this baloney sandwich and eat."

After eating, we spend the rest of the afternoon driving. Rarely seeing a building of any kind, never seeing a power or telephone line, we all take in the changing scenery. Late in the afternoon, after it seems we'll be on the Richardson Highway forever, we stop at Paxson Lodge to fill the car's gas tank.

"Coffee?" asks Mama while my father cleans the windshield.

"No, thanks," says Daddy. "I'll bet they charge an arm and a leg."

Paxson is not as pretty as Meekin's, not by a long shot. But there's something about the way it sits in an endless bog amid the boreal landscape with tall mountains way off to the north and south, the way the lodge's generator hums to make the only available electricity, and the way the building stands at the intersection of the paved Richardson and gravel Denali highways, like a castle or frontier fort. There's something about it that offers an invitation to adventure. *Shall we go down this road or this one? Shall we leave this primitive way station, this outlier of human comfort, behind and strike out on our own?*

We chose to drive on to Big Delta and North Pole, as we head toward Fairbanks.

After a few days driving the highways, staying in flophouses, seeing some moose, caribou, a couple of bears, and eating a lot of sandwiches from the ice chest, we drop off the car in Fairbanks and jump on another Alaska Airlines flight to head home.

＊   ＊   ＊

Several months later, back in Virginia, Daddy is sitting in his worn-out living room easy chair oiling up a loaded rifle when he sees a mouse making its way over the kitchen bar. He kills it with one shot. By now, I'm used to shooting in the house.

"In Alaska, that would have been a moose," Daddy says.

"In the house?" I ask. My father doesn't answer my foolishness.

The next weekend, we make breakfast. "What's that smell?" asks Debbie with a wrinkled nose.

My father digs into the toaster and removes chunks of toasted mouse.

"Didn't think I'd blown it to pieces," he says.

"You and your guns," says Mama. "Let's see . . . a mouse or a moose? I'm not eating mice. Let's move to Alaska."

"Well . . . yeah, the mouse . . ." Daddy's voice fades off. Then, after one or two beats, he says, "Where there's one mouse, there's more. Better set some traps. Wouldn't want live ones getting in the moving boxes."

Soon after, we're committed to Alaska. No airplanes are in the works this time. This time, we will go by car.

Our car is not the perfect vehicle for the Alaska Highway, a road built during World War II to connect the Lower 48 states to America's northern territory. The ALCAN's mostly gravel surface is little changed from when it opened to the public twelve years ago, in 1948. The Studebaker is gone. Now we have a gray Volkswagen sedan. So it's the car we'll use on the forty-five-hundred road miles from Virginia to Alaska. From home to the unknown in a Bug.

I'm excited. Just the mention of travel gets me going. Going far distances by airplane is best. But any traveling beats staying put.

Our trip is on the cheap. As usual. "We won't be staying in motels," says Daddy. "We're camping. And we're going to need supplies . . ."

So in May 1960, we make a quick trip on airline passes

to visit Herter's in Waseca, Wisconsin, to buy those supplies. We've had the Herter's hunting, fishing, and camping catalog in our house for years. To my father, Herter's catalog is a bible of promise, adventure, and possibility. The Herter's store? For Daddy, it's like going to heaven. He goes down the aisles, looking, touching, and even smelling a lot of the stuff. I think it's good to see and smell all the camping and hunting equipment in person too. All the neat stuff is stacked in rows all the way to the ceiling.

For me, though, the best part of the trip has been traveling to Wisconsin by Vickers Viscount, the first turboprop airliner.

Once back from Wisconsin, Daddy packs. My father has everything all thought out. Everything needed for the two-week drive —and for months afterward— we're taking with us on the VW. It reminds me of those Jungle Jim movies about Africa. An expedition is what this is —not a trip. We need a Land Rover. But we have a Bug.

With space at a premium, my father wants everything organized. Everything must be on the car, not in it. "The inside of the car is for people, not stuff," he says.

"You should have been an engineer," says Mama.

My father designs the packing so that things needed on the drive would be most accessible. He packs everything in layers, like one of those fancy layered *pousse-café* drinks Pat used to make at Pohick. When loaded, the roof rack holds, from the bottom up, a tarp, winter clothes, kitchen equipment, tools, and a few toys.

On the very top layer are sleeping bags, air mattresses, and a tent. The four corners of the tarp then fold over each other like a puff pastry and are tied with a bow made from hairy rope.

"See? Look here," says Daddy. "Once in a campground, you peel back the tarp and, from the very top layer, get to supplies we need on the trip. All the stuff on the bottom layers remains stowed for when we get to Alaska."

It's all pretty handy, that's for sure. But with our over packed Volkswagen, we look like a Teutonic version of the Joads.

"You've got to be pretty tall to reach the bow at the top," says Mama.

"Oh, I can reach it by standing on the running board. No problem. And look here," he says, going around to the back of the car. "We can't eat out all the way to Alaska. Too expensive. So, look at this." Daddy points to boxes set over the rear-engine hood.

"I built an outdoor kitchen for the car. That's what I've been working on this week," he says. "See? It's just made of big cardboard boxes and an ice chest. And look. A little cabinet for tins of white gas, drawers for utensils, cutlery, spices, paper towels, pots and pans, and dishes."

He'd built the kitchen's interior shelving out of more cardboard, held it all together with Elmer's glue, and painted the entire thing brown.

He reaches between the boxes and pulls out a sliding counter. "And here you have —a Coleman stove!" Daddy doesn't smile very much, but he's smiling now.

He looks at my Mama and then at us. "Your mother has everything she needs right here for cooking on the road."

We know Mama will have lots of help. How could my father, a pretty good cook, pass up cooking in the wilderness? A chance to be Fess Parker? I suspect Daddy will do most of the cooking.

We've given up our rented house and have been staying with Nana while we get ready to head up the ALCAN. Daddy built his culinary masterpiece in her driveway. Heartbroken, Nana stood by, watching her universe evaporate.

I didn't like seeing Nana's tears. My father must have been too busy getting ready and building gear to notice.

I wasn't that busy. I noticed.

"Nana's crying," I told him.

"Women cry," said Daddy. "They get sad about things. Look at all this new stuff."

Despite Nana's tears, I'm mighty proud of that kitchen, and I can tell Daddy is too. "That'll go for five thousand miles of rough travel. No problem," Daddy says.

Daddy can do anything.

The kitchen is neat. It's an engineering achievement. But to me, the coolest modification Daddy makes to the car is the auto-throttle. He builds it out of a metal shaft, a couple of U-bolts, and an extra VW gear shift knob. It looks like something right out of a Cessna. The shaft reaches down to the car's floor-mounted accelerator.

"The worst part of driving a long distance is keeping your leg in one spot all day," Daddy tells us. "This'll fix that problem. Going down the road, I can set the throttle and take my foot off the gas pedal. Twelve-hour drives will be easy."

I am proud of that throttle. Our VW is just like an airplane. When it's finished, I sit in the driver's seat, engine off, and fly my way to Alaska while never leaving Nana's Maryland driveway.

* * *

Whenever we travel, it seems I'm always awakened way before sunrise. That's the way it is, getting up to go somewhere in the middle of the night. It reminds me of that Errol Flynn movie, *The Dawn Patrol*, where the pilots have breakfast way before sunup. But that's not how it is this time.

I've played all day at Nana and Nornie's big, beautiful house. They must be spectacularly rich to have a house this nice. It's new, clean, and split level. We've eaten dinner, and I'm worrying about my folks calling bedtime, when Mama says, "It's time! Let's go! Let's go to Alaska!"

What? Now? At bedtime?

Okay. Whatever. I'm excited thinking about the long road ahead as my mother, father, sister, and I start to pile into the Volkswagen. Nana reaches for me and smashes her face up against mine as she hugs me goodbye.

I don't like to see her crying in the driveway in the late-setting July sun. Her husband, Nornie, stands with his arm around her shoulder. He looks sad too. As we head out, my face is still wet from Nana's tears.

CHAPTER THREE

My father plans to drive for ten or eleven days, stopping each night to camp. Up through Ohio, Indiana, Illinois, Wisconsin, Minnesota, and North Dakota, the VW —my parents call it "the Snog"— pushes on. Against a nonstop headwind, the engine wide open, we make only forty-five miles per hour.

Camping on the way to Alaska

After camping in Flaxton, North Dakota, on the fifth day out, we try to cross into Canada at North Portal, Saskatchewan. A customs officer tells my father he has to do something with his pistols. "You can't bring them into the country, sir. Sorry. Your rifles and shotguns are okay, though. But, no sir, we can't let you bring the pistols through."

With Daddy grumbling for the next hour, we turn back into North Dakota. We find a Railway Express Agency office, and he wraps his pistols in tape and brown paper. REA mails his guns ahead to their Anchorage outlet. "Damned gimmick," says Daddy. "Rifles okay, but not pistols? Crap. Just a way for somebody to make money."

Daddy is still carping about the delay after we've crossed the border. Our first day in Canada wears on in an atmosphere of complaint. Time stretches ahead like the view to the vanishing point out the front window.

"This is a whole lot of flat and nothing," says Mama, summing up the entire country. "Not much to Canada."

My sister and I squirm. It's been a long ride. We're tired and restless. My father's mood has colored our own. My parents have asked me several times to keep quiet.

"I'm cold," I say.

"Stop complaining," says my father.

"I want a hamburger too!"

Mama promises us a treat for later in the afternoon.

"What is it? A toy?"

"No, it's not a toy," says Mama.

"What is it then?" I say. "Tape to keep our mouths shut?"

Another couple of days go by with much the same; wind and
wheat fields. For a while, my folks amuse all of us by dropping lit
Lady Finger firecrackers onto the endless straight highway as we
speed along. While drinking beer, my folks think this is mighty
funny.

I know what we're doing is illegal, but I have mixed feelings
about us being caught. I don't want my parents in jail, but I sure
would like to see a mountie. If he comes, I hope he's riding a
horse like Dick Powell's RCMP character rode in the movie *Mrs.
Mike.*

Sadly, the only member of the Royal Canadian Mounted
Police I see is on a post card in a gas station.

The road turns to dirt outside Whitecourt, Alberta. It's not
long before the clack and pebble of the tiny stones under the tires
and hitting the inside of our fenders becomes yet more white
noise. Mama asks us kids if we want to go back home

"No," we both reply.

"I'm never going back," I say. "I'm going to born my children
in Alaska, and they're going to be Eskimos."

In British Columbia —my mother says we're in "Peace Mountain"— I'm sick, and we're all tired. But we're seeing snow-capped
mountains and signs —tracks and manure— of big wildlife, so
our excitement grows.

"Somebody at the camp store said they saw a bear yesterday,"
says Mama, putting a bag of ice in our cooler.

"Yeah, and they have a bear fuzzy hanging up there!" I say.

"He means a bearskin," Mama says under her breath to my
puzzled father.

The place enchants Debs. "The outhouses say 'Buoys' and 'Gulls,'" she says.

"Very nice! Clean too, aren't they?" says Mama.

"Yeah! I think they scrub them out with pneumonia!" says Debs.

Mama worries about keeping everything clean. She cleans and cleans our stuff and complains about chapped hands from cold dishwater. Still, hygiene suffers in our camp. I've spent much time since the border with lips pinkish white from drinking Kaopectate.

The view sure has improved, though. We camp on Kluane Lake among the snowcapped and craggy St. Elias Mountains, the highest in Canada. All four of us marvel at the beauty. My parents ohh and ahh. My sister talks about the mountains and the cold blue water.

I am moved, but can offer only the briefest of poems. "Pretty," I say.

After ten days of hard travel, with never a motel or restaurant visited, we finally arrive, almost broke, in Anchorage, Alaska.

We look for houses to rent, but, according to my mother, they are "too high or dumps." But then my folks remember a place called the Alaska House. We stayed there on our vacation scouting trip nine months earlier.

"They had a cabin for rent out back, remember?" Mama says to Daddy.

Sure enough, the cabin they remembered from last October is still available. No lights or water. The bathroom is down a path. But the price is right. Twenty-five dollars a month.

*   *   *

I sit on the floor flying my airplanes at our new rented shack in Anchorage. We don't need the lantern since it's a clear July night and still light out. The midnight sun gives the place a science fiction feeling. All that's needed is creepy music and a tin robot to complete the scene. It's like we're marooned without resources on a planet with two suns.

My folks discuss finances and employment opportunities. We've been in Alaska for about a week, and a flying job hasn't materialized. But it will, "any day now," according to Daddy.

"As a matter of fact, I'm going to see a 'Bud Root' tomorrow," he tells Mama.

But it's three days more before Root comes in from Fairbanks, and the mood is getting a little tense around the shack. However, Root offers my father a job, on evaluation, as a copilot on a little four-engine, fourteen-passenger de Havilland Heron.

Since we have only one car, all four of us take my father to his first de Havilland trip, dropping him off outside the hangar. Daddy doesn't receive any training. His job is to "yank gear," to sit next to the captain and do what he says; raise the landing gear, make a radio call, get coffee. Regulation required two pilots. Root hired my father to be the warm body.

Mama, Debs, and I putter around all day, going to Safeway and running some errands. We have dinner back at the rented house. Then we drive back to the airport to pick Daddy up about the time he's due back from his first day on the job. But he doesn't come back on time, and we have to wait. We wait a long time.

Even in the land of the midnight sun, it can get dark on wet summer nights like this. The airline manager looks nervous, and keeps looking out the window into the rainy, foggy, inky night. I can tell Mama is nervous too. She's pacing. Those two are making me nervous. And since I can't see any airplanes outside and have no toys to play with, I'm also bored.

My sister is reading a *Woman's Day*. Looking at a magazine seems like a good idea. In the big stack of dog-eared periodicals, I find an old *Flying* magazine. I like the pictures in it. There's a Cessna 180 on skis, a Twin Beech, and a girl pilot with a spark plug.

Finally, three hours behind schedule, the Heron arrives. As the four propellers come to a stop, I see the airplane dripping and brooding out on the ramp.

The drive home is quiet.

Back at our shack, my father drinks a cold one. Then two. He sits there staring out the dark window. "Get me another cold one, hon," he says.

They are never "beers." They are "cold ones." He opens his third Hamms with what he calls "a church key" and finally starts telling my mother about the flight. Sitting on the floor with my airplanes, I refly his trip by Coleman lantern on this dark, wet night as uncomfortable details unfold.

Daddy didn't like the way the captain, Charlie Shockles, weaved and dodged through the mountains from Anchorage to Sparrevohn. "He didn't seem to know where he was," says Daddy.

"'Do you know anything about these?' Shockles asked me," says Daddy. "Then he pointed to the VOR. That's a navigation needle on the Heron's instrument panel. 'We don't use 'em much up here,' that captain told me.

"I didn't like that question: 'do-you-know-anything-about-these,'" says Daddy. "Christ! Now I know VORs are rare here in Alaska —there are only two stations, one in Anchorage and one in Fairbanks— but even so, I think that captain's question shows how much of a moron he is. I don't understand it. He had the VOR in the airplane. He should have known how to use it."

Daddy also didn't like it when, after they'd had dinner in Sparrevohn, they loaded up a construction crew and all its gear.

"That captain worried more about lack of cabin volume than too much weight. There wasn't a penciled weight and balance form anywhere in sight," says Daddy. "Twelve big men and all their gear. That airplane was way too heavy. But never mind that. Off we went, the four little Gipsy Queen engines doing all they could as we staggered off the runway. Then we weaved and dodged climbing through the hills —it was like trying to claw out of a teacup."

Later, when they were flying through icy clouds between mountains, "the first thing that happened was we lost our airspeed indicator. Iced up," says Daddy. "Then Shockles popped the boots way too early. That captain should have waited for the ice to thicken up and get hard."

From my make-believe airport on the floor, I notice that Daddy is calling Shockles "that captain" rather than "the captain."

"He should have waited," says Daddy, pausing. "Waited for the ice to get thicker. That would allow the expanding rubber to shatter the ice to break it free from the wing. Popping the boots early when that captain did just pushed icy slush further back on the airfoil. In some areas of the wing, that created a void. The boots just sat there, pumping in and out, inside an ice cavity, doing no good at all." My father takes another long pull on his cold one. "I thought that captain was going to kill us."

"When was the last time you were in ice that bad?" Mama asks.

"Never. The Heron is the first airplane I ever flew in ice." He goes to the ice chest and gets another can. "I don't like that operation. That Root outfit flies on the ragged edge. They're going to kill somebody."

"The ragged edge" is one of my father's favorite expressions. Most of the time, he enjoys telling stories about flying on "the ragged edge." But tonight, I can tell he's not happy with the day's flying. Has his Alaska flying dream dimmed? My father sits sullen, drinking beer, until he falls asleep in his chair.

Over the next days, another trip is slow to develop.

"When I went to the airport today, Root told me the job is part time! It wasn't part time last week. I'm giving up on Root. I don't want to fly again with Shockles anyway. So I quit," he says, "Let's move to Fairbanks."

Mama doesn't look surprised.

"Let's see what cooks there. It's gotta be better than Anchorage. Drier, not as much rain. Opportunities are richer in Fairbanks too," Daddy says with certainty. He offers no basis for this faith.

So, with its cardboard kitchen still attached, the Snog motors twelve hours up the Richardson Highway toward another new home.

Once in Fairbanks, we find another shack to rent right away. This one has water and lights but comes at twice the price. The landlord requires only a signature and no deposit for a month-to-month rental agreement. Now, in another primitive cabin, with only the food my parents brought from Anchorage, Debs and I play on yet another worn-out rug. My parents argue about whose fault it is that we've gotten down to having only fifty cents.

"That's all that's left! Look! Two quarters!" says Mama, holding open her change purse.

"You've been spending too much." says Daddy.

"Well, you're not making any money!"

Each parent denies hurled accusations. It seems the argument goes on forever and soon becomes the only conversation as the days tick. Each time, the voices are louder. Noise, clenched fists, *stomp*. I play with my airplanes and stuff the family anger into a bag somewhere in me. But I'm scared. Are we going to starve in Alaska?

Somehow though, until now we've eaten. And we're never cold.

But still . . .

One afternoon, my sister and I are playing by the fence in the yard. Debbie is talking to a neighbor girl. Holding a two-by-four, I say to Debs, "You'd better stop talking to that girl, or I'm going to hit you with this board."

She keeps talking, so I hit her in the head with the wood. A nail that I hadn't seen in one end of the board punches a neat little hole in her temple.

Things don't go too well for me after that. I'm glad all Debs gets is a Band-Aid on her head. But I dread my father getting home. I know what's coming.

That night, I get a whipping from my father and his leather belt. It stings like fire. No, worse. It burns like hell. The torture begins before each strike and, upon contact, lights up every pain receptor in my body.

"This is hurting me more than it's hurting you," says Daddy. No, it's not.

"You must pay the price for doing wrong," he says. "My father never 'spared the rod.' I can't either. You hit your sister with a piece of wood! The lesson here for you is that violence is not the answer."

I think he's putting all his strength into the blows. But the welts he makes rise little and don't last. Still, it hurts terribly. It's humiliating too. Mixed in with all that is remorse. I could have badly hurt Debs and can't think of any reason I'd taken that swing.

Our first summer in Alaska is getting kind of weird.

*   *   *

My parents are always talking now about "keeping the wolf from the door." Even though my father gets a flying job with a man named Pete, payday is still at least two weeks away. Somehow they keep going to the store, and I'm glad the wolf never arrives.

How has the stream of money not completely dried up? Maybe the check they expected from the Heron operator arrived in the mail. I don't know.

"Do you think we could pawn the Winchester" asks Mama.

"Not the Winchester," says Daddy. "I'm not pawning the Winchester."

I wonder what pawning is. Is it some kind of shooting? Is it shooting for money?

Daddy got home late tonight, and I'm starving. I'm looking forward to the corned beef hash, even though it comes from an Armour can and looks a lot like cat food. Mama smashes the meat into an iron frying pan. Then she breaks eggs, drops them into divots she makes in the hash, and bakes the whole thing in the oven. With the eggs on top, it looks good, smells good, and tastes good.

At dinner, we don't talk about money. Instead, my father talks about his first trip with Pete's outfit. The story adds to the flavor.

In mid-flight, the oil plug had fallen out of Daddy's engine. He made an emergency landing in his Cessna at the DEW Line ballistic missile radar station at Clear, Alaska.

"No problem," he says. "I was right over the runway. All I did was pull the power off, push the nose over, and land. Pete flew down with a new plug and more oil. I don't think the engine was hurt."

Mama chews her food with no reply.

That night, Daddy pulls my first loose tooth. I try to stay awake to see which wall the Tooth Fairy will come through. No luck. But the next morning I find fifty cents under my pillow. Fifty cents! That's a lot of money —all the money my mother had in her change purse. Thanks to the Tooth Fairy, I figure we have twice as much money now.

"We won't need your tooth money for groceries," says Mama. "Payday is right around the corner."

Payday finally arrives, and my parents start their day in pleasant moods. But the day brings a second engine failure. This one is on takeoff. My father lands deadstick, pushes the airplane back to the hangar, and looks for his check. It's not there, and neither is Pete.

That night my mother says, "What's next?"

CHAPTER FOUR

We spend the rest of August 1960, picking blueberries and rose hips for jelly. We make an occasional trip to Fox, outside Fairbanks, to fill up five-gallon jugs from a cold and delicious artesian water well. Roger Conn, the Avis rental car agent we met on our vacation last year, and his wife, Sue, have become friends with us. Roger fishes a lot and gives us pike and salmon. He also gives Mama some part-time work.

My father's flying job brings home no money, but it does provide a flow of stories about student pilot no-shows, lousy maintenance, and poor weather. I'm thrilled by all of it, except the part about no money. Debs and I play hard and call our mother outside to watch ducks flying south for the winter. Mama says those ducks sound a lot like geese. Daddy continues to work for Pete, while getting either no checks or checks that bounce, and he looks for another job.

A man named Hawley Evans saves the day. He gives my father work out of Phillip's Field in Fairbanks.

The rent is due, the electric bill lies unopened on the kitchen table, and blood-sucking Safeway charges too much for groceries. The villain is never Piggly-Wiggly, never Joy Grocery, always Safeway. Regardless, somehow our family survives until my parents cash the first paycheck from Hawley Evans.

After a few months of my father working for Hawley and having a paying job, in the spring of 1961, my parents get a loan from the bank to buy a semifinished house. Its builder was a "crazy Englishman," who according to my father, "didn't own a level or a square."

My father is critical of sloppy construction. The latest in seven generations of skilled carpenters, Daddy says, "Your granddaddy could frame a house, plumb and true, in only three days using just a handsaw, a hammer, a level, and a square. You should have seen him. He looked like a human tornado on the job. Could've made something of himself if he hadn't drunk so much." After a pause, he adds, "His drinking was bad. He'd get drunk and use my mother as a punching bag. That's why she left him when I was eight."

The crazy Englishman shared no such carpentry skill, gave up on the house, and moved back to London before putting up siding, installing a furnace, finishing the flooring, or painting the walls. Seeing our new house for the first time, I find the concrete floor looking like a rough ocean, frozen in time.

"Flimsy heating-system ductwork lies under that concrete, useless and smashed under that lousy slab. Useless. But I can fix it all in no time," says Daddy. "And who can beat the price for this house, huh? Only $3,500."

We now own waterfront property in McKinley Acres, right on the banks of Deadman Slough.

The crazy Englishman's unfinished work includes the lack of windows. We have the holes for windows, just no glass. The first night we sleep in the house, our new insect neighbors try to bleed us to death. My father pitches our tent in the master bedroom. He hammers the pegs into the rough concrete floor and screws a hook to the ceiling. To that, he attaches the tent's peak. We go to bed with the Coleman lantern glowing, its combustive voice singing a satisfied hum.

"That'll keep those 'skeeters from eating us alive," says Daddy. "Snuggle in, everybody. Gets a little cold here in Fairbanks. Even in the summer."

Our bathroom is the crazy Englishman's "crooked little out-house" perched by the edge of the slough, and swatting mosquitoes is part of its charm. Was he a "crooked little man" like in the nursery rhyme? That's the way I picture him.

We have no television or radio. No lights either. The power company hasn't hooked up electricity yet. In the tent, which has been our off-and-on home since we left the East Coast, my parents get out the old Roberts' family Bible. This is our evening entertainment.

Debs and I find our names inscribed on the flyleaf amid a complete family history.

"Who are these people?" Debs and I ask about the names we've never heard of.

"This is your grandfather, Roy. Daddy's daddy. And see 'Lena'? That is Nana. Her real name is Lena."

"Who are Nana and Nornie?" I ask. "Why are they in our Bible?"

Until now, I'd thought they were merely the world's nicest and greatest old people.

"What do you mean 'who are Nana and Nornie?'" asks Daddy.

I shrug in embarrassment, obviously having asked something stupid.

"Nana is Daddy's mama, and Nornie is her husband, Daddy's stepfather. They are your grandparents. You didn't know that?" Mama looks shocked.

"No. Nobody ever told me. They're my grandparents. Wow! That's good!"

Nobody told me that "Nana" was another name for "Grandma" or how Nornie —Norman is his real name— fit in. For grandparents, Nana and Nornie couldn't be beat. We'd rarely seen our real paternal grandfather, Roy. On the three or four occasions we did see him, he was drunk.

Since Nana is Daddy's mom, no wonder she was so upset and crying when we packed up and left. It all made sense now.

Turning back to the Bible, Mama says, "Here you see where Nana married Nornie." Then she points to names in different ink. "And here is Daddy's first family."

"His first family?" This night is full of revelation.

"Yes. See? Here is his first wife, Charlotte."

"Daddy married someone named Charlotte before marrying you?" asks Debs.

"Yes, Charlotte and Daddy got married and then had a boy and a girl," says Mama.

"Why don't we know them? Where are they?"

"I don't know where they are," says Daddy. "I had to leave them behind."

My name, Russell, is the same as my newfound half-brother's name written in the Bible. My father tells me the only way he could bear the pain of losing his children, Jeannie and Russell, was to replace them. He replaced them with us. Daddy begat Russell. And then he begat Russell again.

The next morning, my father installs a heating system from parts on hand. A good Alaskan, the crazy Englishman threw little away, and the back of the house is like a salvage yard.

Daddy drags a twenty-gallon metal drum from a pile, brings it inside, and places it by a kitchen window hole. He props the drum up on four cinder blocks. He salvages stove pipe from another cache. He sticks one end of the pipe out the window with its other end in the drum. With the crazy Englishman's pink leftover insulation, Daddy chinks the window space around the pipe. With plenty of wood available to burn, this proves a serviceable, if far from elegant, solution to the summer cold.

We still don't have spare money, and must do everything on the cheap. The wolf is allegedly always close, but never comes to the door.

One night, instead of the wolf, new neighbors show up with a hot, homemade apple pie. Charlie Ruggles and his dachshund, Bunky —maybe passing for a very short wolf— had heard we'd moved in and walked over to meet us. They live down a dirt lane on the other side of Deadman Slough.

"In ancient times, Athabascans used the slough as a water route to wild potato fields," says Charlie, the pie having been served up after introductions, hand shaking, and small talk.

"But it's full of slime and weeds," I say.

"You're right," says Charlie. "You couldn't float a beach ball in most of it now. Kind of a mess, isn't it? All silted up. But man, it's got history! You'll like this, young man. Russ, isn't it?" I nod. "It's been called Deadman ever since Vuko Perovich killed a man and burned the body in his cabin beside the slough in 1907. You could almost see his cabin from your backyard if it hadn't burned down," says Charlie.

Charlie kindles my imagination while we eat still-warm pie and Bunky, close to the floor, licks his chops. It's the first time I've had cheddar cheese with pie. Alaska is full of new discoveries.

"With very little flow, you've probably already noticed, Deadman Slough is a mosquito paradise," says Charlie. "And, you know, in Alaska, that's really saying something!"

We all laugh, and I show the bites on my arm. "Prodigious," says Charlie, who uses big words. He's a professor or something at the university up the hill.

We finish dessert, and Charlie says goodnight. It's been an evening of pie, gruesome stories, and a dog. I like Charlie Ruggles.

Our house is only a couple miles from Daddy's job at Phillips Field, a small general aviation airport. Hawley Evans bases his outfit at Phillips —an airport he co-founded— in a hangar beside the Piper dealer. I like the dealer's big and bright, red-and-blue Piper sign.

Hawley operates some Cessna 180s, one Republic Navion, two Super Cubs, and one of the first Cessna 210s with its retractable landing gear. Thinking about that high-wing, high-performance airplane excites me.

The classic image of an Alaskan bush plane is one on floats, but all of Hawley Evans' airplanes are on wheels. Fairbanks does have a lot of float planes. But they're found mostly on the Chena River or two miles southwest at the international airport, tied up at that airport's water runway.

I get most of my flying "experience" in Alaska through proximity to actual flying. In my play and imagination, it seems real, and I live the life of a pilot. Sometimes a bush pilot like my father. But most of the time, I'm an airline pilot.

Once in a great while, though, I get to go to the airport and actually fly.

One night, Daddy takes the family for a ride. Rather than ask Hawley if it's okay, he doesn't tell anybody he's taking the family for a joyride. My father has a charter from an airport about sixty miles southwest of Fairbanks. Ferrying —that is, flying empty— from Fairbanks to Usibelli, he'll pick up two passengers there and take them to Cantwell near McKinley National Park. Then he'll fly back to Fairbanks. Daddy figures the two empty legs are perfect to give his family an airplane ride.

We climb in and take off into the long lasting golden hour light of Alaska's September. We fly for about half an hour. The Continental engine purrs and makes me dreamy. The motor never misses a beat, the slipstream outside —the relative wind— brushes the side, and I ride along in bliss. The airplane smells of new avgas, old oils, and vapors of past cargos soaked into the upholstery.

"There's Lignite," says Daddy after a while, breaking my meditation. He points down to a runway beside a black hill. "That's where we'll land. Right there on that runway next to the Nenana River. See it?"

We're close before I pick out the runway from the surrounding terrain.

He lands and taxis off the gravel runway to park the Cessna 180 near the only other airplane on the field. There don't seem to be any other people around. We pile out of the airplane and breathe in the near-freezing autumn air. A weak, yet sharp, smell comes from the nearby hills.

"That's the lignite, the brown coal," says Daddy. "The smell's coming from the inactive mine. They say there was gold here too. All gone now."

In spring and summer, we'd be swatting bugs while standing outside in Alaska so close to the river. But as Daddy talks, we don't have to swat. This late in the season, most of the mosquitoes are dead.

Daddy opens the door of the other airplane, a Cessna 175. "Okay. Great, I'm glad it's not locked. You all climb in here and wait. I'll run down to Usibelli and over to Cantwell. I'll be back in, oh, I don't know," He looks at his watch. "Not more than a couple of hours. Your mother has a book to read to you kids. Here's your flashlight, honey."

We climb into the tied-down airplane. Mama waits to begin the book. The 180 fires up, its engine noise a lovely, satisfying six-cylinder rumble. It taxis out and departs in an air-ripping roar. There's no sound like a wide-open Cessna 180. We watch my father's airplane recede to a flashing red dot. Light from his beacon blinks down near the low southern hills and then disappears.

With my father over the horizon, Mama begins the story.

I wonder if she's reading her journal. It sounds like our story. "What's the name of this book?" I ask.

"It's *Five Little Peppers and How They Grew*," says Mama.

Like us, the Peppers have no money, and Mamsie struggles to keep food on the table. As Mama reads more, though, the Peppers' story and our story diverge. In our house, there's no romantic kidnapping and later rescue by a rich guy. Unlike with the Peppers, our money struggles never seem to end.

But I'm not scared. My parents keep us warm and fed, and, like tonight, I always have airplanes. Airplanes are the thread that stitches my life together. At irregular and unpredictable times, they swoop in to carry me up and away to fresh worlds. Like tonight.

Lignite should scare me. But it doesn't. I'm secure sitting in an airplane I've never met before. This one, a clunky old Cessna 175 —and, yes, it's a good thing it hadn't been locked. This is my airplane, my friend, while we sit here. My father will be back to get us soon. Soon, I will hear his airplane return. Once again, his airplane will be my airplane.

And sure enough, Daddy and his Cessna 180 come back right on time. He finds the runway in the dark, even though the runway lights are unlit. We load up, take off, and fly in the subarctic night back to Fairbanks. Hawley Evans is never the wiser that we've taken a family trip.

CHAPTER FIVE

Soon after the flight to Lignite, my father takes us on another trip. There isn't any flying on my father's schedule for the weekend. We can get away. This time we use the family's VW.

"It's time we get these kids up to the Arctic Circle," he says to Mama. "How can they be real Alaskans if they never cross the Circle? We don't want any *cheechakos* in this family!"

The trip to Circle, Alaska, is a whim, and there's no preparation other than packing lunches and an ice chest of cold ones. The Snog fires up and leaves Fairbanks late Sunday morning. We chug up the Steese Highway toward the settlement of Circle, 158 miles to the northeast. The cheap little car that took us over the Alaska Highway now *putt-putts* us down yet another lonely, dusty road.

We're about two hours down the Circle Highway, and I'm flying my hand in the slipstream from the open driver's window. Up here, we're in the taiga. The rolling landscape shows few trees, just lots of short scrub. In those bushes, I know we'd find lots of low bush cranberries.

With no warning, the engine shuts off, the relative wind drops along with my hand, and the car crunches to a halt on the gravel road. Silence. It's the type of silence only heard in cool, still air when there's not another person for miles around.

My sister and I know to not make a peep. Without a word, my father reaches back to the space below my feet and grabs his .300 H&H rifle. I peek around his seat through the windshield and see a big bull moose standing in the middle of the road. It's not more than two hundred feet ahead of the car.

Silent now, Daddy opens his door, creeps out behind it, and kneels down. He rests the rifle on the door's top hinge. He steadies, takes aim, and fires. *Ker-pow!* Ptarmigan and ravens shoot up from the bushes, feathers and leaves fluttering in their wake. The moose looks startled too, and then crumples in slow motion. Steam comes from his nose and mouth. In a few seconds, a thousand pounds of moose lies in the highway's right lane, cud, green and slimy, still hanging from its mouth.

The silence returns. Or maybe we're deaf from the rifle shot.

"Wow! Look at all that meat!" says my father. "We can eat good all winter. Safeway's not getting all our money. Not this year. Where's my knife?"

"What are we going to tell the police if they come by?" Mama asks. "We gonna tell them that the moose wandered up onto the road after you'd shot it?"

Even I know you aren't supposed to hunt on the road.

"Ah, they're not gonna be by. And we'll worry about it then if they do. Look at all that meat." He grabs a cold one from the ice chest and strops his Herter's hunting knife against a leather band he's gotten from a toolbox.

How did all that stuff get into the Volkswagen? All we packed that morning was lunch and the ice chest. Where did the rest come from? Rifles, knives, tool box, leather strops? Somehow, Daddy equipped the car for an expedition.

For the rest of the daylight hours, Daddy butchers the steaming moose into manageable chunks. From the VW, he takes a bow saw to whack off the hindquarters. Then he grabs a regular carpenter's hand saw and cuts around the ribs and other parts. He pulls out tarps and sizable pieces of sheet plastic —we call it "Visqueen"— in which to wrap the moose parts.

As darkness falls, he hands Mama a shotgun and says, "Stand in front of the Snog, right between the headlights there, honey. If a grizzly smells the blood and approaches us —shoot it."

The last time Mama touched a gun was at Pohick. But never mind her firearms competence or currency. She takes her post as the car's puny six-volt headlights shine on the butchering, an occasional tendril of steam twirling up from a fresh cut of meat. Daddy has me start the car once in awhile to "keep the battery up."

For hours, my sister and I play in the back seat. The sharp, repugnant smell of moose blood, the slurp of the knife cutting meat, and the rasping sound of sawing bone fill the otherwise empty background. The hands of the windup alarm clock taped to the VW's dash move very slowly.

From the stillness comes a loud rustling in the ravine next to the car. Mama muscles the shotgun into firing position, with luck not pulling the trigger en route and shooting my father. Daddy races back to the front seat to grab his loaded rifle as the thing rustles again. He points the gun into the scrub. Wide-eyed, we all expect the rush of a grizzly.

"Look!" says Mama. "It's not a grizzly! It's just a bird!" She lowers her gun, and a great horned owl flies up and over the dis-membered moose.

Hoo-hoo-hoo, hoo-hoo, it says, turning its head and ear tufts toward us.

Mama laughs, sounding relieved. "I guess owls like fresh meat too," she says. "Would've been funny to see that owl try to pick up a moose!" We laugh.

Around 11:00 p.m., the carcass now in liftable pieces, my father packs the car with moose. He puts wrapped moose in the back window-space. Our feet too short to reach the car's floor, Debs and I rest them on wrapped moose. Daddy ties moose to the roof rack and stuffs moose into the VW's forward trunk. The rifle, shotgun, and tools all wind up wedged and crammed wherever they can fit.

"Aw, crap! We have no room for the hindquarters," says Daddy. "I hate to leave them behind. That's a lot of meat. But there's no room. Shit." I'm always shocked when he uses that word.

He smashes the trunk lid closed, mourning the lost value and winter's precious funds migrating to Safeway's corporate coffers. Then lights appear down the road. A flatbed truck, the only vehi-cle we've seen all day, pulls up and clatters to a stop.

"You folks okay?" asks the driver.

"Well, we've got this moose here and the hindquarters won't fit in the car."

"Going back to Fairbanks?"

"Yup," says Daddy.

"Well, throw 'em on the back there. Tie 'em to that pump. You can pick 'em up at my shop in the morning. I'm off Cushman Street." He scribbles the address and says nothing about how goofy it is to be stuffing a moose into a Volkswagen.

"That's great," says my father. "A big help. Thank you much! Sure didn't want to leave all that meat behind. That's a lot of good winter eating. Prices at Safeway . . ."

The driver nods in a cloud of cigar smoke and drives off.

We squeeze into the smelly VW. The bloody moose remnants —the skin, offal, blood, and bones— stain the road.

"What about the antlers?" I ask. "We're taking the antlers, aren't we?"

"Well, Son, we don't have room for them."

I cry. What self-respecting moose hunters wouldn't take the rack to nail over their front door? Isn't that why we've spent all these hours in the bloody Volkswagen?

"Can you . . . ?" asks my mother.

"Where will we put them?" says Daddy.

"Where there's a will . . ." she replies.

My father gets out, opens the trunk, and takes everything out again until he finds his axe. He takes the saw out again too, grabs another cold one from the ice chest, and sets to work separating the antlers from the skull. *Bang, bang, bang. Scrape, bang, saw.* It takes a long time, but I'm happy. My father can do anything.

Finally, well after midnight, he straps the antlers and the bleeding skull top to the Bug's front bumper, and we drive two hours back home.

*   *   *

The flying with Hawley Evans is steady but spaced wide. The paychecks are small. Daddy tackles his financial shortfall by taking matters into his own hands. "I'm not going to let Safeway and the electric company win this year."

He and Roger, the Avis man, cook up a plan to buy an airplane on time payments. It's a four-year-old, two-seat Luscombe 8F Silvaire, which they think will be a great platform for flight instruction and air taxi.

Roger and Russ Roberts' father in Luscombe N9900C,
Fairbanks International Airport, Alaska (1961)

"Let's not tell Sue, though, okay?" says Roger. Roger's wife sometimes babysits us.

Daddy and Roger get the sales contract arranged with the Luscombe's owner, Xen Moore. Over dinner one night, this one special because of her homemade beeswax sheet candles lit on the table, Mama pulls out a note from an earlier phone call. Daddy takes a bite of moose steak and washes it down with a cold one, an Oly. Olympia has replaced Hamm's as my father's cold one of choice.

"The insurance company says the premium for the airplane will be one thousand dollars a year. That's a lot!" says Mama.

"Yep. So, that's it, then . . ." says Daddy.

"No insurance!" says Mama.

Days go by, and, according to Daddy, students are "getting lined up." But it's a slow start for Interior Air Taxi and School. Somehow, before the first student flies, somebody named Dale "gets" the airplane's propeller.

"Did he steal it?" I ask.

"No, he bent it. Hit a ditch," says Daddy. "We have to send the prop to Anchorage to get it straightened. It'll take a little more time before we get this business off the ground. Please pass the string beans." He forks a piece of moose, cubed steak he'd earlier processed with a homemade wooden meat mallet.

While they wait for the propeller, and between trips for Hawley Evans, Daddy, Roger, and the Luscombe guy, Xen, now a new friend, spend many days "spotting for moose." Daddy comes home late from these excursions smelling of what I take to be the Alaska bush: a mix of malt and alcohol.

The propeller might be fragile, easy to bend, I think. But like all newer Luscombes, ours has a new "Silflex" landing gear design.

"The new Silflex design is strong," says Daddy, over another dinner.

I eat while he tells my Mama all about our new airplane. "That new gear design mitigates airframe damage when ground loops occur. Luscombes are hot little numbers, and ground loops are common," says Daddy.

He gets my attention with the word "loops." My mind wanders back to my first memory, from way back when I was little. I rode through a regular loop —a loop the loop— with my father in an Aeronca Champ. The mention of loops takes me back all those years . . . back to my very beginning. How old was I? Three? My fork stops halfway to my mouth as I remember.

"Ready, Son?" Daddy yelled over the roar of the Champ's engine, a few minutes after we'd taken off from Beacon Field. We didn't wear headsets. I thought only Pan American pilots over the Pacific wore headsets. *"Rangoon, Rangoon, China Clipper . . ."*

There was no intercom, no radio, in the Champ.

"Yes! Ready!" I yelled back.

He pushed the airplane's nose down to make the Champ go faster. The airplane's fabric skin moaned, and the struts screamed in the wind over the tiny engine's puny roar as Daddy pulled back on the stick. The stick on the floor in front of me moved back too. I grew heavy for a three-year-old as the load factor increased. My face sagged. My tennis shoes pulled my legs toward the floor. I wasn't sure I would survive the strain. Was I going to die? How exciting!

We were up, up, and up. How far up could we go? Up, up, up, and over the top. With the world upside down, I rose off my seat and, for a moment, floated in the too-loose seatbelt. The trees and cars were above my head, and my body had no weight. Just a second before, I'd been so heavy. My stomach wondered if it should be sick. But it decided right away that, even though unmoored and untethered, it and my other floating organs would be okay.

With the world upside down, the deafening engine noise stopped as my father pulled the throttle to idle. Then with a groan we headed straight back for the ground, and I grew very heavy again. Within seconds, the world righted itself, and Daddy looked over his shoulder to me in the back seat. He grinned. I grinned back.

Though brief, that experience was a lot for a three-year-old to take in. I guess that's why I've never forgotten it.

But now, I think about a ground loop in a Luscombe. It sounds like an exciting maneuver. Do you go upside down? How do you go upside down on the ground?

The airplane's propeller is back from Anchorage and the airplane ready to fly. Ready to make money. Our airplane, November nine-nine-zero-zero Charley —I've already memorized the registration number— was the prototype for the latest Luscombe production run. It has the touted-up strong landing gear my father told us about, optional wing flaps, and a full electrical system. Having sat outside during its four-year life, it also has an unattractive natural aluminum skin and peeling red paint.

"We need to do something about its looks," says Daddy. "Something to make it look more professional."

My father has no desire to polish aluminum to make the airplane look better. His alternative to hours of hard labor sanding and rubbing to bring a shine to the oxidized metal is a fresh paint job. "We're going to cover up all that dull aluminum," he says. "Yep. Paint it. And why pay someone else when you can do it yourself? So that's what I'm going to do."

Of that I am sure. He is confident in every skill. There is nothing he can't do.

Before he got into aviation, Daddy built beautiful houses and cabinets for people. His carpentry skill ranks high. His building projects glow in perfection. His taste in paint colors, however, leaves us wondering. To him, bright yellow houses with green shutters look terrific. He wonders why George didn't paint Mt. Vernon yellow and green.

He doesn't choose yellow and green for the Luscombe, but . . .

Daddy buys three gallons of decent-quality airplane paint and puts the cans on the living room floor. Based on the colors on top of the cans, they must have been a good deal, I think. But I'm only a little kid. What do I know?

Mama is looking at the cans too. She looks up at Debs. My sister is staring at the cans. Since my father is often mean to her —he says he needs to "break her will"— Debs offers no opinion on the paint colors, but her face is grim.

On Saturday morning, Daddy gets up before dawn. He gathers masking tape, paper, air compressor, hoses, and spray gun, and heads to the airport. I rub my eyes, watching him drive off, and wonder where all that stuff came from. Had he packed it all on the VW when we moved to Alaska? The car is like a magician's hat. No matter how much stuff is pulled out, there's always more.

In Alaska, the sun never reaches zenith as it drifts around the compass at this time of year. The resulting perpetual golden hour paints a pleasing, even romantic, glow on the land and everything else it touches. Daddy works in this beautiful light, out in the open air of the airside parking area at Fairbanks International.

The first day, Saturday, he tapes and masks. He takes care to keep the lines straight and the tape tight. He wants no jiggly trim, bleeding, or over spray. That evening, in dimming light, he shoots the first color.

On Sunday, he masks for the next color and sprays in the calm morning hours while many people are in church. Before noon, the paint is dry. He calls my mother from the airport office. "Call Roger. You all come on out to the airport. It's ready."

Within an hour, we all gather at the Luscombe's tie-down spot. The sun, now at its highest, projects the day's most unflattering light. That's not to say the noon sun casts a harsh light. But for artistic revelation, the light could have been better.

My father, in his role as the Michelangelo of airplane painters, readies to unmask his Sistine Chapel. He pauses for effect, as if waiting for an angelic host that doesn't come. Then with a flourish rips away tape and paper to reveal —ta-da!— a mistake.

It turns out that purple and turquoise don't look good on a Luscombe. We all turn to Daddy and wonder what he was thinking. Hadn't the first burst from the paint gun signaled "stop!"? We watch him and wonder when he'll speak of his results. But he only goes, "Humph." The grunt is so loud we can almost see a speech bubble floating over his head.

Ugly it is. But it's flyable and the four of us have some good times in our two-seater airplane.

One day, Daddy put us in the airplane with a nice picnic basket Mama packed. I sit in the tiny luggage space behind the two small seats, and Debs travels on the hat rack above. We don't wear, nor did we need, seat belts. The confines wedge in my sister and me so tight we can't move even in the strongest turbulence.

"You kids duck down as we taxi past the tower," says Daddy. "We don't want the FAA to see four people in a Luscombe!"

Duck down? Already smashed as far as I can go, how can I duck down further? The Luscombe is a tiny airplane. On the hat rack, Debs' chance of compressing further is doubtful too. With Debs and me in sardine class, and my parents not much better off in the airplane's two tiny seats, we take off and fly to an abandoned gold mine way out in the Thules.

Tailings are the gravels left over from gold-dredging operations. Before the miners left, they flattened out the tailings and made a passable runway. From the landing strip, there are good views of mountains and a river. My father has found a good place for a family picnic. There are no wheel marks or footprints. Nobody has been here in a long time.

In Alaska, fliers often get lost forever. It's wise to file flight plans to tell others where you're going. But most of our family flying trips are clandestine. We'd told no one we were flying this time either. It's unwise to advertise putting four people in an airplane certified for two. Nothing stops a flying career quicker than an FAA violation. The entire purpose of coming to Alaska is for Daddy to build flight time for an airline job.

But never mind all that. Regulations have nothing to do with me. We are having a splendid adventure with our airplane. Out on the tailings, we eat, admire the view, and watch for bears. We harbor hope of seeing a moose. A lot of fresh sign —game droppings— dot the runway. It's been a delightful afternoon, with everybody eating Lebanon bologna sandwiches and drinking soft drinks. A real treat. No cold ones lay in sight.

With the food gone and the novelty growing thin, my folks pack up for the trip back to town. I sit on the airplane's tail drinking a bottle of Coke. My father turns and sees me. He turns white.

"Son, what are you doing?" His voice is loud and firm, but measured, like he's speaking to someone holding a grenade in church. "Be very slow now. Get off that tail! Don't jump or move quick. Easy now. You could break it."

When off the Luscombe's tail and away from the airplane, I really catch it.

"Don't you know that we could have been stuck out here?" Daddy yells. "Nobody knows where we are! That tail could have got bent or broken off! Jesus Christ! Sometimes you can really be stupid! Do you know that? I don't have any tools to fix anything out here!" He rubs his hand over the stabilizer, checking to see if it is still okay to fly.

No tools? How can that be? The man who carries two guns, three saws, tarps, sheet plastic, and an axe in a Volkswagen doesn't have any tools? *Not my fault, man. I'm a kid.* But I feel terrible anyway. I've done something dumb and gotten yelled at. I almost broke an airplane. Doing something stupid with an airplane is, for me, unforgivable. Even if our airplane is ugly, it's still an airplane.

Purple and turquoise is the way November nine-nine-zero-zero Charley remains, an eyesore until the crash. An eyesore on the flight line pre-crash, after the wreck, it's an eyesore in our driveway for two years. In our yard, with the wings off, it's a derelict parked beside our garage, next to the Volkswagen's rotting cardboard car-camping kitchen.

CHAPTER SIX

Every day at school, right after lunch, Mrs. Brimsmaid reads to us. Every day. Without fail. After eating and the fun of our twenty-minute recess, her reading makes coming back to class almost a treat. The books she chooses make second grade special: *Old Bill, the Whooping Crane* and *Rascal* are two of my favorites. So is *The Wonderful Flight to the Mushroom Planet*, a book about two boys like me who build a rocket that flies into space. Imagine that.

Today, she says, "Let me read a part of this."

On Fridays, she likes reading poems.

As soon as she finishes reading her poem, something about a prickly pear —it's a weird poem, and it seemed she read it only to herself— she's says, "Okay now, what would you like to hear?"

I raise my hand. Mrs. Brimsmaid smiles, sighs, and says, "I think I know what you want to hear, Russell. But maybe you'll surprise me today."

I don't. I request "High Flight," a poem by John Gillespie Magee Jr.

So once again, with a big pull of breath, for the umpteenth time she reads about the teenage fighter pilot in his Spitfire.

"Oh! I have slipped the surly bonds of earth . . ." It's another Friday in second grade. I close my eyes and rest my chin on my

hands. In my mind, I chase the shouting winds along, dance the skies on laughter-silvered wings, and do *"a hundred things you have not dreamed of . . ."*

I never tire of it.

Later, the class is in the school's library to pick out books to take home for the weekend. Friday is personal book day. Mrs. Brimsmaid asks me, "Russell, are you sure that's the book you want?"

I nod.

"My, but that's a big book," she says. I clutch it to my chest. Ever since I'd seen Gregory Peck in *Moby Dick* on TV, sailing vessels rank almost as high as airplanes. Call me Ishmael. Nothing to do with sailboats and ships —or airplanes and space— gets past me now. If I weren't already an airline pilot, I'd be a sea captain.

The university up the hill from our house shows movies on Saturdays at the student union. Last week, I rode my bike and paid a quarter to watch a documentary about a guy named Thor Heyerdahl, who had sailed a homemade balsa raft across the Pacific. I wanted to know more. Building a raft is something I could do. My friend Donald built a canvas canoe that we paddle around Deadman Slough. The best part is that it's a secret our parents don't know about. Scaling up a vessel to build and then sailing the Pacific is something we could do too.

"Are you sure? That's such a big, thick book," says Mrs. Brimsmaid, slowly shaking her head. "Maybe you'd be happier with one of these." She points to a row of picture books.

I shake my head. "This one has some pictures too. See?" I show her. Heyerdahl's book, *Kon-Tiki: Across the Pacific by Raft,* has a section of photographs in the middle, and besides, the words that I can't read might somehow soak into my head. What's it called? Oh, right. Osmosis.

I'm ashamed, because I know that Mrs. Brimsmaid knows I can't read. I am the dumbest kid in the class. I haven't been able to fake her out. With her arms folded, Mrs. Brimsmaid watches as I check out my book. My jelly legs feel like running away. The librarian stamps the card and looks over her glasses at me and then at Mrs. Brimsmaid. The librarian knows I'm a fraud too. But *Kon-Tiki* comes home with me anyway. I crave the story. Even if I can't read it.

Fridays are special because of "High Flight," personal book day, and because 3:00 p.m. signals the beginning of the weekend. And this weekend, there's more than *Kon-Tiki.* This weekend at home promises to be explosively good.

The crazy Englishman who built our house without using a level or a square proved to be a worse plumber than he was a carpenter. Like the furnace ductwork, most of the plumbing pipes lay crushed and useless under the wavy concrete slab floor. And Daddy has discovered the house's wastewater system is of similar quality. But he has a plan.

Yesterday, he came home from work with a brown paper bag. Normally, he hides his brown paper bags. But this time he smiled and said, "Look what I have here."

This time the bag didn't contain cold ones or a bottle of liquor. Instead, it held three red tubes.

"Dynamite," he said.

I smiled back. I knew about dynamite. They use a lot of dynamite on TV's *Rawhide* and *Wagon Train*.

"What are we going to do with the dynamite?" I asked, getting excited. I said "we" on purpose. I wanted to include myself right away in whatever pyrotechnics might be afoot.

I didn't much like household work, but I was always eager to burn trash. Even though it said "Do not incinerate" on aerosol cans, one often sneaks into the bin. I didn't care about the warning and couldn't read it, anyway. But my folks told me about it. I'm supposed to dig out the aerosol cans and give them to my parents.

But I never dug them out. I liked to arrange the cans to explode in the burning trash with the most dramatic effect. I liked to put the cans in a milk carton or cardboard box so the explosion looked like I'd blown up a building. My parents called me a pyromaniac. I loved fires and explosions. I always considered myself a fireworks aficionado.

And this dynamite project looked like the big leagues.

"We're going to start fixing the plumbing."

"With dynamite?" I asked.

"Yes. I'll show you on Saturday morning," said Daddy.

Friday would have been an endless day if it hadn't been for Mrs. Brimsmaid's serial reading of "High Flight" and bringing home *Kon-Tiki*. That night, I find it hard to go to sleep with all the thoughts of adventure on the Pacific, Spitfires over London, and explosives in the paper bag.

Saturday morning dawns bright and clear. Even though I like to sleep in on Saturdays, today I jump out of bed, eager to get started with the dynamite. Daddy is already up and in the backyard.

In Alaska, wastewater systems usually rely on cesspools. "All the places we had 'outside' never had cesspools," says Daddy.

I'm thinking it has something to do with our bathroom, which is outside in the backyard.

"We didn't have cesspools outside?" I ask like I know what I'm talking about.

"No. We had drain fields. But they don't work well in Alaska because of the permafrost. Here, we have a cesspool."

My father likes to instruct me from time to time.

"You'll need to know this, so listen," he says. "The drain line from the house connects to the cesspool. Instead of a drain field —you know, lines of pipe with holes in them laid in the back-yards— here we have a cesspool. It's a wooden tank with holes in it that serves the same purpose as a drain field. It percolates wastewater into the surrounding soil."

"Percolates" sounds like a coffee pot.

"Do we need to have an outhouse because we have a cesspool outside?" I ask. It's all pretty confusing.

"No, no, no. We're using the outhouse because our cesspool is broken. When I say 'outside,' I mean the Lower 48 states. You know, like back home in Virginia."

Daddy is being super friendly and seems to enjoy having me there to share the project. It's early in the day, and all he's had to drink is coffee, so he's not making me feel stupid when I say stupid things.

We walk into the middle of the backyard, right where we'd

had a garden until a moose came by, trampled everything, and ate all the cabbages.

"See here," says my father, pointing to a wooden hatch on the ground. "This is the 'cleanout' for the cesspool." He opens the hatch. "If you look down in the hole, you can see that it's full."

Yuck! But I don't want to look like an amateur by holding my nose. So, I look and nod, bearing the stench in pursuit of learning. Dynamite guys don't hold their noses.

"It's not percolating anymore. We have to build a new system. But first, we've got to get rid of the old one.

"Back home," he says, again meaning Virginia, "when they build a cesspool, they make it out of concrete or block. Here in Alaska, they use wood. This one has stopped working. It's all rotted and plugged up.

"To make it easier for me to dig out the old cesspool, we're going to blow it up. Bust it to smithereens! Then the chunks of wood will be smaller to handle. Easier for us to dig out of the ground." He points over to a pick and shovel.

I don't like that word, "us."

He rubs his hands together. I've never seen him do that before. I didn't think exhibiting excitement was manly. But he grins and says, "Let's get started!"

Daddy has lots of started —but never finished— projects around our house. Before making a dent in finishing the wreck-of-a-house the crazy Englishman had started, Daddy began an addition on the back of our little place. He'd put up a roof supported not by walls, but by a few four-by-four posts. The plan was to "close it in and make a nice den."

We call the roof —this lean-to, this half-built construction that's already starting to rot— "the cover." This Saturday morning, from under the cover, we run about seventy-five feet of paired insulated copper wire out to the cesspool.

"Is that going to be enough wire?" I ask. On *Wagon Train* and *Rawhide*, dynamite always blows off the side of a mountain.

"Oh, yeah, it's enough. Don't worry," says Daddy.

I nod in agreement.

He presses some things into the dynamite. "Blasting caps, see?" he says. He secures them to the wires with black electrical tape. He inserts the prepared dynamite into a plastic bag and seals it up with more tape. "We don't want the explosives to get wet," he says

"Right," I say.

"Okay, now. You hold the wires, like this," Daddy says. "Don't move around. Be still. We don't want the two ends coming together by accident. We don't want the dynamite going off early."

I'm holding the wires so far apart it looks like I'm hugging a redwood tree.

He nods in approval. "Okay. Now I'm going to lower the package into the cesspool. You make sure nobody messes with the wires."

From under the cover, the lean-to, I see Daddy placing the explosives down the tank opening. Then he replaces the tank's inspection hatch. My strong and quiet father looks up at me and grins. He can do anything: build things, fix things, blow things up. When he's not asleep on the couch after drinking, he's a great man.

After joining me again under the cover, Daddy pulls one of my favorite gadgets from his pocket. It's a rechargeable flashlight battery. I've heard about its money-saving benefits before. "Batteries are expensive," Daddy's told me many times. "This thing replaces two D-cell Evereadies. It saves a bunch of money." But the part I like is that you can unscrew a cover from the end of it and plug the battery right into a wall socket for a recharge. It's like magic. It's wonderful to live in the Space Age.

"Okay, ready? I'm going to touch the wires to the battery. Here goes. Look up. Watch out there. Watch the cesspool!"

He touches the wires to the battery, and the backyard goes off in a big —a really big— *whoof!* The neighborhood cracks with the noise of exploding dynamite. *Ker-boom!* Awesome and sublime. Stupendous.

But my father has forgotten about the Alaskan permafrost. The frozen ground is so hard that it resists even dynamite's energy. Instead of the force going out sideways and breaking up the wooden cesspool —in accord with my father's plan— everything goes airborne.

Our backyard flies high into the air with the cesspool's contents closely in trail. Fifty feet, a hundred feet, more . . . Up it goes. Ravens, robins, and other birds caw, shriek, and flap as they've never flapped before. They escape in clouds of feathers as the sky fills with dirt, pieces of wood, clods of toilet paper, and worse.

After the concussion, we are deaf, and, with the backyard at apogee, all is silent in a timeless moment. The stillness and all the stuff frozen in midair remind me of the poem Mrs. Brimsmaid read yesterday by some guy named Eliot. It was the weird poem about the prickly pear:

> *This is the way the world ends*
> *This is the way the world ends*
> *Not with a bang but with a whimper.*

And then the fallout begins. What goes up comes down. A filthy rain falls in slow motion. This time I'm reminded of the photos I've seen of Hiroshima. Duck and cover. I retreat further under the lean-to. My heart soars. I never imagined the apocalypse would be so joyful. It's a horrific paradise.

My father turns and goes into the house. I don't understand that, but I smile and delight in the black rain. Glorious.

Fairbanks summers being dry, it's a long time before real rain comes to wash the muck and sludge from the trees and telephone wires. All summer, I have reminders of the magnificent explosion.

You know, it's funny. None of the neighbors come by or call. No one complains about the filth on the phone lines. I remember that man who picked up our moose hindquarters. Alaskans. They're a live-and-let-live people.

CHAPTER SEVEN

Where the Luscombe lay a wreck for so long, now only a dent remains beside the garage. The grass has never grown back. But with the airplane gone, so is my father's plan to build flying time in Alaska. His dream of flying for the airlines slowly evaporates. There's no more talk of it around our house.

Daddy takes a nonflying job at the University of Alaska, just up the hill from our house on Gradelle Avenue. I notice there are more and more cold ones on the weekends, and, even with the steady and secure state job, the arguments about money grow louder.

One late afternoon, there's a knock at the door. We don't get a lot of visitors, but I pay only half-attention when a man in a coat and tie introduces himself. "Hello, I'm Dave, one of Jehovah's Witnesses." He stands, holding two pulp magazines and a thick green book. I go back to my room to play airplanes.

Some serious talk is coming from the front door. Half-listening, I hear Mama say, "My husband is not home right now. But I think he'd be interested in what you have to say. Can you come back when he's home?"

I've never heard that before. My parents always sent away the few salesmen at our door. "We're not interested," my mother always says, that last word in sync with the door clicking shut.

But not today.

My father meets Dave the next Saturday, likes him, and invites him back to begin Bible studies. Before I know what's happening, Dave becomes permanent. Not there one day. Always around the next.

"Dave is really something," my father says over a cold one at our dilapidated wooden dining table. It's the picnic table my folks are borrowing from the neighborhood park across the street. "He answers every question I have. Do you know that, honey? Every single question. It might take him awhile, but he always comes back with an answer. He really knows the Bible!"

The crazy Englishman's house on in Fairbanks (1962).
Shown, the wrecked Luscombe airplane and Debs with
poppies in the front yard.

The Bible is an unfamiliar work for my father. His folks were Baptist, but his family never displayed religiosity, nor were they regular church attendees. And me? Except for my mother's uncle's funeral on a scorching day back in Crozet, Virginia, I've never been to a church.

I remember seeing my first glacier, the Matanuska, on our first trip to Alaska. It's down the valley from Meekins Lodge on the Glenn Highway, about a hundred miles from Anchorage. Since then, I've learned a lot about it and Alaska's many other glaciers in school. Glaciers, the teachers say, are slow moving, kind of like the way a tree grows. But over time, giant glaciers can cover miles and miles. While beautiful, they move and crush everything under them, grinding great boulders —and even mountains— to powder. That's the way the Jehovah's Witnesses are to our family. Glacier Dave moves in, slowly but steadily, and soon our family landscape is unrecognizable.

And my mother? She doesn't seem to care a whit about biblical answers or solutions to life's mysteries. Mama likes being with people. She seems to relish the new social life. There may not be booze and guns like at Pohick, but there is now a whole new group of people, something she hasn't had since we moved to Alaska. This religion thing is another avenue to socializing. If she has any misgivings, I don't hear them. She likes a crowd. And saying nothing avoids arguments with my father.

Before Dave's knock, my father contemplated moving back outside, to the Lower 48 again, to pursue his flying dream. The bad luck with paychecks, the wrecked Luscombe, a tendency to quit too early, and, finally, the Witnesses divert those thoughts.

The Witnesses have "all the answers" about a New World Order —the Witnesses love creating proper nouns from common words. They promise a never-ending human life, and offer the warmth of an embracing congregation. And how can an airline job compete with eternal human life?

"Imagine. We'll all live together on Earth —forever," says my father.

I believe in Santa Claus. I still believe Daddy too. What my father tells me is always true.

Dave and his wife, Audrey, become our best friends. My parents make lots of new friends in the congregation. They've never swum in such a big community pool. And we're in the pool a lot. My father takes to it like heroin. The Witnesses seem to answer a yearning, a need. They give him a narrative, a story upon which to cling, and a network of like-minded, supportive people and organizing authorities.

The congregation gathers two times a week for "fellowship and learning." In smaller groups, it meets twice a week, once for Bible study and the other for door-to-door evangelizing.

I have to go to all the meetings. Within a few weeks, it feels like a chronic toothache. But over time, amid the dull misery, I can't help but learn a lot about the church. But they don't call it church.

"A church, according to the apostle Paul, is not a building. It's a gathering of people," says Dave.

But they don't call the congregation a "church" either. They want to stand apart and have a set of rules, an unwritten and unofficial code, about what not to say.

There's a slow trickle of propaganda too. The Witnesses are the only religious group with the truth. Or, as they call it, the Truth. I may chafe at the time devoted to religion, but I puff up with pride that my family has discovered the inside track. The rest of Christendom is an evil part of the "outside World." I come to think of Christendom in the same way I think of cannibals or Nazis.

I hear, over and over, like the same never-ending tapping found in Chinese water torture, that the Witnesses —and only the Witnesses— have the truth and live "in the Truth." The Witnesses discourage social contact with those "in the World outside the Truth." They do not serve in the military and do not allow singing of patriotic songs or pledging allegiance to anything other than God.

They've cracked the code to being on a first-name basis with the English-speaking creator of the universe. Rarely in the Kingdom Hall is "Jehovah" called God. God is for Baptists, Catholics, and the others. We have Jehovah. We alone stand apart from the evil of the soon-to-be-done World.

I learn the only thing Jehovah wants us to celebrate is Passover. But celebration of this, the "Lord's Evening Meal," doesn't involve gifts, festivity, or even a meal, for Christ's sake. If the date of the "Last Supper" does not coincide with a regular meeting, they shoehorn it into another day of the week. For me, this crammed-in extra meeting only means yet one more boring night at the Kingdom Hall. Another night to hear a senior member of the congregation drone on about how lucky we are to live in the Truth.

But I remember God mandated us to celebrate this special day. So I must bear another night to hear about the importance of only the "anointed ones" partaking of the cracker-like unleavened bread. Only the "remnant" may drink the purple Manischewitz wine made from New York Concord grapes. Since my parents tell me it is so, I believe all this stuff. It's the price of salvation. I just hate having to spend so much time scaffolding belief with the endless meetings. It's like they can't let up for a minute lest the faithful lose steam.

In the crazy Englishman's house. Last Roberts family Christmas. Note the "tiger-striped" floor. The plywood subfloor was never finished.

So, except for the Lord's Evening Meal, Jehovah's Witnesses celebrate nothing. This includes children's birthdays —and Christmas.

"No, kids," says Daddy with Mama sitting quietly on the couch beside him. "Jehovah does not want us to celebrate Christmas. It's a pagan holiday."

"What about Santa Claus? What about our tree?" Debs asks with dripping tears. She doesn't cry often.

"We'll celebrate," my parents agree, nodding at each other. "We'll have a December party!"

No, we won't.

My sister and I, at nine and seven, respectively, have Christmas jerked out from under us by my father and mother and their Jehovah's Witness accomplices. Our family goes from celebrating Christmas with gusto to celebrating nothing at all.

My first six years, I'd enjoyed our family's big Christmas celebrations. The whole family reveled in them. Mama loved decorating the house and planning parties. We'd have, what seemed to me, lavish doings at Nana's mansion-like house in Silver Springs. She had a stairway and a silver Christmas tree!

One time, my folks took Christmas 8 millimeter movies of my sister and me walking down Nana's steps in our airline uniforms. I'm a captain, and my sister is a stewardess. We're holding champagne glasses. My parents thought the idea of an airline crew drinking before flying was hysterical. We liked the ginger ale in the glasses. A rare treat. Especially in the morning. "Why can't we drink soda more often?" I asked.

"It'll rot your teeth," said Daddy.

Nana and Nornie not only lived in the best house I'd ever been in, but had a pipeline direct to Santa's workshop. Getting piles of gifts on Christmas morning seemed like we'd fallen into the pages of the Sears Christmas catalog.

But now we are Witnesses, so no Christmas for us. We celebrate nothing now, unless one counts the triennial homemade Mexican dinners. Every three years or so, my folks try to recreate the exotic tastes of a Washington, DC, restaurant called El Mexico —one of their old haunts— with an all-day cooking and eating extravagance.

But even those glorious days, when they made everything right down to the tortillas, wane now that my father isn't drinking so much beer. By becoming allied with the Witnesses, my father has mostly given up drinking alcohol. That's a plus, I guess. At least he's not so mean anymore.

Before long, my father is an upstanding elder in the reclusive, repressive "theocratic organization." He, like the other Witnesses, believes that they are God's one true organization on earth.

To believe the Truth, we must all believe some off-the-wall teachings.

"What's the point of a college education? God is bringing Armageddon, total destruction to Satan's followers and to earth. At the same time, he will give everlasting human life to his followers. Us!"

I hear this from the stage at the Kingdom Hall and from my father. Discouraging college is something my parents can support, since it's one more child-raising expense, like braces, that they won't have to pay for. My permanent teeth have come in like a mutant corn cob. At least that's how they look to me.

"We'll fix that," says Daddy. "Here, take some vitamin D. Do that every day, and your teeth will straighten right out."

My father follows *Prevention* magazine almost as faithfully as he reads *The Watchtower*.

Don't the people writing for *Prevention* have college educations? I can't figure out why someone who will live forever on Earth wouldn't want to get all the education possible. Daddy takes umbrage when I ask, "Isn't the planet going to be full of a bunch of ignoramuses?"

"What a dumb question."

The Witnesses take a bare-bones approach to life. No higher education, few new cars, no concentration on bettering one's financial position. This hope for surviving an imminent Armageddon and then coasting through to an everlasting human life seems to trump the immediate knowable, predictable, routine future. It even trumps living in the here and now.

Living forever as physical human beings on Earth gives me pause. "People's ears and noses never stop growing," I say, a fact I learned on a *National Geographic* TV special. "So by living forever, aren't we all going to look like elephants?"

My father shakes his head.

I love *National Geographic*.

"What about our teeth? We're not like sharks. Our teeth don't regrow. Aren't our teeth going to wear out if we live forever? Are we going to gum our food for eternity?" I wish my teeth would fall out and regrow, since the vitamin D isn't whipping them into line.

Daddy gives me a patronizing smile. A fake smile. "You're too smart to learn, Son."

But I don't stop. "What about man 'created in his own image'? Are you telling me God goes to the bathroom? If I'd designed people, I'd have made us solar powered, like plants," I say.

Illogic and discomfort keep me wobbling with the Witnesses' philosophy. I believe it all, of course. My parents tell me to believe it. But the Witness structure of thinking seems off to me. I believe my parents, believe what they say about the World, the promise of Armageddon and the New World Order. I believe them as I've always believed them. They've given me lots of good advice: "Don't put your hand on that frying pan! You'll get burned!"

But the Witnesses' message never sets. A place in my brain, just above thought, isn't buying it. And ever since seeing *The Manchurian Candidate*, I've begun having nightmares about brainwashing.

I continue to believe my parents in all that they say. I go to the meetings and face the embarrassment of witnessing by going door-to-door. But it all keeps me off balance. I must be the one who's in error. My feelings must be wrong. My parents —my parents!— say the Witnesses are right.

I have the idea that Witness children must be proud, righteous, and believing. "No, not proud," says Daddy. "Pride is a sin."

But pride, or bumptiousness as my father would call it, seems a part of a normal Witness's attitude. It's rooted in exclusivity: being in the know, having the Truth, and being on the only path

to everlasting human life. Imagine that. I know I'm proud of
being one of the chosen ones. Maybe I'm missing something and
the real Witnesses aren't proud. There must be something wrong
with me. My father always tells me I'm prideful and that I fall
short of righteousness and even believing.

"People will live forever in a human body? Is that really true?"

"Of course everlasting life is possible. Methuselah lived to be
nine hundred sixty-nine," says Mama, using a Bible verse to prove
the Bible.

Well, never mind. I know I am proud of having my parents'
inside skinny on eternal life. But I don't feel superior, righteous,
or particularly convicted for being one of Jehovah's Witnesses.
I'm embarrassed and off balance.

All the Witness kids I know go to public school. While the
Organization —the Witnesses like thier proper nouns— discour-
ages the beliefs taught in secular education, it doesn't pony up
for a church school. I think it should, since the price of being a
Witness kid in a public school is high.

I enter the fourth grade by introducing myself to my new
teacher. "Hello, Mrs. Morrow. I'm one of Jehovah's Witnesses.
We're not allowed—"

"I know about you people," she snaps. I want to run away. I
have made her mad. This year, she'll have one of "you people" in
her class.

Sorry, Mrs. Morrow. I stare at the floor. She must now
tip-toe around me. She must compromise normal school stuff
because one of "you people" is in class. Standing in front of her
desk, thinking about religion, martyrdom, and persecution,

I want to turn into a pillar of salt —immobile and silent— like Lot's wife.

In my head, I have a big list of things I'm not allowed to do. I'm ready to recite it to Mrs. Morrow, but she appears to know all about "you people" and is staring at me. My list, the things I'm primed to tell her, includes not singing the national anthem or any patriotic songs, not singing religious or holiday tunes, not saluting the flag, and not saying the Pledge of Allegiance. I'm not to make any holiday, religious, or patriotic artwork. But I need not list them to her. She's made it clear to me she already knows about "you people."

I feel bad, like I've done something wrong. I want to be somewhere else. I wish she would tell me to get lost. I wish I'd melt into the floor. Mrs. Morrow might know about "you people," but she doesn't know about me.

She doesn't know I want to do the prohibited things. Not doing them is not my idea. It is their idea, my parents and the Organization. Me? I'd love to be a normal kid. I hate being a Jehovah's Witness.

At the first school assembly, I lip-synch the Pledge of Allegiance with my hand over my spleen, halfway between my stomach and heart. I know all the words to every holiday and patriotic song, and I lip-synch those too, mouthing out every other word. "—dreaming—a—Christmas—like—ones—used—know—." No sound comes out.

I figure with my on-the-fly editing, God and the Organization —and maybe even my parents— couldn't be too upset. Besides, how will they ever know? God might care enough to know. But I'm hoping to find a loophole as I navigate the eye of salvation's needle.

It's an enormous relief when the music teacher says, "Let's sing *Home on the Range*." I take a breath and sing. Off-key and unpracticed, I sing. Next comes *Old Folks at Home*, the Swanee River song. Both the range and the river become special places to me. Safe places.

Back in church, I have a sense the congregation members are honest and good. I feel safe with them too, while fearing their displeasure should they discover my covert apostasy. Dave and Audrey, and the others, are nice people. They pay Caesar's things to Caesar, but don't vote or serve in the military. They endeavor to be truthful and do good, peaceful works. But even the new Peace Corps is off limits. Several times a week, I hear we are among the few humans on the true road to salvation. Everlasting physical life is the promise for us and our offspring. Wow. We're off to see the wizard.

In the church that we're not supposed to call a church, the overseer says, "Let's now sing from *Songs to Jehovah's Praise!*" So we sing. Or rather, everyone else sings. I lip-synch those songs too. I dislike the music and lyrics. The Witness tunes feel like a cheap substitute, margarine akin to butter. Kingdom Hall singing sounds embarrassed and hollow. Besides that, I worry my singing voice might be as bad as my father's. *Don't sing, Daddy. Lip-synch like me.* But he sings.

In the Kingdom Hall, my mind always wanders. The environment exercises my imagination and memory. It's a survival response.

Today, I think of a robin I saw when camping. The robin hit its head over and over against the car window, attacking its own reflection. I tried to minimize its reflection, including breaking off the limb he used as a perch. I tried newspapering the whole windshield, but all afternoon the robin attacked his own image, over and over and over. Nothing worked. All day the robin returned to attack his rival, his own mirrored self.

Nightfall finally came, and the robin gave up. Thank god. But at sunup he returned to pummel his own reflection. How long would he go on? Until he died? We saved him by driving away. Later, I cleaned the robin's smeared blood from the window. I couldn't get it all. Robin gore remained in the rubber at the edges of the windshield.

Why do I connect the robin to my time at the Kingdom Hall?

CHAPTER EIGHT

We're pacifists. Daddy says that means I will go to prison instead of fighting in a war. I will be happy to go to prison, he says. "It's what Jehovah wants us to do." Well, if he says so, it must be true.

But I've become a big fan of B-17s and World War II thanks to the television show *12 O'Clock High*. Brigadier General Frank Savage, the show's hero, reminds me of Bob of the Pohick days: chiseled, stoic, awash in a cloud of cigarette smoke. Like Bob, Frank Savage spends a lot of time drinking whiskey.

Daydreaming about *12 O'Clock High* gets me through the endless hours at the Kingdom Hall. In misery, I squirm in my seat, immersed in the promise of everlasting life and how to get it. But in my mind, I fly with General Savage as we attack, with extreme prejudice, Nazi Germany from our heavy bombers. Bombing the Nazis keeps me sane until the *drip, drip, drip* of torture finally ends with the evening's last prayer.

At school, I meet Danny. He's a big fan of *12 O'Clock High* too. Together, along with a squadron of other kids in formation, we bomb the playground each recess. We make the most of our twenty-minute breaks. Since we need someone to shoot at, one of us, either Tommy Johnson, Billy Mendenhall, Don Lange, Danny, or I volunteer —as a community service— to be the Luftwaffe. When it's our turn to be the enemy, each of us usually choose to be a Focke-Wulf Fw 190, a much manlier ship than the more ubiquitous and compact Messerschmitt Bf 109.

Danny lives nearby, an easy bike ride down Geist Road. I lie to my parents and tell them Danny wants to learn about the Truth. This is the only way I think they'll let me ride down to his house.

"Here, take this book. It's easy to read. It'll be a good way for you boys to study the Truth together," says Daddy.

Good luck with that. Danny might read, but I'd have to proselytize using the pictures. Or I would if I had any intention of proselytizing.

So with a happy cover story and *From Paradise Lost to Paradise Regained* in my basket, I'm allowed to visit Danny about once a week. During our visits, the book never leaves my book bag. I wouldn't want Danny or his parents to see it and have no interest in sharing the "Truth."

My parents are all excited about my witnessing to Danny, since his father is a Methodist preacher. Danny and his folks live in the church parsonage. It's called the Wesley House.

At the Kingdom Hall, the word gets out that I've invaded an enemy camp. I become a celebrity in the congregation until the novelty wears off. I'm the kid who penetrated the very core of Christendom. I enjoy the attention almost as much as I enjoy playing war at Danny's house.

Besides my Eighth Air Force dream world, there isn't much aviation at the Kingdom Hall. Several congregants have little airplanes —ones that fly, not wingless in the backyard like our Luscombe. How I wish they'd talk about airplanes in church.

But congregant pilots talk only of the glory of the Good News. If they knew anything about real fellowship, they'd talk about airplanes.

Tonight, I'm enduring another Thursday night meeting. It's another endless hour of Ministry School and one more hour of Service Meeting. Ugh. I sit in my coat and tie, looking good and feeling miserable. Among the congregation, I see the back of a head, an aviation oasis named Sig Wien. Just seeing the back of his head resurrects my imagination from the sludge of religious glory. For a moment, the religious airplane drought ends.

Sig and his brother, Noel, are Alaska aviation legends. They pioneered commercial air routes all over the territory back in the 1930s. Those were the historic days of Alaska flying. Sig and his brothers founded Wien Air Alaska. "Sigwien," as native Alaskans called him, was an important role model for Inupiat boys along the coast from Nome to Barrow. He is for me too. Sigwien is a man who, like my father, "could fix anything." According to his legend, "he flew the skies like a bird."

Having transported many outlying people to the hospital for emergency visits, Sig is a bona fide savior. His airplane witnessed the birth of many babies when the call came too late to make it to the hospitals in Fairbanks or Anchorage. A lot of mamas have named their babies after Sig. There's a whole pack of twenty- and thirty-year-old Alaskans named "Sigwien."

Sitting in the Kingdom Hall looking at his bald head, I admire Sig. He's an aviation paragon like General Savage. But Sig is real. He's right there in front of me. And not only does he fly for an airline —he also owns an airline. I'm amazed the quiet legend attends our congregation. This man conquered arctic skies with his own pluck and ingenuity. This man personifies airborne independence. He is unafraid to tackle alone the skies above the arctic wilderness. Yet Sig Wien agrees to the teachings of some pretty hard-line and dictatorial people. People who tell him how to live. He is a loyal Jehovah's Witness. If Sig tolerates the rigors of this religion, well, maybe I should too. I squirm in my seat and ponder paradox.

Tonight, still and reserved, Sig sits like a statue of a saint in our church. That is to say, he might if we had saints. No idolatry here. One must worship only God, the one true god whom true followers know as Jehovah.

But tonight, I do worship Sig. He doesn't know I'm here. He can't feel my eyes on him. I'm an acorn sitting behind an oak tree. But boy, do I know him. Tonight, amid the endless intonations from the Kingdom Hall's stage, I'm off with Sig in his Hamilton Metalplane. We're somewhere over the frozen Alaskan tundra, droning along in an endless winter night.

Droning. If only I really were with Sig in his droning Hamilton. A lot of unpleasant droning goes on in my life here on the ground. Droning in church, droning in school. Without holidays to punctuate the time, life at home drones on too.

CHAPTER NINE

Despite the illumination of "the Truth," despite the warm embrace of his congregation, despite that he's moving up and is already a Ministerial Servant, my father's frame of mind deteriorates. His mood meshes with the interminable Alaska nights. Before the advent of Dave, he treated those dark times with alcohol. Since Dave arrived, he has treated it with religious zealotry. But now, after several Alaska winters, his mood grows black. No longer flying, he views his job at the University of Alaska as mundane and ho-hum.

One black night, Ed Sullivan is on the TV screen. We'd returned from the evening church service. My father turns to my mother and says, "Let's move back home."

I pause as I play on the living room floor, my toy Viscount paused in mid-flight at the end of my outstretched arm. I quit squeezing the levers that make the motors work, and the propellers wind to a stop. My father is talking about moving back to Virginia.

In only a few months, my parents sell the house they've just built, but not finished, next to the never-finished crazy Englishman's place. Two more children, both daughters, Jenny and Polly Ann, joined the family in Fairbanks and my folks figured we needed a bigger house. Apparently the new house didn't add to happiness, though, and soon after Daddy decided we needed to move.

We pack another Volkswagen, this one a microbus, and now with four children, a German shepherd, and a toy poodle, set off for the East Coast in search of sunshine and a fresh start.

My father rigs the bus's interior with a stretcher laid fore and aft over the back seats. This is the off-duty driver's rest facility. He's not planning to stop on the drive. "We're not camping, and we sure aren't staying in expensive motels." says Daddy. "We're going to drive twenty-four hours a day. All the way from Fairbanks to Virginia."

"Nonstop?" asks Mama.

"No stopping except for gas," says Daddy. "The ride up to Alaska in the Snog took ten days, remember? We'll make it to Nana's house in Maryland in five days this time," he says. "Maybe six if we take a break. We might want to stop off and see a couple of sights. We'll need to stop at grocery stores too, to fill up the ice chest."

He gives Debs and me each a one-hundred-dollar bill. "This is from the house money. I figure you two could use a little spending money for the trip."

"What about Jenny and Polly?" Debs asks.

"The little girls don't get any money," says Daddy. "They're too young. They're only four and two. They don't need cash like you older kids."

Too bad for them, but Debs and I have money with a picture of Benjamin Franklin. In all of my twelve years, I've never seen a hundred dollars before and feel rich beyond dreams.

In May 1967 we're off once again along the ALCAN gravel highway, the trip fueled by gasoline and bologna sandwiches on white bread. The long May days light up the scenery, and I spend my time looking out the second-row window. Mountains, moose, and the occasional bear dot my brain like pictures from my Kodak Brownie. I save actual picture taking for the rare or exotic.

"Don't take too many pictures, Son. Film developing is very expensive," says Daddy.

I'm allowed one twelve-exposure roll for the five-thousand-mile trip.

In a couple of days, we've crossed western Canada and reentered the United States. Waking up from a nap, I see the steepest road I've ever seen. It looks like we will topple right down the mountain into Lewiston, Idaho. While we twist and turn, switchback after switchback, a burning smell develops. "Brakes," says Daddy.

"Will they catch fire? They smell like they're burning." I'm hoping the brakes will hold out for the remaining miles of vertiginous road. The town below still looks like we're viewing it from an airplane at altitude.

"Oh, they'll be okay," says Daddy. Mama looks concerned.

I'm relieved when we get to the river bottom. We've avoided flames, and the bus pitches up, so I no longer feel like I will dump to the floor. The road had been that steep.

We continue down Route 12 along the Clearwater River into Lewiston. This is a nice-looking town. Hamburger joints, taco restaurants, an arcade or two. Too bad we don't stop.

On this trip, the days click in slow motion. We are in dark, we are in light, night falls, and the sun comes up again. Instead of the passage of time, there's only the passage of miles and scenery. I tune in to local radio stations on my new transistor. Each town has a local announcer playing a changing collection of tunes. The radio programs echo the view out the window, evolving with the geography —the local water, whether rivers or lakes, the fortresses of mountains, and the richness or poverty of the local economy. The land lies either parched or wet. The towns are neat and trim or down at the heels. The music is mournful or festive, whiny or hopeful. The announcers are either homespun or sophisticated.

Across Idaho and into Montana. Before long, we're making a slight detour to the straight-line course to the East Coast. We've left US Highway 12 and are heading south. My mother says, "This is the road to Yellowstone National Park!"

Wow. An excursion. Yellowstone is a place I have longed to see. I wonder if we'll stop. We're approaching Mecca, the place of Old Faithful, Grand Canyon of the Yellowstone, Mammoth Hot Springs, and the Fountain Paint Pot. These are places I've worshipped from the pages of *National Geographic*. I don't mind it'll cost us added time on the way east

But then my parents ruin it.

"Hey! See the sign? Jellystone is just up ahead! Ha, ha! Russ, you've made it to Jellystone Park!"

I fume. Yes, Yogi Bear was my favorite cartoon when I was a kid —I'm twelve now— but to besmirch hallowed Yellowstone with a Hanna-Barbera moniker is sacrilege. Religious people like my parents ought to understand this. They ought to know better. But they don't.

Pointing to the park's entry hut, they say, "Hey, there's 'Mr. Ranger, Sir!' Ha, ha! Jellystone! Hold on to your 'pic-a-nic' basket! Ha, ha!"

In a flash, the infidels in the front seat pop my reverence. They should shut the hell up. Could they give me a moment to respect the sanctity of Yellowstone?

No. They keep at it. Now I'm torqued off and sit with folded arms and a sour look on my face.

"Ha, ha! What's wrong, Russie? Looks like you're sucking a lemon!"

How dare they laugh? My parents are having a sock hop in a cathedral. Laughing at sacredness at my expense.

It's just as well we drive straight through Yellowstone, only taking enough time to see Old Faithful spout. Man! I'm spouting too and wish I had my own supply of burning sulfur. The Jellystone talk never stops, and, even if it had, they've ruined my time.

I promise to return one day, without my apostate parents, so I can enjoy the park's glory in blessed silence.

Another day down US Highway 26, and we're in Nebraska. I break my hundred-dollar bill with the purchase of a neato felt cowboy hat at the big western-wear store in Ogallala. Now I support my imagination with a hat just like Sky King's. I can now fly the rest of the way to the East Coast in my imaginary *Songbird*. That's the name of Sky's twin-engine Cessna. On my flying trip east, I'll only stop to check on my imaginary holdings at the Bar Double R Ranch.

My brand hangs over the ranch's log entry gate. A purlin at the top supports hanging back-to-back wrought-iron Rs. RR for Russ Roberts. I've cribbed the general idea from Roy Rogers, but hey . . . we have the same initials.

But wait —the imaginary ranch is in Wyoming. I'll have to fly back to the west to get there. But that's okay. The Cessna 310 is a fast airplane. It'd be great to spend some time at the ranch. Even with the backtracking and the visit, I'll still get to Nana's house in Maryland about the same time as my parents as I travel by air. I love the ranch that I've built in my mind. It's beautiful, lying as it does in the shadow of the Grand Tetons.

Wearing my new hat as we leave Ogallala in the VW bus, I've got my life figured out: I'll have lots of cows. My life will be just like Sky's life, with high-plains crime solving and nonstop adventure. I won't have some bothersome niece hanging around like Sky's Penny, but I will have a Jeep for ground transportation. Lots of cowboys and airplanes too. Who needs girls? Cattle drives don't have girls. The only girls *Rawhide*'s Rowdy Yates deals with are in bars.

When I grow up and have the money, I will be a big kingpin, putting my mark on the next chapter of the airborne west. *"Out of the blue of the western sky comes"* not Sky King, but Russ Roberts.

We bump over a seam in the highway, and I'm bumped back into the bus, making our way over the boring flats of Nebraska. Outside the little rectangular window, I once again fly over the spread of my dreams, reclaiming a fantasy that feels alive.

My imagination is important. My imagination is sharp and clear. My eyes? That's another story. The landscape outside the bus looks blurry to me, not because we're speeding along, but because I can't see.

CHAPTER TEN

In Alaska, I'd assumed I was a bad student. In second grade, Mrs. Brimsmaid worked to help me read. In third grade, Mrs. King put me in a special reading class. Stepping out of the regular class to go to a special class for dumb kids embarrassed me. So did going to the nurse's office for daily milk and cookies. I wasn't malnourished. I was just skinny. Evidence to the contrary, I didn't think I was stupid either.

While the special reading class helped, and I learned a lot, I still had trouble. In fourth grade, math became a problem, and I didn't seek help because Mrs. Morrow hated Jehovah's Witnesses. In fifth grade, I wasn't able to take notes from the blackboard for social studies. *Oh no*, I thought, *the stupidity must be real . . . and it's spreading.*

Then, in sixth grade, Mrs. Cunningham got it. She figured out I couldn't see.

She sent a note home to my parents recommending I see an eye doctor.

"Oh, we can fix that," Daddy said. "It's all that darkness in Alaska and the fluorescent lights the kids are under all the time. It ruins their eyes. Poisons them. I just read an article about it in *Prevention*."

The article in the Rodale's health magazine recommended eye exercises and vitamin A.

"That'll fix you," Daddy said.

Even though vitamin D hadn't straightened my teeth, as per Rodale's prescription, I didn't doubt my father. He could fix everything. He rarely needed outside help to do anything. He'd often take the back off the television to remove every single tube. We'd take them to the RCA tube testing machine at Safeway. He identified the broken tubes and fixed the problem every time.

"No need to call an expensive TV guy," said Daddy. My independent, self-sufficient Daniel Boone father loved helping himself. He hated spending money. And he looked down on people seeking help.

"Nornie can't fix anything," said my father, speaking about his stepfather. "No, Norm doesn't know how anything works. He always hires somebody to come in to make repairs or fix things up. That's just crazy. A man should know how to take care of himself."

I didn't like it when he talked about Nornie that way. Nornie could never be a better or more generous grandfather to us. He worked in a successful job at Kodak and gave my grandmother, Nana, a beautiful new custom house. Hmm. Let's see now —we lived in unfinished dumps with junk everywhere. The man who "can't do anything" lives in a new, clean, beautiful mansion . . .

Regardless, under my father's knowing self-help gaze, I pretended to devote myself to the eye exercises. I said I'd take my vitamin A and exercise.

"That'll work," I said. That's what I said, anyway. I didn't believe vitamin A and exercise would help. Nothing in our life ever improved. So I lip-synched the bad eyesight cure too.

* * *

After arriving in Virginia, in the summer of 1967 my folks buy a farm from the estate of a pair of dead old-lady sisters. It's a run-down place. Seven fixer-upper buildings on a hundred acres of fields and scrub.

"I can turn this into a real showplace," says my dad, knowing he can, using his talents and native ability. He could make it a showplace. "This whole farm only cost ten thousand dollars. And we have money left over from the sale of the Alaska house. We'll buy some materials and whip this place into shape," says Dad.

I feel a wave of hope. Maybe this will be the first time in my twelve years he ever makes our home beautiful, or even presentable.

After we move to the farm, in late August I start a new school, again without being able to see the blackboard. But right after that, something changes. Did my mom speak up? Did she put her foot down? I couldn't imagine her putting her foot down. But my older sister, Debs, has been wearing glasses for as long as I can remember. Why not me? What keeps my father from letting me have glasses? All the talk about self-help eye cures disappears overnight. Somehow, without an argument, Dad allows Mom to take me to the eye doctor.

I sit in a big chair in a darkened room. The office is dark and cool, with wood paneling. Pictures of smiling people wearing glasses decorate the walls. The eye doctor twists and clicks various lenses in front of me.

"Is this better?" Click. "Or is this better?" Twist. "This?" *Click, click.* "Or this?"

In a few minutes, Dr. Marks says, "Well, you have terrible vision! It's no wonder you can't see the blackboard!" Turning to my mother, he says, "It's time we put this boy in glasses."

Two weeks later, the eye doctor calls, and I get my first pair of corrective lenses. They have brown plastic frames that fade to clear at the bottom. Studious.

Leaving the eye doctor's office, I hear snapping at the top of a flagpole. I look up and see the American flag, waving in sharp relief against the blue sky. It shocks me: the loud colors, the distinct edges, the wrinkles in the cloth. The snap I hear coincides with the new sharpness I see in the fabric. Even though I must live under my Jehovah's Witness parents, looking up at that flag now, I'm proud to be an American.

I also see treetops, their skinny brown branches covered with green leaves razored against a bright blue sky. Even from the ground, I see individual leaves, not the glob of earth tones I'd viewed before. Amazing, this new world. Who knew it could look like this? Until now, I'd been living in an impressionist painting. Now it's a crisp world created by Ansel Adams.

I only need my new glasses for distance. I can read books and work up close without them. But, except while sleeping, I keep them on all the time. Being without them is unthinkable. They become as much a part of my body as my nose. With the glasses, I become a permanent Clark Kent. Without glasses, it's like being without pants.

*   *   *

On the farm, we soon have a bunch of sheep, cows, chickens, and two horses. By watching *Rawhide* television reruns, I learn how to handle livestock. I don't like our pigs. They're a mess. I don't like our sheep either. In his book *Lone Cowboy*, Will James calls sheep "sniveling woolies." I call them that too. I'm a horse and cattle guy. A modern cowboy.

On the cheap, my father purchases an Allis-Chalmers farm setup: tractor, plow, side sickle mower, and a 1950s model Roto-Baler, a real Rube Goldberg contraption that clanks, chunks, and rattles at it rolls hay bales like GIs roll cigarettes. The farm-implement kit includes a hay rake manufactured in the nineteenth century and designed to be horse drawn. Seven hundred dollars is the price for the whole shebang, all the equipment needed for our farm.

At twelve, I quickly learn how to work the tractor and drive our two-ton farm truck.

"That Model B tractor was manufactured in 1937 during the Great Depression. The Depression started the year I was born," Dad says with the pride of the downtrodden. "The tractor has an electric starter, but it also has a crank, like a Model T Ford. That's your backup in case it won't start."

About half the time, I use the crank starter, because the six-volt battery doesn't have the punch to spin the engine. Tending to backfire on the compression stroke, the crank often flings me backward. It never breaks my arm. But it comes close, and it sure hurts.

Dad gives me free rein with the farm animals and equipment. Mowing the entire farm with the tractor and sickle is a good job for a twelve-year-old. I have the responsibility for routine maintenance too. Oil and fan-belt changes are on me. Other repairs too.

About once every two weeks, I hit a stone and break one of the mower's sickle bar teeth.

I need wrenches and a ball-peen hammer to remove the blade. I have to be careful, because when the blade is banged loose, there's a real chance it will cut off one of my fingers. It's scary. But once the blade is out, I install a new tooth by hammering in two steel rivets using the ball-peen hammer and a sizable piece of steel as a buck.

Did Charles Dickens write about my childhood? Or was it Sinclair Lewis? Those are both good writers, and, thanks to the special reading classes in Alaska and the glasses that allow me to learn from the blackboard, I'm now reading those authors. I identify with David Copperfield and *The Jungle's* Stanislovas Lukoszaite. Dangerous child labor is normal to me here on the farm. There isn't much coddling. I learn a tremendous amount about machines and their maintenance. I make mistakes, take the licks, get scared, and press on. I'm on intimate terms with the box of Band-Aids and the Ben-Gay ointment.

While working on the farm, bouncing over ruts, and scaring up bugs, my imagination roams. Round and round the dry summer fields I go, cutting grass and baling hay. The grasshoppers I've scared up land on the tractor to ride along with me, as I think I'd rather be in the air. With the airlines a faraway dream, in my imaginings I fly for the military. In my mind, I am somewhere over Europe —the tractor is my B-17, the field ruts the flak that bounces me around. Turning on the fescue, I line up at the initial point, the IP, for another bomb run on the Nazi enemy.

CHAPTER ELEVEN

Dad has to inspect a Beechcraft Musketeer at Charlottesville-Albemarle, an airport forty minutes away through Virginia's backcountry. Since it's a Saturday, I get to come along. I'm up front with Dad in our green-and-white Volkswagen bus, and excitement buzzes in my mind like a low-voltage current.

We pass corn fields and oak forests. An oak tree, standing alone in a farm field, grows tall and wide, a giant compared to the trees I'd grown used to during our seven years in Alaska. There, the white and black spruce and birch trees stood stunted, their roots battling the permafrost. They could not grow tall.

On the ride to Charlottesville, I see horse farms with slumping wooden fences and cow pastures with barbed-wire fences. Rusted-out farm equipment dots the landscape. It sure is nice to see these things now.

I pull the bus window open —it's a warm early June day in 1968— and the chemical odor of the bus mixes with the fresh woods, the fields, and cattle smells of the countryside. We left Alaska a year ago but I still haven't acclimated to Virginia's high humidity.

"What's wrong with the airplane at the airport, Dad?" I ask.

"Nothing's wrong. It's just an annual inspection. We got

behind in the shop last week, and they asked me to come in and get it done today," he says.

Living on the farm, he's looked for work. But he only found a few construction jobs: putting doors in new buildings and stuff like that. So, after the familiar arguments with my mother about money, this year he's fallen back on his airplane mechanic experience. He got a job with Marty Macy, the owner of Horizon Aviation in Charlottesville.

Marty, descended from the founder of Macy's department store, is the richest person we know. In our family, there's no end to money with Marty.

"For a rich man, he's really down to earth," says my father. Dad says, "Marty actually talks to me when he comes through the hangar." This amazes my parents.

Mom mentions Marty often, always remarking, "He seems to be so nice," even though she's never met him.

I don't care so much about Marty. I care about the airplanes in his hangar. I haven't been around airplanes since I was eight. For the last five years, I've been living my pilot life through the few flying magazines and books that turn up. I've flown only in my imagination. Today, we won't be flying, but at least I will experience real airplanes: smell them, feel them, touch them.

We're going to an airport. My dream of becoming an airline pilot, unfertilized since those long cold years in Alaska, is sprouting again today.

Dad isn't a licensed airplane mechanic, even though he's capable through years of experience and natural talent.

He's competent, but not qualified. He must do inspections under supervision. Even at Capital Airlines, he was only a line mechanic, always working under a licensed A&P mechanic or authorized inspector. He never got his mechanic's license, because he wanted to fly. "I don't want to turn screws on the ground," he said.

But today, he is my hero. He's taking me to see a real airplane again. He's stoking my dreams, even if he doesn't know it. During the drive to Marty's hangar, I bombard Dad with more questions, and he answers every one.

"Will the lead mechanic be there?" I ask.

"No. He'll be in on Monday to do the checks and sign the logbooks," says Dad.

As we pull into the airport, I sit up straight, and my eyes zero in on the metal hangar with "Horizon Aviation" in blue letters on a white field. A red arrow shoots through the word "Horizon." It's the most modern, exciting sign I've ever seen.

I jump out of the bus, and Dad shows me how to open the hangar doors. "Pull the pins out of the concrete, and then push the doors out to each side. Careful to keep your fingers clear," he says. "Get your fingers between those doors and they'll cut 'em right off."

The doors are dangerous, like the sickle blade on the tractor. Dad pushes one big door, and I push the other. Placing one hand above the other to avoid crushing my fingers as the doors overlap, I lean my thirteen-year-old weight into it. The door rumbles and clatters like a freight car along the gritty metal runner and clangs when it hits the stop.

The morning sun shines through dusty windows on either side of the hangar, covering the two airplanes inside with a soft yellow light. Warmth seeps through my body. All that's missing is an angelic choir. This is real religion. The Kingdom Hall? That's phony compared to this.

A blue-and-silver Cessna 172 sits in the back corner. I know Cessnas well —they were everywhere in Alaska— but the Beechcraft Musketeer I've seen only in magazines. I've never laid eyes on one in real life. Like the Cessna, it's a four-seater. White with a maroon stripe and tail number, the Musketeer stands front and center, its nose facing out. To my eyes, it's gorgeous. I'm like a man on a desert island with the only woman in a thousand miles. The past few years I've been in an airplane drought. Today, any airplane would be beautiful.

I walk over to the Musketeer and run my hand along the leading edge of the wing. The feel of the smooth curve of the aluminum and the bumpy rivets where the metal sheets overlap works from my fingers to my heart, and right into my permanent memory. Walking around the wing tip, I run my fingers over the red navigation light screwed to the end and touch the inward swoop of the wing tip. At the back of the wing, I push down on the aileron, feeling the bends of the little strengthening ridges in the aluminum.

The wing feels light yet strong. It's a curious thing about airplanes. They hold up under extreme forces in the air. They're almost impossible to break in flight. But if you drop a hammer on one, or you push on something the wrong way or too hard, you'll damage the airplane. I remember sitting on the Luscombe's tail out in the Thules.

I step back and take another look at the whole airplane, trying to burn it into my memory, letting my eyes reinforce what my
hands have already started.

Up at the nose, Dad has laid out his wrenches and screw-
drivers and is taking the cowling off the engine. He looks at me.
"Go on, crawl up in there."

In three steps, I'm at the wing, where a surface of black anti-
skid tape leads to the airplane door. The door is ajar. I put my
left foot up on the step and grab the brushed aluminum handle.
Pulling myself up onto the wing, I'm careful to keep my feet on
the black anti-skid. I don't want to mark the white paint with my
shoes. Pushing the door open with my right foot, I step into the
pilot's seat.

The ivory-colored yoke, the steering wheel, is right in front
of me. Beyond that is the vast array of instruments. It feels so
exciting, so exotic. So overwhelming too. But somehow it feels
just right. Comfortable. This is my place, my home. This is me
in context.

The instrument panel extends high across the front of the
cockpit. Above it, I see only treetops and sky out through the
hangar door. One propeller blade slices through my view. I hear
Dad working on the cowling, popping open the metal fasteners.
I hold the smooth, curved edges of the yoke and turn it left and
right. I see the aileron moving on the left wing: up as I turn left,
down as I turn right.

When I examine the instruments, I recognize several from
my books and magazines. The needle sits at zero on the tachom-
eter. The artificial horizon is dead in front of me. The altimeter

shows a thousand feet. There must be a million switches, dials, and circuit breakers.

I settle back and reach down to feel the cool, smooth vinyl on the side of my seat. Looking up at the ceiling covered in the same vinyl, I notice cracks and chips in some plastic trim. They're not defects to me; everything about this airplane is perfect. The cracks and chips show this airplane has flown.

In my mind, I take the Musketeer onto the ramp and taxi out. I line up on the runway and place my right hand on the throttle. I imagine pushing that throttle forward and taking off. Up in the air, I see the clouds against the blue sky. I sit tall for the best view.

Each time I touch an instrument or inhale the smell of the old vinyl, my body fills with strength. Being in contact with this airplane is building my muscle, strengthening me, and lifting me up with its power.

Nudging the yoke, I fly back into the traffic pattern. I line up on the runway and bring the Musketeer in for a landing, nice and easy. Parked back in the hangar, I come back to reality. With one last deep inhale of airplane smell, I gaze around the cockpit. Then I step out of the Musketeer to check on my dad.

He's squatting under the nose. He reaches up under the engine, and liquid pours out in a thick, unctuous, black stream. "I'm changing the oil," he explains.

I can smell the used oil, roasted and nutty.

"And after I've changed the oil filter, we'll have to address the plugs," he says.

While the oil drains, he shows me the spark plugs, one on the top and bottom of each cylinder. He points out the fins around the cylinders. "That's part of the cooling system —that's how the cylinders keep from getting too hot."

Walking around to the front of the airplane, I grab hold of the propeller. I run my hand over the sculpted metal. "Watch out," Dad says. "The propeller picks up little pieces of gravel that chip the leading edge. You can't see the nicks, but they can give you a good slice. It feels like a paper cut."

I wander over to the Cessna. Unlike the Musketeer, it's a high-wing airplane. I don't have permission to get in, so I peek through the window to see the instruments. "What's wrong with this airplane?" I call over to Dad.

"Nothing's wrong with it. A lawyer owns that airplane. He just keeps it in here."

Behind the Cessna on the back wall are metal counters and cabinets, a drill press, a vat of parts cleaner called Varsol, and a small lathe. Five Snap-On calendars hang on the wall, displaying girls wearing bikinis and tool belts. Another vat holds carburetor cleaner, something I know well from working on the farm. The chemical odors mingle with the metallic smell of the counters. The industrial smells of tools, airplane tires, and fuel mingle to create a blissful aroma.

"Why don't you go get a drink?" Dad says. "The machine's around the outside."

I get my soda —another treat today. I get about one soft drink a year on average. Standing beside the drink machine, I take in the scene outside the hangar. Small airplanes, mostly Cessnas, taxi out and take off. One pilot stays in the traffic pattern, practicing touch-and-go landings. He finishes, taxis in. Now the sky is clear of traffic.

Walking back inside the hangar, to check on Dad's progress, I hear a much larger airplane come in for landing. Thrust reversers scream as it thunders down the runway. My heart races. I run out and around the back side of the hangar in time to see a Piedmont Airlines 737 turn off the runway.

It pulls up to a small terminal about a hundred yards from me. I watch through a chain-link fence as the airstair floats down from the forward door. The passengers descend and walk across the ramp to the terminal. It's unreal, like a movie. The last time I'd been this close to an airliner was in Alaska.

In 1962, my grandmother, on her way back to DC after visiting us in Alaska, had boarded a Boeing 707, a Pan American Clipper, at Fairbanks International. After we got hugs and kisses from Nana, she passed through an open gate. We stood beside that fence and watched her climb the stairs and disappear into the jet.

When the Boeing started up, Mama yelled, "Wave at Nana!"

"How will we know it's her?" yelled Debbie.

"Watch for her gloves," Mama shouted. "She's wearing white gloves. Watch for her gloves!"

As the 707 began its taxi out, a dozen white gloves waved from every other passenger window.

Today in Charlottesville, even parked at the gate, this smallest of Boeing jetliners captivates me. Romance seems to radiate from the jet. I see constant activity: first the baggage offloading, then the fuel truck. After that, the first officer comes out for a pre-flight inspection. He wears his black hat with its shiny brim, black shoes and pants, and a white shirt with three stripes on the shoulder. Although it's daytime, he carries a flashlight to shine up into the wheel wells.

That's my future, I say to myself. I won't fly for a little outfit like Piedmont, but something first rate like Pan American or TWA. I feel it right down into my toes: Flying for the airlines is where I belong.

New passengers come out and climb aboard, and then the stairs retract into the airplane. The guy on the ground gives the captain a thumbs-up and twirls his right hand over his head, and the right engine turns. Soon it screams. The left engine turns. Now two banshees shriek. The air shimmers behind the engines' exhaust. Despite the din, I don't cover my ears. The sound fills my body with a life-affirming vibration.

The flaps come down, and the ailerons move. The elevator, the horizontal control surface, on the tail goes up and down. The rudder goes right and left. The airplane taxis away toward the end of the runway and turns into position. I hear the engines spool up. After a beat, the 737 accelerates down the runway. An enormous cloud of black smoke shoots out from each of the two underwing engines. Faster and faster the jet goes. Just as the Boeing passes me beside the hangar, the nose lifts, the wings flex up, and the 737 lifts from the ground. I wrap my fingers around the chain-link fence and watch the airplane split the air. The noise cracks like thunder on rock. The sound rattles the fence and rumbles my body, echoing in my chest.

Oh my god, this is the best. The power of it. Energy rushes

through me and shoots back out to the airplane, a feedback loop that turns me into a stronger, happier version of myself.

I walk back around to the front of the hangar, my heart still racing.

"What did you think of that?" Dad asks.

"Pretty neat," I say, downbeat. I've read enough to know pilots don't get excited.

"Make a lot of noise, don't they?"

"Yeah, pretty noisy."

My mind bursts with possibilities. I want to be home, alone, to let the sights and smells from today fill my imaginary world. I want to fly the tractor to Pago Pago and Nagoya. I want to be a captain with four stripes on my shoulders, getting the thumbs-up from the ground crew and taking my airplane to the runway. I want the controls to respond to my touch. I want to pull back and lift the machine into the sky with a deafening roar.

I reach up to adjust my glasses, and I'm back on earth. My euphoria slowly leaves like a leaking balloon. I'm just a kid standing in a hangar in Virginia. But even so, there's something that feels real. Unquenchable.

Buttoning up the Musketeer's cowling, Dad says, "Well, that's it. We're ready to go." We rattle and bang the hangar doors shut and climb back into the Volkswagen bus.

I have different and better questions to ask on the way home. I've been in a Musketeer now. I've been close to a working Boeing. "What about the Beechcraft, Dad? Is it better than the Cessna? Is a high-wing better than a low-wing? How come most airliners, other than the F-27, have low wings?"

Dad talks about the six-cylinder Continental engine on the Cessna in the hangar and the advantages of a high-wing airplane in the bush. He doesn't ask me to stop talking, and something in his voice makes me think he likes answering my questions. I remember that Dad loved airplanes too. Maybe he still does. It's the one thing in life we've shared.

CHAPTER TWELVE

I'm wearing my glasses as I do math homework at the kitchen table. It's dark outside, and the harsh ceiling light makes the kitchen look even dingier. The worn vinyl floor is curling up at the corners, and the walls are bare —there's not even one cabinet. My father has them planned out, though. He's made a sketch.

It's funny. He builds beautiful things for other people, but never gets around to building nice things for us.

My grades have improved, and not only thanks to better vision. School is not much of a challenge here in Virginia. It's much easier than the schools in Alaska, where we'd done term papers in the sixth grade. Seventh grade in Virginia is like fifth grade in Alaska. But the glasses and the country school give me a boost. I feel good now that school is just another task rather than an impossible mountain to climb.

Mom, in a white dress covered with big autumn leaves, cooks hamburger patties at the stove and fixes a simmering pot of gravy to go with them. My mouth waters. I love hamburger steak night.

The porch door creaks and slams as Dad walks into the kitchen. From the fresh wood smell, I can tell he's in from the woodworking shop he set up in the old tenant building on the farm. It's a wonderful shop with top-of-the-line equipment. With his professional setup, it should be easy for him to make cabinets for our kitchen.

He pours a cup of coffee, and I'm relieved he hasn't gotten himself a beer. He's been drinking a lot since we moved back from Alaska. But my relief at his sobriety tonight is likely unfounded, since he probably had a good snort from the vodka bottle under the truck seat before he came in. Now, in the kitchen, he drinks coffee as a smokescreen. He looks around the room, pausing to stare at our dishes and cups stacked on the counter. The place needs cabinets. But then I feel his eyes on me.

I keep my head down, focusing on a math problem. "I'm really sorry you got those glasses," Dad says, casually, like he's letting me know I have ketchup on my shirt.

His words hang in the air. I freeze and tighten the grip on my pencil. Mom stops cranking the can opener. He has been drinking. We can both tell. As the silence continues, I feel pressure in my stomach that sends my shoulders higher, and I feel my head recede, like a turtle.

I know the glasses are my fault. I'm too lazy to do the eye exercises the way I should. And maybe I should take more vitamin A.

I'm sorry I have glasses too, I answer in my head. *I'm the one who has to wear them.* At least now I can see. But I still don't look up to see him.

Finally Dad says, "You know, don't you, that you'll never get hired by the airlines with glasses?"

Now I do look up, meeting his eyes.

"They don't hire people with less than 20/20 vision," he says in a matter-of-fact way. His dispassionate words knife my gut.

Can this be true? I want him to correct himself, to offer me another opinion. In shock, I hold his gaze. He must see the hurt in my face, because his eyebrows raise and his jaw relaxes, almost like he's surprised I didn't know.

My body disappears. I float in the air with this news. My dream is gone. Murdered. This information comes from Dad, the ultimate authority on flying, so it must be true. But it can't be true. Not for me. Like when he fixes the broken TV tubes, he has to have a solution for this problem too, a way around the rules or a way to fix my eyes for real.

When I find my breath, I ask, "Unless I do what? What can I do?"

Dad looks away. My mom has resumed her cooking, scraping the corn niblets from the can into a pot, her back to Dad and me. I keep my eyes on him, all my hopes directed at his plaid flannel shirt and khaki pants, his leather shoes coated with wood dust.

He sighs and tilts his head at me. "Well, you know, you don't have to worry about that. Armageddon is just around the corner. All bodies will be made whole, and you'll be able to see."

Dad looks off at some faraway picture in his mind. His voice softens, and he talks about the lambs and the lions in the field of a new garden. It's weird that in Jehovah's Witness literature, nobody ever has a house. My father is not talking to me anymore. He's got a funny look on his face. He might as well be behind the podium at the Kingdom Hall.

I turn the page of my homework. My mind races. This is

an emergency. What am I going to do? More exercises? More vitamin A? Oh god, maybe the fluorescent lights in Alaska did poison me. Is there a cure for that? Was I stupid for not taking the vitamins and not doing the exercises? Or was I stupid for thinking I could be an airline pilot?

In my head, I hear Dad's old refrain: "You are too smart to learn. You are arrogant. You're not above the rest of us. With your bumptious attitude, you're headed for a fall." I never really believed him. But now? Now I know it's true. I'm no better off than he is, because now neither one of us will be airline pilots.

Did Dad know all along that those eye exercises and vitamins wouldn't work? Were glasses a kind of surrender? Had he known from the beginning that my vision problem would keep me from flying the line? Is this the fall he's predicted?

After his sermon, Dad puts his cup in the sink and goes out onto the porch. The closing door sends a whoosh of cold, dry air through the kitchen. Mom doesn't turn around or talk to me.

Waiting for Armageddon doesn't help. I don't care about the lamb lying down with the lion if I can't fly a jet. Armageddon or not, my world ends if I can't fly for the airlines.

Slowly, I refocus on my math book. I won't solve this flying problem today, but I will solve it. Even though I've never been at the controls of an airplane in flight, I've always been a pilot —an airline pilot. It's who I am. If Dad doesn't have the answer, I'll find one for myself. I reach up, adjust my glasses, and get back to the work in front of me.

*   *   *

In my bedroom tonight, I read *Fate Is the Hunter* for about the fifth time. Ernest K. Gann wrote that destiny —he called it fortune— is an active force. He wondered why he succeeded as a pilot, flew the world, and survived, while other pilots —pilots he knew were better than him— failed and even died.

I wonder at my fate: why I'd gotten rotten eyes, why I'd been born on the cusp of Armageddon, why my Worldly desire to fly might end when the Witnesses survived destruction to live like agrarian Luddites among the vegetarian lions and credulous lambs.

The airlines, the airlines, the airlines.

There must be a way.

PART TWO

CHAPTER THIRTEEN

I turned fourteen in December. The next month, in January 1969, my parents take over operation of the Orange County Airport. Marty Macy suggested they might want to operate his satellite facility there as their own. He's downsizing Horizon Aviation. The millionaire is trying to make his outfit profitable.

The airport is thirty miles from the farm. My folks put our hundred acres up for sale right away. I guess we're finished being farmers. I leave *Rawhide* reruns and my cattle career behind. Dad never finished the kitchen cabinets.

I work hard around the airport every minute I'm not in school: washing airplanes when it's warm enough, cleaning hangars, mowing tall weeds left over from last summer. Working at the airport, I learn the meaning of the expression "a labor of love."

In exchange for my free labor, Dad said he will give me flying lessons, and today is payday. In a few hours, I'll be airborne.

*   *   *

I sit in the cockpit of a Piper Cherokee 140, holding the smooth, curved yoke, the plastic "steering wheel." I can see where somebody's rings have scratched it. I feel good. It's the same sensation I had in Charlottesville sitting in the Musketeer last year. But today is different, and I can feel an unusual pounding in my heart, a little lump in my throat, an extra rush. Today, I will fly. Despite the frigid January air, I feel warm.

My imaginary flights my entire life have been leading to this. I will fly an airplane today. It feels natural. I've been a pilot my whole life. I've been a pilot only temporarily on the ground. But the reality of my first lesson electrifies me and frightens me a bit too. What if I screw it up? What if I just can't cut it? What if I'm a two-dimensional creature unable to operate in three? What will that say about me and, thanks to my crummy eyes, my unrealistic dream of becoming an airline pilot? Or becoming any kind of pilot?

It's a Saturday, and Dad and I agree that we'll go up after lunch. I'm trying to not be eager. No, I can't show that. It wouldn't be cool. But with hours to go before flying, I do the preflight check. I inspect the outside of the Cherokee, a low-wing four-seater, white with blue trim. I walk all the way around the airplane, drain some fuel to check for water in the tanks, and check the oil quantity. Even the tire pressure gets checked.

I've always been more of a Cessna guy. I admire the look of high wings and Cessna's bush plane reputation. But the Cherokee, which we lease from its owner for rental and lessons, looks perfect to me today. What is the best airplane? The one you have. In this one, I will be airborne. Today. And airliners have low wings, don't they? Some people call Cherokees' low, rectangular wings "Hershey Bar wings." Despite the pejorative, for me, the airplane is a charmer in aluminum. My first kiss. My first date. But I know the pugnacious airplane will never win a beauty contest.

I come back several more times during the morning for additional pre-flight checks. I circle the airplane, looking for missing pieces and parts. On the second time around, I guess I'm just looking because I want to spend time with my new love. I check the propeller and look again at the tires. Then I climb into the cockpit. Anticipation excites me, but I keep it under wraps. I've been around enough pilots to know to keep it cool and calm.

After lunch, I head back to the airplane, my hands in the pockets of my jacket. I circle the Cherokee one last time, running my hand over the cold metal. Oxidation in the paint causes a bit of chalkiness. A slight resistance meets my stroking palm. The airplane needs a wax job. I'll do it in spring. When it gets warmer.

Dad walks over carrying a clipboard, wearing his khaki pants and a heavy jacket lined with red plaid flannel. "Ready?" he asks.

I nod and step my 120 pounds up onto the wing. *Don't screw up*, I tell my tall, skinny self as I come through the right-hand door and climb over to the pilot's seat on the left.

Settling onto the fabric and Naugahyde-covered seat again, I grab a handle between my legs, pull it up, and slide the seat forward until my feet touch the rudder pedals and there's a slight bend in my knees. For years, my parents told me, "You'll get to fly when you can reach the rudder pedals." I remember visiting the cockpit of the Northwest Stratocruiser and how big it looked, the rudder pedals way down what seemed a dark tunnel, way beyond my feet. Today, I reach the Cherokee's pedals with ease. I let go of the handle. With a snap, the seat latches in place.

Dad sits down and pulls the airplane's only door closed. He checks the primary lock at his right elbow and reaches up to snap the safety latch at the top of the door. We're locked in now. This is it. I can't believe it's happening. I don't drink coffee, but there's a caffeine-like buzz running through my nerves as Dad launches into our pre-start checklist.

"Exterior pre-flight?" he reads. It's a command. He only questions that I am alert and in the loop.

"Complete," I reply.

"Master switch on," he says.

I flick on the master switch, and needles on my instruments come alive like somebody yelled "ten-hut!" The electric turn-and-bank indicator's gyro spins and hums.

"On."

Next, we prime the engine. Because of the frigid weather, Dad pauses reading the checklist. "Give it fifteen strokes of primer," he says.

I do, and hear the fuel swishing through the pump each time I push the knob. A little gurgling *whoosh* as I pull it out. A *wheesh* sound and pressure as I push it in. Fifteen pumps.

Then he says, "Magnetos?"

"On both."

Dad tells me to open the small window on my left. "Yell 'clear' to warn people to get out of the way of our propeller when we start up."

"Clear!" I yell through my four-by-five-inch window opening and, in a moment, push the starter button with my left thumb. With a clang, the starter engages the ring gear flywheel at the front of the engine, and the propeller turns. One blade passes the windshield. Two blades. Three. After I see about five blades pass in front of me, two spark plugs ignite the fuel, and two cylinders fire off, then gasp. The engine almost stops. But then, *blap, blap, blap,* the engine catches. Two cylinders fire; the engine bucks a bit as the other two misfire. After a moment of indecision, the one-hundred-fifty horsepower engine smooths to a four-cylinder rumble.

The airplane vibrates like a horse shivering, and my body syncs to it. My senses flush with the noise of the engine, the array of instruments in front of me, and my father's loud voice giving instructions over the lovely, lovely loud sound. My heart races and my body tingles.

I've spent years studying airplanes in magazines and books. Since we took over the airport, I've been in daily contact with them. But at this moment, I know I am a total rookie. *Don't . . . screw . . . this . . . up,* I say to myself again.

"Oil pressure?" Dad reads the after-start checklist.

I respond to each item, and I test the radio and check to see the oil temperature is rising. Now, with the after-start checklist complete, it's time to taxi out. At the top of the rudder pedals are the airplane's only brake pedals. My father's side has no toe brakes. Keeping my toes pressed on to the brakes, I click off a button that releases the black parking-brake handle. That handle is under the middle of the instrument panel. If he needs them, if I screw up, my father can apply both brakes at the same time by pulling on that handle.

I ease my toes from the pedals and let the propeller's thrust pull the airplane forward, pushing a bit on my brake pedals to test them and to try out my foot-pedal steering. I'm impressed by the direct connection between my foot movement and the immediate response of the airplane. The rudder pedals at my feet connect directly to the nose wheel, so any pressure on either pedal turns the airplane.

We taxi out past the fuel pit, past the bristly winter grass on the edges of the pavement. We park just short of the runway, turning the nose of the Cherokee into the wind. But the wind-sock on the far side of the runway is almost limp. Calm winds. Turning into the wind today is pro forma.

With the throttle a pinch forward of the aft stop, the engine idles at a thousand revolutions per minute. I follow the checklist, let the oil temperature come up a tad more, and push the throttle up to eighteen hundred rpm to check the magnetos: Two clicks left on the ignition key to check the right-hand magneto. Two clicks right to go back to both mags. Then one click left to check the left-side magneto. Then back to both. They check good.

To test the carburetor heat, Dad tells me to pull the carb heat knob out and look for a slight decrease in the rpm. "If the carburetor has ice, the engine will run rough as the heat melts it to water, and, with the engine bucking as is swallows the water, the rpm will rise," he says.

I pull the knob. "Looks good. Right?" he asks. "About a fifty rpm drop —and smooth. No ice. Getting ice in one of these Lycoming engines is rare. But you have to look for it anyway."

We check the oil pressure —again. We also check the oil temperature and fuel gauges and make sure the fuel tanks are in balance. I double-check the fuel tank selector on the pilot's side wall, ensuring the selector is in the detent notch for the left tank, the default selection if both tanks are equally full. If they weren't, we'd select the fullest tank.

Dad reaches up and adjusts the trim tab to the takeoff position with a little crank handle mounted on the ceiling between us.

Using a big lever between the seats that looks like a Volkswagen's parking brake, I test the flaps in all positions —*click, click, click*— and then return the lever to the first position beyond up with one final click. Now they're set, ten degrees of flap for takeoff.

Now it's time to talk to UNICOM. I already know what to say over the radio. I've been running the transceiver inside the airport for the last month and have learned the lingo by listening to pilots come and go.

Dad gives me the go-ahead. I pick up the radio microphone. "Orange County Traffic, Cherokee nine-five-nine-zero Whiskey, taxing to runway two-five for takeoff." Nobody replies, because the normal UNICOM operator —me— is in the airplane. Electricity crackles through me like static on the radio, animating the realness.

We release the parking brake and the little tires rumble on the pavement as we taxi east to the end of the runway.

"Always line up to the runway in the opposite direction of the traffic pattern. Then look for traffic as you turn," says Dad, pointing to the way he wants me to go.

I make a right turn, looking for any traffic in the pattern.

"See? Turning right in a left-hand traffic pattern leaves no blind spots. You saw the whole sky in the pattern. Now line up. Make sure you put your nose on the centerline," Dad yells over the engine as we get into position on the runway. "Not *left* of the line. Not *right* of the line. *On* the line!"

I see the big, white number "25" and the half-mile-long white stripe of the centerline in front of me. "Wrap your right hand around the throttle," Dad yells, "but I'll be right behind you, and I'll actually push up the throttle. I'll show you the proper rate."

I already know not to push the throttle in too fast. A placard on the instrument panel says, "Do Not Open the Throttle Rapidly. Two Seconds Minimum." I've spent hours memorizing that panel.

"At sixty miles per hour, I'll start a little back pressure on the yoke, and you'll follow through with me. Keep your hand on the yoke. Once airborne, we'll climb at eighty-five miles per hour. Okay, let's go," he says, loud over the engine noise.

I lift my feet off the brakes and place my hand on the black, round throttle knob at the bottom center of the instrument panel. Dad puts his hand on top of mine and applies pressure. I push a little too, and we take the throttle all the way up, as far as it will go. All the way to the firewall.

CHAPTER FOURTEEN

The airplane makes a big racket as we speed up. The wheels rumble on the pavement and send vibrations through the seat and into me. I feel those rumbles more than hear them. The engine noise is loud. A high-frequency whine comes from the wheel bearings. Dad pushes the rudder pedals back and forth in quick movements —*left, right, left, left, right*— as the light breeze and engine torque try to move us from the centerline. I can feel my set of rudder pedals move under my feet. His small adjustments are natural. I'm sure he doesn't even realize he's making them.

"Okay, here's fifty," he yells. "And, as sixty comes up, I'm applying a little back pressure on the yoke. Look inside to check your speed. Look outside to stay lined up.

"Here's sixty."

Our nose lifts off the ground.

"Okay, airborne."

The wheels quit rumbling, and there's a fluidness now to our motion. The airplane feels like it's floating on a soft, soft pillow. But it feels to me like it wants to fall off that pillow. An image of a guy spinning plates on *The Ed Sullivan Show* flashes in my mind.

"Now we're going to accelerate to eighty-five as we climb out. Stay on the controls with me," Dad yells.

Out of my forward window, the white stripe on the runway

shrinks and then disappears below and behind. It's clear up here, no haze. I see fields unfolding for miles in front of us as we climb. With each second, I see further. The Blue Ridge Mountains stand brown and gray in the wintry distance. But yes, I see a blue tint too.

Dad brings my attention back to the cockpit. "Okay, we're at five hundred feet. I want you to bring the flaps up. As you push the button to release them, *gently* lower the flap handle down all the way to the bottom. *Gently.*"

With great care, I push the silver button with my right thumb. With slight bicep pressure, I keep the airflow from slamming the flaps up and the handle down. With my remaining four fingers, I lower the handle gently to the floor.

Dad turns us left to take us out of the traffic pattern, turning forty-five degrees off the runway heading. "We'll climb up to two thousand feet AGL and do our practicing there."

"AGL?" I ask.

"Above ground level. That'll be twenty-five hundred feet here on the altimeter." He taps the instrument's glass face.

Up at two thousand feet above the ground, we're no longer climbing. The airspeed needle jiggles a bit, but I see we're going over a hundred miles per hour. On the climb, Dad's been reaching up to the ceiling to reset the trim tab every so often.

"See? I've lowered the nose," he says.

I hadn't noticed.

"If you don't set the trim properly, the airplane has a tendency to climb as we accelerate," he shouts. "As you increase in speed, you need to trim forward to keep the nose down . . . to keep it from rising. But don't fly the airplane with the trim. Set the nose where you want it, and trim the pressure off the yoke."

Huh?

My attention wanders to the unfamiliar world around me. I've entered an extra dimension. The airplane is up in the air, but I've entered a vortex. I'm like Dave, flying through that phantasmagoria in *2001: A Space Odyssey*. My mind swirls in this amazing universe. Everything flashes in front of me. But there is no time for amazement.

"Okay, now notice your wing tips," says Dad.

I jerk back into aerial mechanics and look out on each side.

"You see how the tips are equidistant from the horizon? The same distance between tip and horizon on both sides? Okay. Now look forward. See where the nose is right now?"

I nod.

"Okay. Right there, you see how straight-and-level flight looks at this power setting —I want you to maintain that. I'm taking my hands and feet off the controls."

I glance over and see his hands in his lap.

I put both hands on the wheel. Sitting taller, I regrip my fingers on the smooth plastic grooves of the yoke.

"No death grip," he says. "One hand only. Two fingers. Thumb and forefinger on the wheel." He shows his left forefinger and thumb and squeezes them together.

I do the same on the yoke.

"That's it. That's all it takes. No need to manhandle. Handle it like you would a—" He stops there. I'm only fourteen. "Hold it easy. Gently now."

The yoke is alive, like an animal. It feels good to the touch, but I'm unsure how it will respond. Will it purr, or will it bite? I'm nervous and ready for it to bite and leap out of grasp.

I see the round gold logo in the center of the yoke. Letters spell "Piper" over an arrow-shaped check mark. Below, "Cherokee" shows in red.

"Look up! Check your wing tips. Now look at the nose on the horizon. See? You're descending a bit. Raise your nose. Just a bit."

I pull the yoke back, feeling slight vibrations coming through the plastic into my arm and into my body.

"See? You're climbing back up to twenty-five hundred. Good. Remember. You tend to fly where you look. You looked down, and you started down."

We fly in a mixture of engine vibration and uncongealed random air motions. A mechanical, hard tone translates through metal skin and cables while the air contributes a softness. I've never before felt this. This is a machine in thin air.

"Notice how your left wing is down a little bit there —a little more distance now between the horizon and the wing on the left side? See that? That means you're not level anymore, so what are you going to do?"

"I'll turn right," I say.

"What?"

"I'll turn right!" I yell. We don't wear headsets, and there's no intercom in the airplane. I turn the yoke slightly to the right. Tied together with mine, the yoke in front of him —his "steering wheel"— moves too. I don't want to change the airplane's direction. Just its attitude relative to the horizon. But my motion is the same one as turning, and the right wing comes down.

"Don't forget the rudder," he says. "Every time that wheel moves, I want to feel the rudder —the rudder pedals— move."

I press on the right rudder pedal.

"Yes, that's the way. But do it when you're turning the yoke. Do it again." He bumps the yoke to the right. "Okay, make it level again."

I push the left rudder pedal and turn the wheel to the left.

"Okay now. See?" says my father. "The nose wants to come up as you roll out of a turn. Apply a little forward pressure as you roll out."

I push on the yoke, and the nose of the airplane returns to its original position on the horizon. With slight adjustments, I've leveled the Cherokee. There's momentary mastery, a shot of power, a punch of adrenaline, and a flash of wonder.

I learned to drive on the farm when I was twelve. So far I've driven tractors, trucks, and cars around the farm and the airport. But this airplane? It's a whole new thing, a marvel. My body is fluid, and strength builds, and it feels as if the airplane and I grow together. Though unsure, challenged, and overwhelmed, I sense something more. Somewhere amid the nervousness, I know I am where I belong. If a person wants to know who I am, he will look for me here.

"Now let's do a left turn," Dad shouts. "Lower the left wing. The rudder trims the wing, remember? So every time that yoke moves, I want to feel the rudder move too."

I nod.

I guide the yoke with my hands and press the rudder with my foot.

When I get to what he thinks is the proper angle of bank, Dad says, "Now neutralize the controls and turn the yoke back to the middle position —the neutral position. That'll stop your roll."

I do as he says.

"The airplane will want to lose altitude anytime you're turning. So what do you do? You bring the nose up a little to keep from descending. Once established in the turn, you can trim a little." He points to the silver trim handle in the ceiling.

I reach up and crank.

"Whoa!" I say as the nose jumps down and my weight lessens in the seat.

"Wrong direction! Crank the other way. And put the nose where you want it. Then trim off the pressure. Don't let the trim fly the airplane —and don't let the airplane fly you!"

I try to do as he says, even though I don't understand.

"Okay, that's good," he yells. "Now you've got to climb a little to regain that altitude you lost."

I can't believe all the things I have to remember. Man, this is complicated. It feels like patting my head and rubbing my stomach while riding a pogo stick.

"Look at the altimeter. You're losing altitude. Pick your nose back up."

My nose is the airplane's nose. I pull back on the yoke, and there's an immediate response from the Cherokee.

I take my eyes off the horizon for a second to look at the

winter green hills against a blue sky. Sure, I've seen all this from the air before. As a passenger. Now it's different.

There's something about holding the controls, seeing the world outside change as I move the yoke, that makes this different. Here in the air, with my hands and feet on the controls, even the familiar landscape around my home is new, exciting, fresh, and unreal. This is an unknown country. Another planet. An alternative universe.

Dad keeps shouting directions and instructions. There's always something to adjust or maintain. I need to pay attention. Having Dad next to me is good. He's the best pilot in the world. He's flown in the Alaska bush, and now he's my teacher. This is what dads are for.

After I practice slowing down and speeding up —to eighty miles per hour and back to a hundred— he says, "Let's head back home. Do you see the airport down there?"

"No," I yell.

"There," he points. "Just to the right of town. See the town? Follow Route 20 out to the right."

I see the road and, after too long, spot the runway. Dad explains the landing procedure —I will work the flaps and keep my hands on the controls with him.

"I want you to set the power once we get into the pattern and as we land. But don't worry —I'll be right there with you."

On the downwind leg, on his direction, I set eighteen hundred rpm and reach down to pull the flap handle up to the first notch. *Click.* The handle grabs and locks. The airplane balloons up with the added lift.

"Don't worry. We'll work on that next time," says Dad. "Now we'll start a left turn to the base leg. Give me fifteen hundred rpm and the next flap setting. Don't try to hold altitude now. Let the airplane descend."

I pull the power back and set the flaps to the second notch.

"Let's maintain this descent, and when we start to come in line with the center of the runway, we'll make our final turn and set full flaps."

We fly perpendicular to the runway, then turn left and position our nose right down the centerline on final approach. I bring the flaps to the last click.

"Final approach now. Good," he says. "When we get close to the runway, I'll ask you to pull the power all the way off. I'll pick the nose up a little bit, and we'll *flare* the airplane so we don't hit hard," Dad yells, emphasizing the new word.

I follow through with him, and when he says, "power off," I pull the throttle knob all the way back to the stop. There's a little backfire from the engine. Dad adds back pressure on the yoke to bring the nose up. The engine goes *bucketa—bucketa—bucketa*. For a pregnant moment, we glide in relative silence. A blanket of warmth wraps around me.

One wheel touches with a slight bump, *dut-da-dut-dut*. Then, *screech*, the right tire touches. The nose bumps down, and all three wheels rumble. The engine idles: *tuckata—tuckata—tuckata*. The wheel bearings' whine pipes down as we slow.

I'm relieved I didn't screw up. I didn't freeze. My father didn't get angry with me. I'm in love with this airplane and the fresh new world aloft.

We're back to earth. I'm back to earth, but I immediately long for the sky.

The peaceful, fluid feeling leaves me as soon as the yearning hits me. Even before we're off the runway, I can't wait to get back up in the air. Dad turns the airplane one-hundred-eighty degrees, and I taxi us to the tie-down spot. We run through the after-landing and shut-down checklists.

"Well, good job," says Dad like it's been nothing. He sounds like I've flipped my first burger or gotten a good grade on a report card. There is no congratulatory tone. "There was a lot to learn, right? How do you feel?"

"Yeah, good," I say, keeping it cool. All in a day's work for a pilot.

"Are you ready to go again?"

"Yeah, anytime," I say, cool like.

The sooner the better. I've found my vehicle to joy, and I will count the seconds until I can fly again.

CHAPTER FIFTEEN

At our airport, Hubert Compton is a fixture. While the world changes around him, Hubert stays put. I expect he will always live in Orange County, Virginia. I admire that. There must be something nice, something grounding, in being content in one's place. But for me, ever since my folks hauled me to Alaska when I was five, staying in one spot too long makes me itchy.

Hubert was the first to greet us when we took over the operation back on that wintry January day. Over the next months, he was there, giving support and patronage when my folks put in a new restaurant at the airport.

Hubert is in the insurance business. According to my father, insurance's purpose is to bleed people. Hubert is successful. He has a pleasant house and a nice airplane. Because of his relative affluence and the insurance agency, in my father's estimation, Hubert is mighty close to being "The Man" —a shark.

Is Hubert one of the sharks? You can't have money without being a shark. My father has no money, because he is not a shark. Having no money has nothing to do with his choices. He's a victim of circumstance. He can't see the possibility that Hubert is in the insurance business because he's a people person and offers an important product to protect peoples' finances. Does my father not remember our wrecked Luscombe? Can't my dad see that Hubert is interested in others' well-being, curious about his community, and eager to lend a helping hand?

While I still believe my father's assertions, still have faith in him —my skepticism as yet not entering consciousness— I admire Hubert and realize the airport is full of people of value. They might be people of the World, but I'm learning a lot from them. Dairy farmer Silas Nixon teaches me kindness. Navy officer Billy Graves —only ten years older than me, and close enough to my age that I can easily see myself in his shoes— gives me the opportunity to learn empathy when I worry about him when he's at war in Viet Nam. Mick and Bernard, two pilots from our neighboring airport in Gordonsville, demonstrate how dedication to a hobby —flying for the joy of flight— can be one of life's lodestones. How could one not admire, trust, and even love such individuals?

My father's religion supports his distrust of people. The Witnesses preach a lot about the people of the World. They must not be trusted or admired. Until they accept the Truth as one of Jehovah's Witnesses, people of the World are the enemy. Is the Kingdom Hall the only place from where my father's distrust and suspicions of people grew? Or has he always seen himself as the oppressed underdog, the victim of the bourgeoisie?

Whatever. I like the pilots at the airport. I like Hubert. Although frugal, he's a good customer and a good friend to me, the airport kid.

Some pilots have tables and sofas in their hangars. All us pilots —since I'm flying now I include myself in that group— feel welcome stopping by open hangar doors to shoot the breeze.

It's not unusual to flop down on a dusty couch for an hour or two of "hangar flying."

Hubert's hangar, in contrast, is his *sanctum sanctorum*, reserved solely for his airplane and him. While a person might stop by to say hello, Hubert's hangar is not a place to linger.

"How's it going, Hubert?" I ask, walking by his open hangar door.

"Going good," he says.

"Anything happening with the Mooney?" Hubert's airplane is a lovely Mooney Super 21.

"Nope," he says. "Just out here cleaning a bit. I changed the oil over the weekend, and I wanted to check for leaks. Had a chance this evening to clean up any drips before buttoning her up." He turns back to the airplane and sticks a screwdriver on a hose clamp.

I haven't stepped over his hangar's threshold, its frontier. As I turn to walk across the ramp, Hubert calls, "Hey, Russ. Were you here when the governor flew in today?"

"Yes, I was," I say. "That King Air was great! Did you see it?"

Around noon, Virginia's turboprop Beechcraft King Air, November one Victor Alpha, landed. A local Republican contingent met the passengers and crew, while several cars stood by for a motorcade. While I was sticking chocks under the wheels of the airplane, our commonwealth's governor, Linwood Holton, joined me under the wing. "We're going to be in town for a while. Can you watch my airplane while we're gone?" he said.

"Yes, Governor. I'll be happy to do that. It'll be safe and ready for you when you come back."

Colonel Willard Plentl, the airplane's pilot and director of Virginia's Department of Aviation, in the process of closing the airplane's door, looked over and grinned. He lowered the door and left the airplane unlocked and open.

After the dignitaries left, the bystanders at the airport went into the restaurant to talk about the big day. I climbed into King Air one Victor Alpha. It was my charge, my responsibility. The governor said so. From a crouched position, necessary because of the four-foot-ten-inch high ceiling, I marveled at the passenger cabin. The seats lay against the side walls with an aisle to the cockpit between them. An aisle! The cockpit had a door just like a mini-airliner. I duck-walked through the cabin, past the miniature galley with its tiny oven and electric coffee warmer. The instrument panel seen up ahead through the open cockpit door pulled me forward like a magnet. The cockpit, the control center of the marvelous machine, glowed like a throne room.

I swung myself into the pilot's seat, enraptured. Out the side windows, I saw the feathered propellers and the heat burnished stacks of the turboprop engines, some black exhaust soot visible at the openings. Jet turbines lay inside those cowls. Jets! I placed my hands on the black throttles and imagined advancing them as the Pratt & Whitney PT6 engines screamed to life outside. I looked down at the parking ramp. In the airplanes I flew, I always looked out at the ramp. From the King Air, I looked down. A wave of superiority washed over me.

My father always said I was bumptious. Sitting in the King Air reinforced the trait. Put fertilizer on it. Can an airplane make one feel superior? Or is it one's thought about oneself in a situation —or a machine— that does it? Whichever, the King Air dripped grandeur. This thing smelled like an airliner: leather, cloth upholstery, and stale nicotine mixed with the perfumed aroma of burned jet fuel.

For a good part of the afternoon, until Governor Holton returned, the King Air rarely left my sight. I fueled other airplanes as they arrived. I swept the hangar. But the governor's King Air sat on the ramp like a dazzling magnetic diamond. With each spare moment, I crawled under, in, and around it until I'd etched the placement of each rivet into my mind.

God, I prayed, *if you let me fly something this nice, I will never ask for another thing the rest of my life. God, do you read? Over.*

"No, I didn't get to see the airplane," says Hubert, jerking me back to the present moment. "I stayed in town for the meeting with the governor."

"Well, you really missed something," I say, my voice trailing off as I remember running my hands along the King Air's cool, smooth skin.

CHAPTER SIXTEEN

The days roll on. School days go slowly, and the days at the airport go quickly. "When are you going to solo?" Pilot acquaintances ask when they see me. The question kills me. It'll still be seventeen months before I'm old enough. One must be sixteen before flying alone in a powered airplane.

But I keep taking lessons, and my flight hours build.

Pilots fly in from all over to drink coffee, eat a burger, and swap stories. Stories are a way to learn. I pull the details from the pilots. I need to know the engine power settings, a flight's weather, and the minute techniques they used to stay safe. The pilots use salt and pepper shakers to set up the terrain and their hands to re-fly the maneuvers. With my endless questions, the pilots probably fly their hands more than they fly their airplanes. But from my point of view, the pilots are there to teach me.

*   *   *

This morning, I'm bleary-eyed and charged with nervous energy. There wasn't much sleep last night. I pull on gray pants and a white shirt and clip on my navy-blue tie with intentional solemnity. I slip on black loafers, grab my blue blazer, and let myself out the door. These are my church clothes. But today, better than church, they are my charter pilot uniform.

The airport is still and quiet when we arrive. In the bluish light before dawn, I see the outline of my dad next to the Piper Cherokee Six. A shiver runs through me, and my steps lengthen. I'm Dad's copilot today on an important flight.

"Help me get these seats out," Dad says, opening up the large door on the left side of the airplane. He looks like a larger version of me in his charter uniform.

We're due in Fredericksburg in an hour to pick up an injured woman and fly her to New York's John F. Kennedy International Airport. Dad said she was in a car accident and wants to get back home to her doctors and family. With a broken back, she can't handle the bumpy roads, so we will fly her there.

The Cherokee Six has three rows of two seats each. We pull three of the seats out of the back to make room for the woman's stretcher. Her nurse will sit in the one remaining passenger seat, and Dad and I will sit in the two seats up front.

He could do this flight on his own. He only asked me along because he knew I would want to come. I'm supernumerary. Without a pilot's license, I'm a passenger by law. Still, I feel the pressure of pulling my weight and not messing things up.

Kennedy International. Flying into that airport as a commercial passenger would excite, but I'm going to fly into that behemoth as a de facto crew member on an air ambulance flight. The prospect thrills, but I feel a little fear too. I'm like a rock climber facing a new cliff.

Dad already told me I'll handle the radio communication and

follow along with the navigation. We filed an instrument flight plan, so I'll be talking to air traffic controllers the whole way.

I'm hungry for the experience I will have by the end of the day. I have only about twenty-five hours of flight time and today wish it were ten times that much. I hope I don't screw up.

At fourteen, I've never flown in the cockpit of an airplane this big. It looks massive to me. When I climb into the right-hand front seat, the long nose of the airplane extends way out in front of me. It's strange and thrilling to see the propeller so far away.

The rest of the airplane, now missing half of its seats, stuns me with its enormous size. This thing goes on forever. There will be plenty of room for a stretcher and patient, a nurse and luggage.

The sun rises in front of us as we take off and fly east toward Fredericksburg. During the short fifteen-minute flight, anticipation fills me with an eager tension, heightening my senses. Soon we will pick up our passengers.

The Cherokee Six is bigger and heavier and fifteen knots faster than the smaller Cherokee airplanes I've flown. Taking off, I love the extra power. Our size seems to fit our important mission today and better fills, it seems to me, the enormous scale of our destination —Kennedy Airport.

We arrive over Fredericksburg airport to find a thick ground fog in the river bottom and no visibility for landing. Not reported when we took off, the fog must have developed quickly, right after dawn. This happens often on cool, moist mornings.

"It's pea soup down there," Dad says. "We're at zero-zero. Call the airport. And tell the ambulance to meet us over in Orange."

I make the call and slump back in my seat. Have we already failed in our mission? Now the poor lady will drive over the bumpy roads to get to our airport. The whole point was to spare her from road travel. Is this turning into the Keystone Cops? I'm frustrated. We're supposed to be saving the day.

Back in Orange, I pace as we wait for the ambulance to arrive. Finally, I see the flashing red lights coming through the airport gate, and hurry to the Cherokee.

The paramedics open up the back of the ambulance and roll the patient on a gurney to the airplane. All I can see is her dark brown hair against the white pillow, her brown face lined with pain and misery. Blankets bundle her body.

The medics angle her in through the side door. It's a tight fit. The woman groans as they set her stretcher down. They use spare seat belts to fasten her bed to the airplane. The stretcher's own straps secure her body. The nurse climbs in and takes a seat. She's right next to the patient. The tail of the airplane dips down as the landing-gear nose strut extends with the rearward load.

Dad secures the aft passenger door from the outside. He climbs on to the wing and gets in before me through the only pilot's door on the airplane's right side. I settle in next to him. With a groan, the nose lowers with a motion like a hobby horse. The weight balance is better now that Dad and I are in the front seats. We then run through the pre-flight checks.

"I'm going to keep us as smooth as possible," Dad says. "You handle the radio as best you can and do your own navigation. Tell me when you are confused or don't know something. We'll compare notes along the way."

I nod, looking down to make sure my charts, pad, and pencil are all within reach. This is a whole new ball game, flying into Kennedy. It's the busiest airport in the world, and we'll be flying through the busiest air corridor in the world: Washington, DC, to New York City.

Maybe we'll see a new 747, aviation's latest and greatest. No, I remember it won't be in service until next year. But we're bound to see several 707s. Kennedy is the big time, and I'll be a part of it.

I know all the radio lingo for instrument flights from books and listening to other pilots, but I've never used it in action. A few minutes after leaving the familiar rolling hills of our town, it's time to talk to Washington Center, the air traffic controllers for the DC area.

"Washington Center, Cherokee three-six-three-zero Whiskey. We'd like to pick up an IFR clearance to Kennedy," I say, using my steady, confident pilot voice like I hear and use over UNICOM at the airport.

"Roger, Cherokee three-zero Whiskey, stand by." There's a pause.

"Cherokee three-six-three-zero Whiskey, Washington Center. We've got your clearance ready. Are you ready to copy?"

I get my pad centered on my lap and grip my pencil tight. "Cherokee three-six-three-zero Whiskey ready. Go ahead."

The center reads off a route clearance that takes us, as planned, over the Delmarva Peninsula and over eastern New Jersey.

"Roger," I say, and read back the route.

"Climb and maintain nine thousand feet," Washington Center says.

Is Washington Center curious why a Cherokee Six would fly this busy commercial route? In the Six, I'm in the big time. That's how I feel. But to the controllers, our airplane is a pipsqueak. I wish they knew about our crucial mission, that we're transporting an injured passenger and her nurse. My dad could have added the prefix "Lifeguard" to our call sign to alert the controllers we've got a sick lady on board. I don't know why he hasn't. Does he know about it? He must. He knows everything about flying.

The green trees below give way to big buildings and more highways as we approach Washington, DC. To my right, Chesapeake Bay shimmers in the morning sun. On the left, I see the Potomac River curving through the city. The Washington Monument looks bright white but tiny, a small toothpick against the dark and light greens of trees and grass on the Mall.

"Cherokee three-zero Whiskey, you have traffic at ten o'clock and ten miles, United 727. Report him in sight," the controller says.

Out the front of the Cherokee, I see an airliner above us. "Three-zero Whiskey has the Boeing in sight," I say. Even though it looks small from our distance, it feels like I hooked a big one. Wow. A sense of belonging warms me. I'm flying with the major leaguers now, where I'm supposed to be. That I'm up here doing a job makes it even better.

As we head north toward Philadelphia, the green forests disappear, and I see lots of buildings and concrete. The Delaware River looks beautiful snaking beside trees, fields, roads, and buildings.

Now we hear airline pilots talking about us on the radio.

"Continental four-seven-five, you've got a Piper Cherokee at one o'clock and ten miles, nine thousand. Report him in sight."

"Continental four-seven-five has the Cherokee."

I can't believe they're talking about us. We're up here in their territory, and we're real to them.

I have only minutes —sometimes seconds— between radio transmissions. I scribble down notes in my own made-up short-hand and read back instructions. Sometimes I miss a number or a heading, and I turn to Dad. "What did he say?"

"I got it," he says, taking over for me on the radio.

Dad's not angry. We're both focused and working hard —we're a team. There's no teenage sarcasm here. No crossed religious philosophies. The vodka bottle under the truck seat is miles behind.

When we get a quiet moment, Dad turns his head toward the back of the cabin.

"Everything all right back there?" he shouts over the engine noise to the nurse.

"Yes, we're fine," she yells back.

It's been a smooth ride so far, with clear weather, and I haven't heard the patient make any noise since they loaded her into the airplane. But even if she made noise, it would be hard to hear over the roar of the two-hundred-sixty horsepower Lycoming engine on the nose.

As we near the Philadelphia area, the controller says, "Cherokee three-six-three-zero Whiskey, contact New York Center on 124.2."

My face flushes as I confirm the message. The big time keeps getting bigger —now it's New York Center.

I scan the horizon, looking for a first glimpse of New York City. It starts small, but I can tell something's different up ahead. I make out spiky rooftops. Sunlight glints off glass towers and my eye catches the spire of the Empire State Building, still the world's tallest. The Hudson River comes into view and then the East River. All the waterways are busy with big freighters. I see an ocean liner too. Is it the brand-new *Queen Elizabeth 2*? Or the old *SS France*? We're too far away to see markings, the shape, or number of smokestacks.

We see more airplanes too. Most are big airliners maneuvering to line up for approach at one of New York and Newark's three major airports. The air traffic controller chatter picks up. These New York controllers talk fast. Lose focus for a second, and I'd be sunk. My body tenses, and I tilt my head with concentration as the instructions come rapid-fire. It's not only the speed of the talk. It's that accent. In Virginia, we don't hear much Yankee.

"Cherokee three-six-three-zero Whiskey, descend to and maintain five thousand feet for traffic," says the controller. We descend, and a few minutes later, a 737 flies overhead. It's clear that the principal job of the controllers in New York is keeping us separated from the big jets. Never mind hitting one.

"Even being too close behind one might cause us major trouble with wake turbulence," says Dad.

As we descend to three thousand and then two thousand feet, the details of the city become sharper, but I have little time to notice. Gatling gun directions from the controllers come nonstop. Between their thick New York accents and their speed, I'm way out of my element. It's like going from middle-school Spanish class to negotiating multiple deals in Mexico City's central market.

With unfamiliar navigation fixes and constant traffic on the radio, Dad and I both focus to hear our airplane called. If we miss it, we have to ask the controller to repeat it —"Say again," we'd request, and then the controller would be behind on his next call. I don't want to throw in a monkey wrench. I don't want to screw this up.

"Whoever sees the airport first calls it out," Dad says. "Do you see it?"

"No. I don't see it yet." From the map that's in my lap, I project where the airport should be. I look out again and spot the lattice of four crisscrossing runways surrounded by gray low buildings and water.

"There it is at one o'clock," I yell. I suspect Dad has already spotted it. He probably said nothing to give me a chance to call it out.

We fly the Canarsie arrival procedure to runway one-three right. To help keep airplanes away from Brooklyn and Queens' buildings on approach, Kennedy installed a system of lights that guides airplanes over Jamaica Bay. Staying on the lighting system seems to me like threading a needle —with turns low to the ground and little room for error. Dad is focused, but cool and calm, as always while flying. He's never flown into Kennedy before either, but he's a bush pilot. I figure if you can fly in the Alaska wilderness, you can fly anywhere.

We come in along the line of strobe lights sticking out of the swampy water of Jamaica Bay. It's the first time I've flown low over water like this, but I have no time to look down to enjoy the view. Seeing the weeds, grass, and water on the periphery, however, is still thrilling.

We're following a 727 on the same approach. But he's going to the parallel runway, one-three left, a good way north of us. On our runway an American 707 taxis into position for takeoff.

"We'll have to touch down before his takeoff point to clear his wake," says Dad.

I don't understand. But there's no time to ask.

As we turn onto the final approach to line up on the runway, the scale of the airport overwhelms me to insignificance. The runway is three times as wide as the one at home and way longer. It feels like we'll never touch down. The Cherokee Six, a giant to me at the beginning of our trip, loses scale and now feels like a bug.

Our wheels finally contact the massive runway. In rapid staccato the air traffic controller advises, "Cherokee three-zero Whiskey, turn left and contact ground control."

We've used not even a third of the runway for our landing. No, not even a fifth.

The general aviation building appears in front of us as soon as we turn off the runway. We pull up as an ambulance with its lights flashing comes through the gate. I puff with fourteen-year-old pride for delivering the patient safely. Flashing lights have that effect on teenage boys. The team of paramedics unload her in reverse order of the way she came in. They unhook the stretcher from the restraining straps and maneuver with care, grunting through the left-side rear door. The number of uniformed people and the ambulance's red flashing lights add to the feeling of emergency. I feel even more important, standing here in my go-to-meeting clothes.

With the patient riding away in the ambulance, I have the urge to plant a flag. I landed at Kennedy International Airport! There should be a plaque. All the tension of the flight converts to joy as I see the huge airplanes around me —British Overseas Airways, Swiss Air, United. Across the ramp, I see a Pan Am 707, white with blue trim and black letters. Beside its passenger door, I see its name, *Clipper Windward*.

A haji has nothing on me. I've made it to Mecca.

The Learjets and Gulfstreams parked beside us at the general aviation terminal, in any other setting large and elegant, look like toys. Our Cherokee Six, the smallest airplane here, seems out of place. We sit, white and red with black trim, invisible. Several helicopters come and go like bees servicing the hive. They have a place in the busy city. We don't.

The general aviation building looks like something built by the Soviets, boxy and bleak. The little airplane terminal is plain, unembellished. Here at Kennedy, general aviation seems to be discouraged. We walk inside the dingy little building, and Dad orders fuel. We find a sandwich machine and deposit coins for two ham and cheeses. Then we buy a couple of soft drinks and head back out to the ramp and our airplane.

I take one more look around the endless acreage of Kennedy Airport, the noise and busyness of it, and the huge scale of the airplanes. I try to trap it in my memory. I know I'll be back. I just don't know how long it'll take me. Forgetting for the time my poor eyesight, and the impossibility of me ever having an airline job, in this moment I suspect I will have stripes on my shoulders and brass on my hat when I return.

We have no passengers on the way home, so Dad lets me fly. He'll do the radio work. I imagine it's a bit like flying a cargo plane, the back now empty of our passengers and half the seats.

"You're going to notice it's heavier on the controls than the other Cherokees. But just do things like you normally would, just watch your attitude, and you'll be fine," Dad says. "I'll give you your speeds." By "watch your attitude," he's not talking about me being a punk —although that is the usual context. Now he means to mind the airplane's positioning —its attitude— relative to the horizon.

The airplane feels heavier to me, more powerful. I like that feeling. I push the throttle forward. The engine growls, and the constant-speed propeller digs in and cycles a bit as it accepts power. We take off from the same runway on which we landed, again needing only a fraction of the pavement to get airborne.

The ride back is pure bliss. No more talking and sweating over the air traffic controllers. I just fly. Dad does the talking. The single propeller spins way, way out over the long nose of the airplane. My imagination stretches way, way beyond that, to the miles and years ahead.

I'm grateful for Dad inviting me to come today. He's the best pilot in the world; he landed at Kennedy, no problem. He should be an airline pilot. That would make our family complete. I don't think about all his rejected airline applications or his drinking.

In the airplane with Dad, I don't worry about the drinking, the anger, the religion. Here he's patient but firm, wise, even kind of gentle —a great flight instructor. In the airplane, I'm proud that he's my father.

Two hours later, from the downwind leg at our airport, I see the familiar airplanes parked in their usual spots. It's hard to believe, but I really flew a Cherokee Six to the busiest airport in the world —and I didn't screw up. I've taken another step on a path that, here in my waking dream, will take me back there someday.

I can't wait to drop the news of my flying trip to New York to my buddies at school on Monday. "Oh, by the way . . ." I can hear myself saying.

I'm not popular or athletic, and I'm always the last one picked for sports —worthless at ball games— but I have this one cool thing that no one else has. It sets me apart. I'm still different. An outsider.

I'm still embarrassed to be me. I still sting from being a Jehovah's Witness kid back in grade school. Never allowed to take part in any activities —not even school sports teams for some reason. It would be great to be one of the "in kids." But I'm an outsider.

With flying, though, I'm an outsider in a good way.

We land and taxi the airplane back to where we started that morning.

"You going to put it away?" Dad asks.

"Yeah, I'll take care of it," I say.

I put the three seats back in the airplane and push the Cherokee Six back into its place in the main hangar. I walk around to the propeller and look through the cockpit window. I was there today, flying in this airplane to Kennedy International Airport. Next time, I'll be in an airliner.

I reach up and adjust my glasses. I'd forgotten about the glasses.

CHAPTER SEVENTEEN

The warmth from the wood stove, which sits against the long wall that separates the living room from the kitchen in the drafty old farmhouse, is almost too hot. On the other side of the wall, Mom is at the kitchen stove, working on dinner. Dad's six-foot frame fills up the doorway between the two rooms, his head almost brushing the door frame.

Here on Mt. Sharon in the house we rent from Tinsley Mack, my dad is wearing what amounts to his uniform: a plaid flannel shirt, tan slacks, and black leather shoes, his black hair combed straight back. It's about six thirty, and he has a beer can in his hand, right on schedule. This is the time of day when I expect Dad's personality to change.

The Huntley–Brinkley Report plays on the television, a low drone. I catch a mention of the upcoming flight of Apollo 12, but it's mostly background noise. Debs sits on the couch, reading a book. Jenny, a six-year-old with a pageboy haircut, sits next to her and plays with the baby, Polly Ann, four now, but still called "the baby." Jenny makes funny faces with the baby. Their hands go up and down. Stupid play. I have no interest in that.

I'm sitting cross-legged on the floor. In front of me are my Aeronca 7AC Champ model airplane and a hybrid balsa model

I designed myself. They're both due for maintenance. Now, at the end of my day and before dinner, is a good time to do that.

The Aeronca Champ was a gift from Grandma, my mother's mother. The hybrid I cobbled together using parts from at least four different balsa planes I bought at the drugstore: a Strato Streak, the kind with wheels; two Sleek Streaks; and a Sky Streak. They're made of balsa and powered with windup rubber bands. I rigged the hybrid with four rubber bands attached to four red propellers to make it a four-engine airplane, like a balsa airliner.

The last time I flew the hybrid out on the ramp at the airport, it did very well. It even handled engine failures when one rubber band wound down early. But I'd noticed the airplane wasn't quite stable in the air. It could be better. This evening, I take a wing from one of my other airplanes, cut it in half, and attach it to the hybrid to make a larger tail. The half-wing will be my new vertical stabilizer. With airplanes, if it looks like it'll fly well, it probably will. This looks good.

The Aeronca Champ is next —one of the nicest airplanes in my fleet. I'd worked hours putting all the balsa together, covering the wood with paper fabric, then painting the entire thing with yellow airplane dope to make the paper stiff. But now one wheel is slipping off its wire axle. I use needle nose pliers to bend the wire and secure the wheel. I replace the airplane's rubber band with a larger one and find nothing else amiss.

Going back to the other airplane, I lean down at eye level with the hybrid and inspect the alignment of my stabilizer on the tail. What was a curved wing is now a clipped and vertical stabilizer.

The curve should apply a little right-rudder bias to counteract the red plastic props' yaw input. Cool. This should make the flight more stable next time.

Suddenly, Jenny's pink-and-white nightgown catches on the wing of the Aeronca Champ. She's standing in front of me, holding a toy. She must have stopped playing with the baby and gotten interested in my airplanes. Who wouldn't?

Her eyes sparkle like she wants to play. Her bare feet are inches from my airplanes. "Hey, get out of here," I say, reaching up to push her shoulder. "You're going to step on the airplanes!"

Jenny's face drops; she wobbles backward and spins around to face the kitchen.

I check my models, making sure they're okay. Out of the corner of my eye, I see Dad taking long strides toward me. Adrenaline shoots through my body, and instinctively I scramble to my feet.

He's over me in an instant, hitting my shoulder with his hand. "How do you like that?" he asks, pulling his shoulders back.

He stands solid as a rock, looking like a bad cop with his pursed lips under a black mustache. His eyes are black and dilated. All I see is anger.

"You like being pushed? Huh? Do you like that?" He punches me again.

The malty smell of Colt 45 beer hits me. I know that I'm not dealing with my good dad, the man who teaches me to fly. With alcohol, Dad is unpredictable, dangerous, like a rabid animal. I stay silent, keeping my gaze on the floor.

"What do you think you're doing? You think you can treat your little sister like that? You're bigger than she is! How do you like being pushed?" He hits me again, not with his full strength, but enough to set me back on my heels.

"She was about to break my models," I mumble, unable to meet his eyes.

"Your precious airplanes." He picks up the Aeronca Champ with strong, callused hands —the hands he uses to build beautiful cabinets and fix airplanes, televisions, and everything else.

My hands clench into fists, and my stomach tightens. I want to hit him, grab him, and make him stop. I want to take my airplane back. But that would be stupid. He's four inches taller, fifty pounds heavier, and fueled by alcohol. And he's my father.

With one wing tip in each hand, he holds the airplane out in front of my face, like he's about to show me a trick. Nothing up his sleeve.

My insides burn, and my breath catches in my throat. In a flash, he pushes the wings together. Presto! The airplane cracks and snaps as it collapses into itself. The paper cover rips, the fuselage splinters, and the tail breaks off. I feel like he's killed a beloved pet.

I can't believe what's happening. I did nothing that bad. I pushed my sister away. That's it. It wasn't my fault she was too close to my airplanes. I don't deserve this punishment. But I stay quiet, because I know it could get worse.

Dad drops the crushed Aeronca Champ to the floor. Then,

seeing my hybrid, he lifts his foot and smashes that airplane into pieces with one big stomp of his black leather shoe.

"How do you like that?" he says with satisfaction in his voice. "Now you're not going to have to worry about your precious airplanes!"

My hands are still in fists, but there's no strength. I am crushed too. A ball forms in my throat to dam my tears. But he's not finished.

"You think you can lord it over people. You think you're so damn smart." Now he repeats himself, emphasizing each word, "Do-you-think-you-can-lord-it-over-people? Huh? Well, guess what? With that attitude, you're headed for a fall." Tonight, his usual litany comes out of his mouth like shots from an automatic rifle. *Pam, pam, pam.*

The wood stove burns on my left side. I'm too close. I'm scared he'll knock me onto the hot metal. I plant my feet and keep my eyes down. It's not only the stove that's hot. Heat glows from my feet to the top of my head. I worry any insignificant movement or sound will make him erupt.

"You're bigger than your sister," he says. "Well, guess what, big shot! I'm bigger than you!" He shoves me again.

Oh yeah? Screw you, I think to myself. *Bastard.*

Dad continues in his steady, tight, firing pattern. Every word hits the target. "You always think you can get your way. It's all about you! You think nobody else counts? Well, I've got news for you. You're arrogant and bumptious. And you're headed for a fall!"

I let the familiar words shoot through me, concentrating on

the worn gray rug at my feet. If the words hit something vital, I'm finished.

But finally, he's done. I'm lucky he hasn't clobbered me.

Dad walks back to the kitchen, and I lift my head to scope out the room. Jenny is gone. So is the baby. Debbie sits, hugging her knees, tucked deep into the corner of the couch. The book is still there, but the pages do not turn. She doesn't look at me.

I kneel down to the wreckage. It's way beyond repair. What the hell? This shouldn't have happened. I was wrong to push Jenny, but his reaction made no sense. Damn it. Alcohol.

But I sense there's more to my father's craziness than booze.

I carry the pile of balsa wood, paper fabric, plastic wheels and propellers, and rubber bands into the kitchen. I open the lid and toss them into the trash.

My father stands at the counter, his back to me, chopping onions. A new can of high-octane malt liquor, moisture beading its sides, sits beside the cutting board. I walk softly in my high-top sneakers, like a skilled Indian scout on television, noiseless, hoping to escape his attention.

My mom is cooking at the stove and doesn't turn around. I realize that she's been in the kitchen the whole time and didn't interfere. I guess I'm not surprised. She goes along with Dad no matter how screwed up he acts. I know she walks like an Indian scout on *Gunsmoke* too.

Seeing my broken and snapped airplane parts in the bin sends another wave of fury through me. *You son of a bitch. Okay, maybe I am arrogant! Maybe I am a know-it-all. But guess what? I am better than you.* I swallow hard to dampen the rage and keep the tears away.

Mom drops the pork chops into the frying pan, and their savory aroma clears the beer smell. Dinner is uneventful. Mom rattles off the details of her day, the same as always. I eat —I can always eat— but there's a pit in my stomach. I don't say a word. That he had attacked me was bad enough. But he had attacked my "precious" airplanes and that was a sacrilege.

My little models weren't the first airplanes my father had destroyed.

CHAPTER EIGHTEEN

Did my father think about his broken dream when he crunched my models? Was he projecting his disappointment onto me? Was he sending me a message that a Roberts man should never expect to fulfill aspirations or even be happy?

Our first airplane, the Luscombe, spent almost two years as a wreck beside our garage in Fairbanks. It wound up there after my dad balled it up, crashed it. He never got the money to fix it. My folks didn't have the money to make payments on the airplane either.

He'd bought the airplane to go into business doing air taxi operations and flight instructing in Alaska. To my freelance father, customers looked like a stack of dollar bills. There weren't many, but he hoped a lengthy line of students would miraculously form to rescue our family's anemic bank account.

The crash ruined his plans. It happened one afternoon when he and his student were practicing short field takeoffs in the Luscombe. For whatever reason, my dad allowed the student to make his initial climb "on the ragged edge." Dad enjoyed risk. Or did he have a death wish? Whichever, he enjoyed telling tales from flying on the ragged edge. That day, they were climbing out a tad above the airplane's stalling speed. At forty-four miles per hour indicated on the airspeed meter, the wing nibbled at the air, hanging on to flight with a little shiver.

As the Luscombe staggered over the far end of the runway, the tiny headwind blowing straight down the runway quit with no warning. The Luscombe's airspeed, already on the razor's edge of performance, dropped. The wing gave up —and stalled. From not very high in the air, the airplane plunked back onto the ground. Having used up all the runway, the airplane touched down at the very end of the strip.

If there had just been a little more runway —just a bit more— the airplane could have stopped, taxied back, and tried another takeoff. It would have been just another anonymous maneuver —mere background in the comings and goings of the small airport.

Instead, the Luscombe bounced across a perpendicular ditch at the end of the strip and then across a gravel road. The airplane's Silflex landing gear caught the road's second ditch. The gear flexed as far as it would go and bent. The turning propeller caught dirt clods before the engine convulsed to a stop. The airplane, in sickening slow motion, flipped over on its back. *Kah-rump.* The tires spun overhead in the air, useless, like a fly beating its wings in a spider trap. The wheel bearings whirred *err-err-err* as they spun down overhead.

Neither occupant suffered serious injury. They unbuckled their seat belts and bumped to the upside-down ceiling. Neither my father nor his student got more than a scratch.

The purple-and-turquoise Luscombe didn't fare so well. The propeller bent, the landing gear sprung, the top of the cabin rumpled. The wrecked airplane was disassembled and wound up next to our garage. There was no use leaving the wreck at the airport. With the airplane at our house instead of the airport, the local pilots would not have a constant reminder of my father's embarrassment, his screw up.

Daddy hadn't wanted to pay for insurance and didn't believe in it. So there was no money to fix the wrecked airplane.

"Damned insurance companies. All they do is drain the life out of people. Sharks. That's what they are. A racket. A thousand dollars a year for airplane insurance? Ridiculous. I hate insurance companies." Daddy waved an Olympia beer can for emphasis.

Over time, I learned that insurance companies dripped more venom than even Safeway. They possessed more evil than a Luscombe wing.

"All these big companies want is the working man's money. They're sharks. They smell every drop of the little man's blood. They sniff out money like a wolf smells blood. Then they connive and scheme to get it."

With no insurance, there was no airplane, and the business's income dried up. With that, my dad stopped making payments to the former owner, Xen Moore, and the airplane wreck lay beside our garage.

It wasn't out of the ordinary to see airplanes in Alaskan yards. Yards were more junk piles than gardens anyway. Oil drums. Old pickup trucks. Airplane pontoons. Building materials. Antique Cat bulldozers. Dismantled airplanes like ours. All this and more was common junk in Alaskan neighborhoods.

My schoolmates, the Binkley kids, lived across Deadman Slough at the confluence of the Chena River. Their dad, Captain Jim Binkley, ran the excursion tourist riverboat *Discovery*. Those guys had a tremendous pile of junk in their backyard. Their dad even had several old dilapidated Yukon sternwheeler steam riverboats, relics of the Klondike days. Their place was a play day paradise.

Not exactly out of sight, our airplane seemed mostly out of mind for my father as it sat with weeds growing into it. It was hard for me to mow around, and I didn't want to hurt it further with sticks and rocks from the lawn mower. So the weeds grew. They wound around the bent landing gear and through the engine compartment during the airplane's slow attempt to turn to compost.

Over time, there was less and less talk about fixing the airplane beside the garage. My father still talked about the nasty design of the airplane, however. "That wing's chord is so narrow, it's wicked. It'll stall without warning. Like that!" He snapped his fingers.

You might have thought he was talking about a rocket-powered Me-163 Komet, not a tiny little feather of an airplane with an engine only a tad more powerful than gravity.

"It's a wicked little beast. Demonic."

I believed him. Since the Luscombe beat one of the world's best pilots, my father, in my mind the Luscombe design became infamous and deadly. I didn't question that there was never a word about lack of skill or judgment being factors in the crash.

But even talk of evil disappeared as the weeds grew high around the airplane.

Besides the challenge of mowing around it, I enjoyed having

the wrecked and uninsured Luscombe in my yard. It was very convenient for me. Even as the weeds grew through and around, I "flew" it a lot as it sat there. Even though the controls felt dead in my hands, and I heard no wind or engine, my imagination made the most of the opportunity. I figure I accumulated about fifty hours of plucked and wingless Luscombe time before repossession came close to two years after the crash.

Xen, the original owner of the airplane, the mortgage holder —now living in California— showed up one Saturday with a truck and flatbed trailer. He didn't yell or scream. He remained almost pleasant as he loaded his non-insured wrecked airplane onto his rig. It seemed weird he acted so nice. Even though I was only in second grade, I thought he should have been mad. I'd have been mad if I had to come get the pieces of what had been my perfectly good airplane.

Xen and Daddy loaded the airplane. The scene unsettled me. While they labored, my father looked at the ground a lot. He talked about the weather and that season's fishing prospects. He was my father, and I thought of him as a rock of unquestionable strength, ability, and rectitude. It felt weird that he was looking at the ground so much.

As the two men worked, I tried to stay by Daddy's side. To keep him close. And not in some figurative way. I kept him physically close. I knew he was right about insurance and his war with the monied set, the sharks. At eight years old, I was my parents, and they were me. But somehow I felt shaken. That day, as always, I took his side. I knew he was right. And wise. And just. But all morning I wanted to upchuck.

Xen was too nice even as he left sentences dangling. He knocked a bee's nest from under the instrument panel and said, "Bees. Lots of dirt —the plane's been sitting— long time. Wish I'd gotten here earlier, but I was hoping—" He raised his head in my direction and stopped.

In my head I finished his sentence, " —to get my money."

The conversation was one way, and I didn't understand why. The two men lifted the fuselage from the ground, one talking about nothing and the other one spurting half thoughts. Weeds —wet, slimy and twisted, anemic and white from a lack of sunshine— appeared when the airplane parts were moved. Chlorophyll made plants green. To make chlorophyll, a plant needs sunlight. That reminded me of science class. For a minute, I forgot my nausea.

Xen wiped his hands on his pants. Dirt and dust smudged his khakis. He sighed. I bet he thought it would've been good if the little kid, me, hadn't stood there. The guy was being especially polite like I was when embarrassed.

Or maybe nice is just how Californians were. Whatever.

The airplane's aluminum groaned from the unnatural stresses of hand-lifting. It seemed wrong to lift an airplane by hand onto a trailer. And it seemed wrong to not pay someone. And, wicked wing or not, it seemed wrong to crash a Luscombe. Other people flew Luscombes and didn't crash. However evil it might have been, wouldn't insurance have made all this right? There'd been several mentions of insurance among the lifting of wings and other airplane parts.

The men's words sounded like the airplane's groans. I wonder how the airplane sounded when my dad wrecked it? Had it groaned when it hit the ground and rolled across the ditch? Had it screamed? Had it yelled at my father, "You arrogant and bumptious bastard! Think you can bend the laws of aerodynamics? Well, this time you've met your fall!"

It wasn't even noon when the Luscombe departed in Gradelle Avenue's dust. I stood at the end of the driveway and watched, sad to see my airplane go.

Daddy seemed happier, though. How was that? He seemed glad and walked lighter as the image of the airplane disappeared in the cloud of gravel dust. Daddy wiped his hands on his pants, turned away from the airplane and me, and walked away. I watched his back go into the house.

I reached down to pick some white, slimy grass. I decided then I would look into insurance. *I will swim with sharks when my turn comes*, I thought.

CHAPTER NINETEEN

November nine-nine-three-six Charley belongs to an airline pilot. Bill's airplane is a Luscombe Silvaire, almost identical to the Luscombe my dad crashed in Alaska. Three-six Charley lives in the main hangar at our airport in Orange, Virginia. It shares the hangar with two other Piper airplanes, a single-engine Comanche and a Tri-Pacer.

"Wow! Look at that," I said that first day at the airport in January 1969. "A Luscombe! Look at the 'N' number. Nine-nine-*three-six* Charley. We had nine-nine-*zero-zero* Charley. This is our old airplane's younger brother." I loved seeing Bill's Luscombe. I felt like I'd found my old friend's twin.

Each time I see three-six Charley in the hangar, I'm taken right back to the time I'd spent flying in our airplane —both the few times I'd been airborne in it and when I "flew" it while it lay derelict beside our garage.

Our Luscombe adventures seem ages ago. Half a lifetime has passed since then —going on seven years.

Our airplane had been the Silvaire Uranium and Aircraft Company prototype. Serial number S-1. Bill's airplane is S-40 and three years newer than ours. But I feel superior as I sweep the hangar floor. Bill's airplane has no flaps. I suspect our airplane with its flaps would have been better in the bush, getting in short and taking off quickly.

I scratch an emotional scab and realize my superiority comes from jealousy. Bill's no-flap Luscombe is here. Still alive. Not broken. His airplane is not a basket case. His airplane's paint is pleasant to look at too, not irritating like our Luscombe in its hideous purple-and-turquoise livery. I wonder if anybody has rebuilt our airplane by now. My parents told me Xen took it to California, for paint and repair, to fly again. But how would they know?

As I stand in the gray hangar in Orange, with a kind of cathedral light streaming in from the tall, dusty windows, I try to find fault with Bill's airplane. I think about our old Luscombe and envy the flying machine in front of me.

Bill was a Florida State trooper before getting his airline pilot job. An old man for an airline new hire, he'd begun his airline career in his mid-thirties. He's been with the airline now for only two years. Still an airline rookie, he flies as an engineer, the nonflying pilot, on a Boeing 727. But he's a demigod to me, and I wish Bill would visit the airport more often. It seems he comes to the airport about every week or so. I'd like for him to show up every day like Hubert. To me, Bill's visits are of great value. To me, he looks like a grizzled airline veteran. A paragon on the long seniority list to greatness.

"Hey, Bill! Where you been?" I ask when he pulls up in his Volkswagen. Even if I'm busy, I drop what I'm doing to go out to the hangar with him, grab a rag and help him polish, check the oil, or do whatever needs doing. Time in company with an airline pilot, especially one who wants to spend time with me, is invaluable. I hope some of his aura might rub off. I hope the stuff in his brain will leak out and I'll be able to grab it and cram it into my head.

Bill's airplane's twelve-year-old factory paint job looks good. It's not ugly like my father's do-it-yourself Luscombe painting fiasco.

But Bill is unhappy with the design and colors and wants a change. "A Luscombe is a sporty machine," he says, a rag in one hand and a bottle of spray cleaner in the other. "A sporty —even aerobatic— airplane, and I think it ought to look like it."

Over several weeks, I spend many fine hours with Bill planning a new design and then many days prepping his air- plane for new decoration. Bill enjoys talking. While sanding, masking, and rubbing his airplane, he preaches the bene- fits of flying for a major airline. In particular, he praises the security afforded by a big airline whose pilots are the lucky members of the Air Line Pilots Association, the airline pilots' union.

"I can't tell you enough about the importance of ALPA." He pronounces it AL-puh, with the emphasis on the first syllable, pausing with a piece of sandpaper held like the Statue of Liberty's torch. "The airlines wouldn't be near as safe without the union. Far from it! No sir! For thirty-five years, ALPA has insisted the airlines improve safety when management wants to scrimp to save a buck!"

Should I bring a stool for him to stand on? This is a splendid speech.

"ALPA works on stuff like not overworking pilots. We call that 'pilot pushing.' We can't have management pressuring pilots to fly when conditions are unsafe. Or when pilots are worn out. Nope, can't have that! Instead, *ALPA* puts on the pressure. It presses managements and the FAA to keep things safe when the airlines are unwilling or too durn cheap."

Bill doesn't swear. He doesn't drink. I know he goes to church, but he doesn't talk about it. He never tries to convert me.

"After all, the corporations' primary interest is money. Money! The *pilots'* primary interest is safety and quality of life. 'Schedule with safety.' That's the ALPA motto. In the 1930s, when ALPA started, airlines wanted pilots to fly all the time, under any condition. 'Get the mail in on time!' That's all management cared about. Lose an airplane or pilot? Who cares?"

I shrug my shoulders and shake my head at the corporate hubris.

"Fly in all conditions," says Bill. "Don't worry about weather or maintenance. Go, go, go! Let me tell you, without ALPA it would still be like that. Money over safety. Airliners would be dropping like flies!"

He chisels the thoughts into my head. I know I will never forget what he's telling me, like words in stone: union . . . power . . . safety.

Bill stops his work. Holding a piece of dripping, dirty, six-hundred-grit sandpaper, he stands upright, faces me square on, and pokes his left index finger into my shoulder.

"Understand this: Airline management represents a giant corporation," he says. "It holds outsized power. The union is the only way to level the playing field. Jack and the beanstalk? One man against a giant? Forget it. Jack needed an army. An individual pilot holds no power against a monster. No power. Get it? None. But together . . . well, unity, the power of collective energy . . . That's the only thing that gives us strength."

Bill talks a lot. He's kind of like his new paint scheme. Bold, loud, and festive. Pinstripes, lightning bolts, and sunbursts on the wings. When finished, his bright new colors hold the promise of action his airplane's ninety horsepower could never provide. Bill's new paint design looks cool, but it might be like putting a track suit on a chihuahua: One shouldn't expect a lot of performance.

A month later, Bill comes to the airport on his way back from work. He's in his uniform, and I stand transfixed by what I see: the archetype of the steely jawed, disciplined flying professional. My ideal. Except for my eyesight —if I weren't crippled— that would be me a few years. It would be me if there was any universal justice. If I could just see —and if the world wasn't going to end before I grew up.

"Hey, Russ. You want to go for a ride?"

"Yes, I do!"

"We've got this new paint job," says Bill. "It should be good and cured by now. Let's go and wring it out!"

"Let me tell her where I'm going!" I rush into the restaurant to tell my mom —I've taken to calling her "her" most of the time— I'm going flying with Bill.

She shakes her head and smiles. "Okay. See you later." she says.

I'm tall and skinny. Bill is not fat either. Still, it's a tight fit as we climb into the Luscombe. Stepping with his left foot to a peg on the landing gear leg, Bill swings up almost like he's getting on a horse. Then he squeezes his almost six-foot frame into the airplane's tiny left seat and squishes the door closed. The door and frame meet with a thump. The door might have slammed if Bill's body hadn't acted like a cushion. He slides the latch closed with a muffled click.

His face is even redder than normal from the contortions. It's not that he's out of shape —he looks like he could have been a surfer when younger— he's a trim and clean-cut kind of guy who probably dated Gidget in high school. No, Bill's not out of shape. The Luscombe cockpit is tiny and takes a lot of bending and pulling to fit into. They say there's a line of demarcation whether one can fit into a Luscombe or not: before pie and after pie. I have had no pie, and I repeat Bill's gymnastic performance from the right-side door.

"Whew, all in," says Bill as he puts on his seat belt and starts the engine. There's no checklist. The engine finds its breath. *Blap, blap, blap.* Bill finds his breath too. "Hey, I'll bet you I can fly around the pattern in less than thirty seconds. Takeoff to landing. Thirty seconds!"

"What? No. I don't think you can do that. How?" I say. A better question would be why.

"Watch," Bill chuckles.

As the engine warms up, Bill takes his sunglasses off and opens the tiny glove box to pull out some Bain de Soleil. He smears some cream on his face. "With this red-blond skin, I can't afford a sunburn. They say sunburn causes cancer." While the cream soaks in, he does the engine run-up from memory. When the engine's warm and checked out, we taxi out and line up on the runway.

Bill advances the throttle to pour tiny coals to the little Continental engine, and we buzz down the runway like a big bumblebee, all yellow, white, and black. The instant we're airborne, he cuts into a tight left turn. Tight and steep. I worry the wing will drag in the grass or hit the fence. I take a big breath, a huge inhale. He continues the tight turn, never more than fifty feet off the ground. All I can see out the left window is earth. I don't breathe. Around we come, my cheeks stretching down, my rear end pressing hard into the seat from the g-load. We bend a full three hundred sixty degrees to line up with the runway again. Chopping the power, Bill plops the Luscombe down midfield and comes to a stop.

"Did you time it?" he asks. I shake my head. I'd been too stupefied to look at a clock.

"Well, I did," he says, looking down at his watch. "Thirty-three seconds, wheels up to wheels down. Told you we could do it."

He hadn't said we before —he'd said I— but I was okay with the inclusion now that we'd survived the reckless miracle. I didn't quibble that he'd originally said less than thirty seconds.

We taxi back to the end of the runway and take off again. "Let's go see if Betty is back home from the store yet," Bill says. Betty is Bill's wife.

He points the Luscombe toward Clark's Mountain, a hill about a thousand feet high and five miles northeast of the airport.

"Yup, there it is. Clear as a bell. Great visibility today! General Lee used to ride his horse, Traveller, to the top of Clark's

Mountain to keep an eye on McClellan's Army of the Potomac during the winter of 1863 and '64."

I get a history lesson as we fly toward Bill's house on the top of the mountain.

The distinguishing features of Bill's mountain are two: a big peach orchard and a very tall AT&T microwave tower. With the tower, the hill is easy to spot from an airplane.

"Yep! She's back! There's Betty's car in the driveway," he shouts, pushing the nose of the Luscombe down a bit and banking to whip around the north end of the hill. He keeps the tall tower always on our left. Again, we're in a tight bank, pulling at least two gs. He chuckles as he brings the airplane down to the level of his house. Closer and closer we get. Abeam the back porch —we're close enough to see porch seat cushions and a hummingbird feeder— he pushes the airplane's throttle all the way in. Big noise comes from the little engine. Bill pulls the small airplane into a tight right chandelle, a high-performance right climbing turn. The airplane groans a bit with the increased strain on engine and frame.

I look over past Bill. I don't see Betty on the porch. But I do see an enormous grin on Bill's face.

I wonder. Is this what an airline pilot should do on his days off?

CHAPTER TWENTY

I'd gotten off the school bus an hour ago. Then I'd eaten my usual after-school snack in our airport restaurant: a cheeseburger, a big order of fries, and a drink. If I'm not too hungry, some days I'll have an iced tea or a root beer. Today I'd been starving and had a chocolate shake. That should be enough to hold me until dinner. After eating, I'd gone into the airport operations office to check the day's activity log.

My folks had enjoyed a quiet day. A few arrivals needing fuel. One airplane rental. Three unfamiliar names in the visitor's book. I'd already stuck the tanks, using a long wooden dowel to probe the two fifteen-hundred-gallon aviation gasoline tanks. Once a day, I checked that the actual tank level jibed with the arithmetic on the fuel log. After that, I swept the main hangar floor.

My daily chores done, I now settle in and listen to the occasional transmissions from airplanes flying into other airports. The line-of-sight signal allows me to hear airplanes within about fifty miles of Orange County Airport. The radio has one channel, locked to 122.8 MHz. This is the universal communications frequency, called UNICOM. Airports with no air traffic control tower use UNICOM to advise airplanes of local conditions and pass the occasional message.

"Orange UNICOM Mooney six-four Quebec, five miles north. Landing."

The little airport radio crackles in basso, the voice quivering a bit. It sounds almost like it comes from a helicopter. This is an unfamiliar voice, and I don't recognize the call sign.

"Six-four Quebec, Orange County. Wind east at about five, favoring runway seven. No reported traffic. Will you need fuel?" I ask. I am fourteen.

"Roger, runway seven. And no fuel. Thanks."

In a few minutes, an orange-and-white single-engine Mooney Executive 21 lands and taxis to the ramp. I greet the airplane and signal with my orange wands where I suggest he park.

A man with wild hair, more pepper than salt, climbs out and jumps to the ground. He's agile for a large man.

Sister-ship to Kellen's Mooney Executive 21

(Photo credit: Trevor Nelson)

"I'm Kellen," he says. "I hear you've opened a restaurant."

"That's right," I say. "Right through the hangar door there."

"ho, Ho, HO!" he says, rubbing his hands.

In the next days and weeks, Kellen's after-school visits become a regular thing. He flies in almost every weekday when the weather is good. He eats a light snack, talks for one or two hours while drinking coffee or iced tea. Then he climbs back in the Mooney and, after a fifteen-minute flight, returns to his home airport. On Fridays, he has a huge steak. We almost never see him on weekends. In May, he flies to his summer home on Mt. Desert Island in Maine. We see him again in early October.

He's always in his uniform: blue jeans —always too small for his overweight body— blue denim shirt, a blue nylon bomber jacket if the weather blows cool, and black leather Acme Wellington boots. Always polished.

Kellen is an interesting character, and, although we never stop trying, it's hard to get personal information out of him. But over many visits, things leak out.

We learn that Kellen flew in World War II. To me, this elevates him above most pilots who populate our airport. Major airline pilots and World War II aviation veterans, in that order, top my ranking scale.

Kellen tells a lot of stories about "the outfit." "There's nothing like being in a great outfit," he says. "Everybody pulling together. Listening to the boss. Greased machine. You know, getting things done. Getting ready to do the mission. And then *doing* the mission!" Kellen talks like that all the time, but somehow, facts about him remain few.

"The only thing that came close to those days in the Air Corps was up in Maine a few years back. I helped the Caruso brothers put their outfit together. Bar Harbor Airlines." He never says how he helped Tom and Joe Caruso. He does not mention having flown for them.

Most of the people working at the airport are high school students. There are two older ladies who work the lunch crowd on school days, but mostly the workers are kids. My sister, Debs, Chris, Rosemary, and Faye cover most wait staff shifts. Other people come and go based upon demand and availability.

Besides a mechanic who leases hangar space, my parents and I are the only ones who work on the aviation side of the operation.

The young staff seems to suit Kellen. He seems most comfortable with us kids. Adults? Not so much. My father calls him a "blowhard." Listening to Dad, over time I hear about lots of blowhards. It's funny that most of them are people richer than my father, better educated, or more accomplished.

The waitresses guess that Kellen must be over sixty years old. That could be right, but it's hard to tell. Anybody more than thirty-five looks old to me.

Kellen's uncombed and overlong hair sticks up. It waves in the wind of jokes and stories like a field of black-and-gray wheat. Old as he is, when Kellen tells stories, he sounds like a horny teenager. Telling stories is what Kellen does most.

"Are you sure about that guy?" asks Clint, a pilot who flies from Kellen's home airport. "I think he's some kind of fat satyr. I sure wouldn't trust him around *my* daughter."

With all the young girls working at the airport restaurant, I know Kellen makes a lot of adults nervous. He flirts. He makes innuendo. I suspect he might take advantage of a target of opportunity should one fall in his sights.

"Hey, you guys," I say to the two waitresses on duty. "Has Kellen ever stepped over the line with you? I mean, after what Clint said . . ."

"He's a dirty old man," says Chris. "But with me at least, he's never gone too far."

"He always stops when told to stop," says Rosemary. "And he keeps his hands off 'no-man's-land' —from here to here and here to here." She points on her body to her boundaries.

I'm relieved Kellen's ribald and suggestive manner apparently never takes root. But I know the adults watch him like he's a creepy troll living under a slimy bridge.

When he calls inbound on the radio today, as usual Kellen sounds excited and happy. I think he knows I am happy and excited too. Separated by at least forty-five years, we share the bond of airplanes and a love of aviation history and lore. A teenage virgin from a family with no money and a geriatric debaucher with a seeming unlimited money supply.

Sitting at the lunch counter a few minutes later, Kellen has a Wall Street Journal spread out in front of him. Chris brings Kellen a plate of fries and asks, "Where shall I put this?"

"That's what the bishop said to the nun!" said Kellen "ho, Ho, HO!"

Never mind his raw manner. He and I are buddies. Genuine friends. I'm used to his ways because it's the way of my teenage contemporaries. All randy little bastards. The only difference is my high school buddies aren't old and rich.

He eats his fries and order a dessert. Chris brings him a vanilla cone. Kellen says, "Lick me until ice cream."

"You're a dirty old man, Kellen," says Chris.

Kellen waves his head from side to side, looking around with an innocent expression of "Who, me?" on his face. His hair flies and his stomach shakes. "ho, Ho, HO!"

It would seem we're a pair from different planets. But at the airport, the differences fade. We are equals in our love of flying. And we're equals in our juvenile lascivious appetites. I have an excuse for mine. Like all early teenage boys, I'm at peak libido. My powerful energy lies in wait, untried and without fulfillment. I think Kellen's is a case of arrested development.

* * *

After school, the bus drops me off at the airport, as it does each weekday. The airport: My refuge. My university. The brisk October air is still, the sun low and dim in a clear blue sky. A perfect day for flying, although that's not my plan today. This weekday afternoon at the airport is for chores and, if I'm lucky, a visit from Kellen.

I leave my backpack in the airport office and head out to check the levels in our fuel tanks. Once again, in daily ritual, I drop a graduated stick into each tank and mark down the measurement on my clipboard. No one is around as I walk across the ramp, although I'm sure some pilots must sit in the restaurant, sipping coffee and swapping stories.

I need to check the airport lights. It's on my list of daily chores.

A rotating beacon sits atop the hangar. The beacon is surplus from the early air mail days. It used to mark a part of a visual airway that crossed the Blue Ridge Mountains. The county got the beacon as surplus from the FAA. Now, each night, the beacon's big white light and a smaller green one flash, shining mostly to no one. But once in a while, a pilot seeks our airport in the dark. So the beacon flashes all night, every night.

I climb the beacon's tower and check the bulbs and the mechanisms. The old light will be good for at least one more night.

I return inside and set my clipboard on the counter in the office, a small annex to the large, white cinderblock hangar. The office extends out toward the runway. Windows provide an almost two-hundred-seventy-degree view of the field.

Russ' mother, Russ (16), and Billy Graves. Bill is sitting in
Kellen's usual spot in the airport restaurant.

I pull out the fuel records and begin cross checking the amount of fuel in the tanks with the amount sold. Even though this is not flying, I love the work. Dad gave me a few responsibilities at first —sweeping the hangar and such— and I took on more and more. Mom and Dad still do some aviation work. But I consider the airside my territory. Usually now, Mom and Dad work mostly in the restaurant, the part of the airport that holds the best hope of making us some money.

The UNICOM radio, a gray box with two knobs —for volume and squelch— and a speaker, sits on the counter. I have my FCC Restricted Radiotelephone Operator's license, so I'm legal to transmit. Mom, Dad, and Debs can use the radio too, but they have less time and interest. I end up answering the radio most often. I think it's great: I love talking to the pilots and giving them useful information.

We're a non-tower airport, that is, an airport without air traffic control, and answering the radio is a courtesy, not a requirement. There's a speaker on the side of the hangar too, so I can hear calls when I'm out on the ramp. I can break whatever outdoor chores I'm doing to pop back into the office to answer many pilots.

They call in to say they're on approach. I answer, telling them about other known traffic in the pattern and which runway the wind favors that day. This afternoon, a pilot calls in to ask for a favor.

"Orange UNICOM, Aero Commander seven-four X-ray, could you make a phone call?" says the pilot.

"Seven-four Xray, Orange County. Sure, go ahead with the

number and credit card," I answer. I never say "Orange" or
"Orange UNICOM." It's always "Orange County" or "Orange
County UNICOM."

"It a local call," the pilot says. "Coleman's Cab. Going out
to Woodberry Forest School. Tell Simon we'll be there in twenty-five minutes." Being a local call, there is no toll, and he doesn't
need to read his AT&T credit card number over the air.

That's the normal kind of service pilots expect at small airports like ours, but they also know that someone answering on
UNICOM is a crapshoot. Either we're in the office or we aren't.
Often, pilots are on their own flying in and out of Orange County
airport, using their eyes to see the wind sock on the far side of the
runway and look for other traffic in the pattern.

The Aero Commander lands, he needs no fuel, and Simon
Coleman carries the pilot away in his taxi. I hear faint laughter
from the restaurant through the back wall of the office as I stand
at the counter, hunched once again over my fuel ledger. My stomach rumbles, anticipating my afternoon snack: a burger and a big
order of fries. Will I have a shake or an iced tea? A familiar voice
comes over the UNICOM.

"Orange County, six-four-Quebec," he says. It's Kellen. His
voice sounds off, shaky.

I snatch the microphone from the counter, "Six-four-Quebec,
Orange County. Go ahead, Kellen."

Kellen's voice comes back a little high and tense. I hear loud
vibration in the background. Kellen's transmissions always sound
like he's in a helicopter —he has a natural warble to his voice—
but today he's barely readable.

"Engine's running rough as a cob. I don't know if I'm going to make it to the runway."

CHAPTER TWENTY ONE

"I'm five miles northeast, and this thing feels like it's going to come apart. You may be coming to get me out of a field," Kellen says, the vibration almost obscuring the sound of his voice.

My heart stops, and my palm feels moist as I grip the mic.

"Roger, six-four-Quebec. Do you want me to call the fire company?" I want his go-ahead to call the authorities. To me, this sounds serious enough for a Mayday call.

"No, if it quits, I'll let you know. Wind okay for two-five?" Kellen asks, stressed but determined.

"Wind is calm. Runway two-five is good. No reported traffic," I answer.

The UNICOM goes quiet. Other traffic over other airports around the region clams up. I stand at the counter and calculate in my head how long it should take him to get to the airport. In two or three minutes, I should see him on approach. I look at my watch. If I don't see him in four minutes, I decide, I'll call the fire department. If he's not here by then, he'll be in a field somewhere —or worse.

It's too early to see him, but I stare out the window to the end of the runway, willing him to appear. It's impossible to stand still. I pace back and forth at the counter, never out of reach of the mic, looking out over the fields, trees, and hills for the Mooney.

I look for other traffic too, traffic that might conflict with Kellen's emergency arrival.

I want to be out in the air with him. But I'm glad I'm not. I just want to know what's happening. I can hear a plate clatter in the restaurant. The noise is an invasion. Here at our airport, Kellen and I are the only ones who know about his emergency, and to me, it feels like we're the only two people in the world. I wish I could talk to him to learn exactly what is going on.

I know the priorities of flying: aviate, navigate, communicate —in that order. Kellen needs to fly the airplane to the airport. Letting me know how he's doing is his last concern.

Should I go tell somebody? That would mean leaving the radio. And what if Kellen calls back? I see our Volkswagen bus in the parking lot, so my parents must be around, but I'm not sure where. How would it help for someone else to know? I'm not sure, so I stay put. I check my watch. It's been three minutes.

No airplanes appear through the office windows, and no other pilots call in. I wait in silence, hearing only the squeak of my sneakers on the square linoleum tiles as I continue pacing. I duck down to get a view of higher altitudes through the windows. Nothing.

If he has to land short of the airport, I sure hope he makes it to a field. We have a stand of trees on the final approach course, about a thousand feet from the end of the runway. Dad has talked about clearing them to make the approach safer for pilots, but he hasn't gotten permission yet from the county to do it.

Kellen needs a pasture. Landing in the treetops or hitting the trunk of a tree might be the end of him. Not a happy prospect.

Holding my breath, I peer again through my north-facing window and see the orange Mooney in the distance, coming in low. Way low. I freeze, but I feel my heart pumping again. I squint at the airplane —no smoke, a good sign. It looks like a normal approach except for his low altitude and the still retracted landing gear.

Kellen cuts the pattern at forty-five degrees. He doesn't have the altitude for the regulation square turns. He clears the trees by a hundred feet or so. He puts his landing gear down. I let myself take a few tentative breaths. Coming in faster than normal —I can see his flaps are up— he crosses the threshold, bleeds off the extra speed, and puts the Mooney down on the runway. I let myself exhale. While the Mooney rolls to a stop, I dash out of the office and jump in the Volkswagen.

Speeding down the runway, I pull the bus over onto the grass close to Kellen's airplane. It's still sitting in the middle of the strip. The Mooney's propeller stands still. The engine either failed on rollout or Kellen shut it down, not wanting to further damage it by trying to taxi over to the hangar.

Kellen stands at the front of the Mooney, peering down into the engine in front of the cowling. He wears his standard denim shirt, nylon bomber jacket with a fake fur collar, blue jeans, and boots.

I'm wearing jeans and a long-sleeved shirt, not having thought about my jacket as I ran out of the office. I don't need it anyway; adrenaline pumps, and I'm warm.

Kellen looks up when I climb out of the bus. He throws up his arms and waves them in fake panic, "Jesus Christ, that was a hell of a ride! I didn't think it was going to hang together."

"Glad you're here. I was a little worried," I say, not wanting to betray the intensity of my concern over the last ten minutes.

Kellen seems pumped up, almost like he's at a party. He picks up his tow bar and waves it around.

"The airplane was jumping around like a son of a bitch. It must have blown a jug. Maybe it broke a rod," he says, rocking back and forth on his feet and looking down into the engine compartment again.

With the cowling still on, it's almost impossible to diagnose the problem, but Kellen needs to make the attempt.

"I never had anything like that happen before. Jesus H. Christ! It was running so rough I thought it would tear away from the engine mounts. Bouncing around like an epileptic whore! Here, let's push it over to the ramp," he says. "Hey, where's your coat? You need to get a bomber jacket so you look like you're part of the outfit. You need a jacket. Cold out here. Wag-Aero has 'em."

Kellen attaches the light aluminum tow bar to the nose wheel. The airplane weighs about two thousand pounds, loaded the way it is. We leaned into it to get it going, but after it's moving, the Mooney's three wheels roll without strain under the airplane's own momentum.

The airplane is facing the opposite direction from where we want to go, but Kellen doesn't turn it around. He just pushes from the nose. Pushing is easier than pulling. I'm on the left wing and provide a steady shove.

"Looks like I'm stuck here in Orange. I sure can't fly it back home. ho, Ho, HO! Is that mechanic around? This is going to be a big deal. We're sure not going to turn a couple of screws and call it good! ho, Ho, HO!" Kellen says as we push.

"No, he's gone home already. But we'll figure something out."

I apply a little more pressure to the wing. The adrenaline wearing off, I realize we have about a quarter mile between us and the hangar. On a regular day, that would seem too far to push an airplane, but today Kellen and I don't mind the distance. After the action, pushing the airplane is like a cool down.

Kellen continues his description of the flight, talking non-stop. "I couldn't put the power up because the son of a bitch would start running rougher. I couldn't hold altitude to level out on my approach. Just had to maintain a steady descent. I kept the flaps and gear up as long as possible. Glad I didn't run out of air before I made the field! Would've gotten grass in the wheels! Or worse. Trees —leaves in my teeth! ho, Ho, HO!"

As Kellen talks, I recall every detail. Up to now, I've read about and prepared for engine problems only in books and in my mind. I've heard stories around the airport. This is my first direct involvement.

Something clicks in my head. This is why you go through the preparation, the learning, the instruction. This is why you need to memorize all the emergency procedures. Bad stuff happens. Things can be out of your control. It happens even to an old pro like Kellen. Even World War II veterans —pilots ranking high in my esteem— are not immune.

When we reach the hangar, I push the doors open with little effort, still powered by residual adrenaline from the recent emergency. We give the Mooney a final boost to bump it over the door track and steer it into the hangar, tail first. We walk into the restaurant with a story to tell.

"Jesus Christ, what an afternoon! Hell of a high price for a hamburger!" Kellen booms when we walk through the restaurant door. "I'm having a sundae today too! ho, Ho, HO!"

A pilot sits at the counter, drinking coffee. My mother, a waitress, and the cook are the only other people in the restaurant. Kellen's booming voice stops conversation, and all eyes turn to us.

"Why? What happened?" Mom looks the two of us up and down for clues.

"Christ, you should have been there. I thought that son of a gun was going to become a bunch of parts flying in formation!"

Mom crosses her arms and raises her eyebrows. Kellen launches off, describing his emergency landing. I grin and sit down next to him. I've always been proud to know this guy, but now he's really been through something —and I was there. Are we comrades in arms now?

Kellen finishes telling his story, and his audience registers awe. I can't tell if it's real or fake. We order our afternoon snacks as we make our way through the restaurant to the office to call the mechanic. I pick up the phone and reach his wife, who says he's planning to be in the hangar the first thing tomorrow.

"Please tell him we've got a serious engine problem for him," I say. "The Mooney's already in the hangar."

I ask about Kellen about his going home.

"I'm not going home. Not with the airplane broken. Hell, no," he says.

"Hey, I'm sure it would be no problem for my dad or one of the guys to run you home. Not that far, is it? It's only an hour, right?"

"Nah, I'm going to stay with the airplane. Is there a hotel around here?" he asks. I suspect he doesn't want any of us to know where he lives.

"Sure, the James Madison Inn. I'll call and see if they have a room. If not, there's DeVivi's," I say. "The Madison hotel is a neat old place —elegant, and three stories high— a bit out of scale for our tiny town, but better than DeVivi's motel."

"Great, I'll have dinner here and then you can run me into town, okay?" says Kellen. "Oh, that's right, you don't have a driver's license. Well, could your folks run me to town? 'Course, I'll have to stop at the drugstore for supplies. I need a toothbrush and stuff. ho, Ho, HO! Maybe your mom and dad will let me borrow a car."

I call the James Madison Inn. They have room tonight, so I make a reservation.

We walk back out to the restaurant and eat: for him his sundae and then a hamburger; the usual, a burger, fries, and, this afternoon, a chocolate shake, for me. My dad shows up when we're finishing eating, and Kellen tells him about the airplane. This time, he leaves out the profanity and heroics. When he talks to Dad, it's technical.

When Kellen's not around, Dad sometimes complains about him: "He doesn't seem to work for his money. Kind of a lazy slob. Flying around in that airplane . . . More money than he's got sense. I'll bet he's on a trust fund." Dad also doesn't care for the way Kellen talks to the teenage waitresses. Kellen and Dad seem to tolerate each other in the way bull moose tolerate each other. They are not friends.

"Yeah," Dad says, after he hears Kellen's report, "sounds like it swallowed a valve. Doesn't sound like a rod broke, because you didn't lose all your oil."

Kellen never mentions my role in his drama, but that's okay with me. I'm proud that when I found myself in a life-and-death situation, I kept my wits about me. At least to me, it felt like a life-and-death situation. I didn't screw up and didn't abandon the radio to run off looking for help.

Yes. Kellen is a comrade-in-arms now, I've decided. We made it through this together. It's another thing learned from my older friend, another experience under my belt that will make me a better pilot.

CHAPTER TWENTY TWO

Since Kellen flew in World War II, I use him —or try to use him— as a primary source.

"What did you fly in the war?" I ask him.

"Oh, this and that."

"Where were you based?"

"Well, you know, a person moves around a lot in the military."

"Did you ever shoot down any airplanes?" On *12 O'Clock High,* they shoot down airplanes several times an hour.

Kellen looks over the top of his glass of iced tea and waits a minute before answering.

"You know, I've seen guys after they've killed someone. They don't say anything. The first thing they do when they get out of the airplane is throw up. Then they find a bar and drink.

"Killing somebody —that's not something a guy likes to talk about." He takes a long drink of iced tea and looks at me. "And if I were you, I wouldn't ask about it, either."

He's so serious, unusual for him, and I learn the lesson.

The "airport kids" is what we're called; the teenage waitresses, some adult pilots' children who hang around, and me. The airport kids always want to learn more about Kellen. He fascinates us. But even after we've known him a while, he still offers few personal details.

"What did you do for the Carusos up in Bar Harbor, Kellen? Did you fly for them?"

"Man! Those were the days. Nonstop excitement," he says.

"Like what? What kind of excitement?"

"So, there I was at thirty thousand feet with nothing on the clock but the maker's name and still climbing! I threw in the third jet! And oh! Jesus Christ! And a voice said, 'Yes?' ho, Ho, HO!"

His ditty is dictum to not pry.

But even though his answers go missing, the airport's young people never stop pumping him for personal details.

"Where do you live?"

"Up on a farm."

"What do you do for a living?"

"Oh, I take care of business."

"Are you married? Do you have a family?"

"Somebody asked me about that once." He shakes his head from side to side and puts up his hands like somebody had asked if he was a cannibal.

"How old are you?"

"Some question!" Big laugh, "ho, Ho, HO!"

We've learned that if you probe too much, Kellen won't show up again for a few days. But over time, some details have leaked out: A summer home in Maine. A former winter place in the Bahamas.

"I used to go down to Nassau every winter for a few months," Kellen told me once. "But I stopped going when the Mau Mau took over."

When my parents win an eleven-foot Styrofoam sailboat at a Chamber of Commerce meeting, Kellen shows me how best to set it up.

"On my boat in Maine, we've got a lateen rig on the dinghy, just like your boat there. That's pretty neat! It works good!"

"A boat?" I ask.

"Schooner. Been in the family for years," he says.

Whoa! An answer. And to find out he's a sailor too? Kellen's stock rises.

For Kellen, sex lies ever present, like the water under his boat or the air under his wings. When conversation about airplanes dims, tales of pulchritude rise like mushrooms in a damp forest. Sometimes airplane and sex talk mix.

"I had a Cessna 180 once. I had a guy paint some bomber art on the tail. It showed a gal with big . . ." He holds up his hands in front of his chest as if holding two bowling balls. "She had nothing on but a grass skirt and flowers, blowing in the breeze. I called the airplane the *Gay Lei*. That's when gay meant cheerful or carefree, not fruity."

Kellen seems happiest when talking about the two pillars of man: airplanes and carnality. Being a teenage boy, I like both things too. Kellen is a bard, laughing and embellishing each stanza of his lascivious offerings with great care. He composes riveting tales of sex like a randy Shakespeare.

For a while now, Kellen's been working at putting a sharper edge on my chess game. A gentleman player, he tells me to "Guard your queen," alerting me I need to get her out of the way before he kills her. I'm doing that now too. It makes me feel refined.

After losing as usual, I sit eating my after-school snack and drinking a chocolate shake. Kellen goes pensive as a story begins. Paying close attention, I stop eating. I put down my burger and wipe my mouth with a paper napkin. Listening to Kellen is always a priority.

Talking to him is like being in medical school. As yet, I've never done surgery or even examined a patient. Never yet been out of the biology classroom. But I sit on an orange stool at the airport lunch counter with my experienced and august professor, learning what must be graduate-level stuff. With the fine education he's providing through lectures, I know my sexual practice, when granted the opportunity, is sure to be expert and fulfilling. I'm hoping that opportunity arrives soon.

It's early spring, and I direct my affections toward Dornin, another teenager my folks hired as a waitress. She's been working for a while now on weekends. Her mother suggested Dornin work at the airport to gain experience working "at a real job in the real world." A pretty and tall girl, Dornin shares her mother's elegant carriage. Graceful like her mother, Dornin is cool and poised. It didn't take me long to be smitten —not for the mother, but for the daughter. A year or so older than me, and private-school educated, Dornin tolerates my clumsy feelings of warmth but never offers encouragement.

But there's hope, even as I continue to learn through my tutor's discourses.

I've yet to realize Kellen is more Dr. Frankenstein than Dr. Kinsey.

"You know, sex isn't always fun," says Kellen. "Sometimes it can really twist you around."

"How's that?" I ask.

After an uncomfortable pause, during which I've time to eat a bunch of fries, Kellen continues.

"One summer between high school terms, I was staying over at my school roommate's place. Sure as hell didn't want to go home." Kellen looks like he's made a mistake, opened up a crack. He says, "ho Ho, HO!

"Anyway, I fell for his sister in a big way. Huge crush."

His pause is long, and I break it with a bite of burger and long pull on my shake.

"This gal was built," he continued. "Really stacked! I mean *va-va-voom!* Looked like she was always wearing a Mae West. An inflated Mae West! I mean—" He cups his hands way out over his chest, the bowling ball thing again.

I know about Mae Wests. Gibson Girls too. They were World War II life jackets and emergency radios. All that time watching *12 O'Clock High* taught me a lot.

After a moment to bask in his voluminous memory, Kellen says, "I tried everything I could to get in her knickers. Man-o-live! You know what? She flirted back! I knew I was going to lay some pipe. Sometimes you just know, you know? It was just a matter of time —and finesse!" He looked out the greasy window at the back of the kitchen into the pale afternoon light.

"That summer held the promise of paradise. I couldn't eat —believe it or not! ho, Ho, HO! Skinnier back then," he says, patting his stomach. "All summer, I almost exploded with excitement! For the whole friggin' summer I was ten-hut!

"But time was running out! I already had my train ticket. We soon had to get back to school."

He realized he was talking a lot about himself and hadn't cracked a joke in sixty seconds. So he tried to amend the tone. "Yep, a train ticket, and my train hadn't yet made it to the tunnel! ho, Ho, HO!

"Anyway, one night, I made my move. This was it, man. I rolled out of bed. I crept down the hallway to her room, the front of my pajamas pointing the way like a homing needle. They had a big house, and it took me a long time to make the trip. Or so it seemed. That hallway was endless. It had all these paintings of dead relatives and statues and stuff. I didn't let the paintings' glares discourage me, though. I was on a mission. I hoped the floor wouldn't squeak. Didn't want to wake her mother —who, by the way, wasn't bad looking either. I would've done her too! ho, Ho, HO!"

An image of Dornin's mom flashed in my head.

"Were you just going to barge in?" I ask.

"Hell, no! I wasn't going to jump her, if that's what you're getting at! What do you take me for? Hell, no. No, I planned to wake her up and let her know I was there —'Hello, my dear. Nice evening.' You know, be a gentleman. But let her know I was available! You know? I was pretty sure —no, I was sure— she'd wake up, smile, and say, 'Oh, Kellen. Put 'er there, big boy!' Just like the nun said to the bishop! ho, Ho, HO!"

"So, I opened the door. Quiet like. This was it. I was just a few seconds from Nirvana. The moonlight streamed in like some kind of magic ether. It lit the room just enough so I could make things out. I could see her in her bed. With her brother —my roommate— on top of her. Going at it! Like rabbits!"

I can tell this is no time for questions, so I sit through another long pause. This time I don't eat.

"You could smell that smell," says Kellen, his voice soft.

"Jesus Christ, I almost blew chunks —I never got over that. Sick."

No "ho, Ho, HO!" this time. Kellen looked at the window again. "Look there. Geese going north." He sighed.

"I've never been the same since. Ripped something out of me, you know? Changed me. And I had to look at that SOB every day for the rest of the term."

I don't bother him as he watches the geese fly out of sight.

*   *   *

Kellen and I go flying together a few times that summer. Sometimes he comes with me as I move airplanes around from one airport to another. The airplanes I fly are usually Cherokees and other Pipers. So it's always better when I go with Kellen in his airplane. I never pass up an opportunity to fly in his nice, slick, fast Mooney.

Today is a fine afternoon. Kellen says, "Hey! It's a great day! Not a ripple when I flew in. Let's you and me fly down and see what's doing at the beach. We'll make a run down the Outer Banks."

With nothing much going on at the airport, I say, "Sure. Let's go!"

We do the preflight inspection and are climbing onto the four-seat Mooney's wing. I see Dornin, taking a break from the restaurant, come out to stand by the hangar door. She waves. I say, "Hey, Kellen. Can Dornin go?"

What girl wouldn't move toward feelings of love by going flying in a fast little airplane? Especially in a Mooney. I figure inviting her to go flying with us might be like romantic grease, a sure-fire attempt to lube what I hope are Dornin's latent affections toward me. To promote positive conditions that might increase the chances, as Kellen puts it, for me to "lay a little pipe."

I'm hoping Kellen will immediately see the plan and co-conspire. What could be better? A pretty girl with whom I'm smitten, time with one of my best friends, and a cross-country Mooney ride to the shore. All at the same time. Perfect.

"Sure she can go!" says Kellen. "Come on, Dornin! ho, Ho, HO! See you when we get back, Russ."

Off goes Kellen with my would-be girlfriend. Jesus Christ! What a backfire. What a mistake. I am pissed. I've delivered my would-be love to the jaws of the lion and lost an airplane ride. This won't happen again. Lesson learned. Damn it. In mating season, there are no friends.

* * *

But on balance, the great days with Kellen far outnumber the crummy ones. Today is another day, and we are cleaning his airplane on a gorgeous Virginia afternoon. Vacuuming the little cargo compartment, I find three *Playboy* magazines and a fake leather portable travel bar set.

"Go ahead! Open it up!" says Kellen. "That thing is the killer-diller!"

I don't know how I know that "killer-diller" means "neat." Too much World War II television, I guess. Or maybe it's the way Kellen says it. But Kellen's bar set is neat and contains two glasses, a jigger, swizzle sticks, and a full bottle of Cutty Sark scotch whisky. All compact and ready to go.

"You never can tell when you're going to get stuck somewhere, you know, like when my engine crapped out," says Kellen. "ho, Ho, HO!"

"Don't you carry extra clothes or shaving stuff in your kit? A toothbrush?" I ask.

"Nope. A good drink and a good magazine. Scotch, naked girls, and good reading. That, my friend, is all you need . . . ho, Ho, HO!" he says. His eyes are wide and brows arched high like he's made a big discovery. "Hey! You know, those are ideas that might catch on! ho, Ho, HO!"

Leafing through the magazine, Kellen says, "Yes, sir, Hugh Hefner is on to something with this. High culture, man. I think there's an article in here by John Cheever, the 'Chekov of the suburbs.' Good reading." He pulls out the centerfold and smiles. "Mmm, Britt Fredriksen. Oh, but aren't you looking good today, my dear? ho, Ho, HO!"

We finish cleaning the airplane. For the next couple of hours, we sit on the wing enjoying the beautiful afternoon, the perfect air, the flawless light. Relaxing, meaningful, but forgettable conversation fills the time. We cover it all, from the thoughts of Francis Bacon to Britt's bra size.

"All the philosophers denied sex until the twentieth century —Plato, Kant, all of 'em!" says Kellen. "All of them except the Marquis de Sade, and he really wasn't a philosopher, was he? No, he was a rapscallion! A friggin' satyr!"

"That's what Clint called you."

"Me? ho, Ho, HO!"

The rest of the talk, tales of bawdiness and airplane stories, disappears from memory the moment it is spoken. Forgotten words. Words like the summer breeze: warm and gentle. Ceiling and visibility unlimited. Both the weather and the words are stress free. If we were by the shore, this would be a red-sails-in-the-sunset day. An inconsequential day, with inconsequential talk, the memory of which I know will stick with me the rest of my life.

*   *   *

Whitey flies in for lunch on Saturday. He flies pipeline patrol in a little Cessna 150 —looking for leaks— and pops in occasionally to grab a bite. Even though he flies Cessna's basic trainer, he has a spectacular job. He gets paid to fly. Whitey and Kellen have been at the airport several times together and have bantered like old chums, so I assume they are good friends. Whitey is the closest thing to a Kellen intimate we know.

"Hi, Skippy!" says Rosemary, the waitress. The waitresses

call Whitey "Skippy" because he once crashed his airplane in a peanut field. My sister, Debs, who works mainly as a waitress but sometimes as the restaurant manager, comes in from the kitchen to greet Whitey.

"Hi, girls!" says Whitey

He orders lunch. His usual: a BLT and a glass of sweet tea. He takes his normal spot, the seat straight across from where Kellen likes to sit. No other customers are around. Rosemary, Debs, and I begin an interrogation.

"You've known Kellen awhile, haven't you?" we ask.

"Yep, awhile. Not well, but a while. Why?"

"What do you know about him? Where's his farm?"

"Not sure. Somewhere in northern Virginia. Fauquier County. Hume, I think. Horse country."

"How old is he?"

"Not sure. Pretty sure he's older than me."

That tells us nothing. Both men are ancient.

"Does he work?"

"Don't know."

"Is he married?"

"Well, about that," says Whitey. "I heard he murdered his wife."

"He what? Murdered his wife? And . . . ?"

"That's it. I heard he murdered his wife. Somehow there wasn't a case. Dunno. Acquitted or something. Judged an accident, maybe. Some kind of mysterious Agatha Christie kind of thing. Dunno. He didn't serve any time, though. That's what I heard."

We let Whitey enjoy two bites of his BLT.

"Wow. That's weird. Children? Does he have kids?"

"Don't know. Maybe. Yeah, I think maybe there were one or two kids. Yeah, the farm and a couple of kids with horses. Maybe."

We never ask Kellen about his wife. And none of us kids tell my parents about the rumor. We don't want Kellen banished.

CHAPTER TWENTY THREE

My dad and I spend little time together now. He's drinking a lot again, and that's making any regular time with him, well, difficult. The only good times we share are when we fly together. I have some interactions with him at the airport, but I try to avoid him.

The holidays approach, yet one more season holding nothing for me. Even though drinking now trumps faith, my father still swears allegiance to the Watch Tower Bible and Tract Society. So again, there's no Thanksgiving. Even though lights decorate the town and carols fill the radio airwaves, there will be yet again no Christmas for us, either.

But this year, I have reason to celebrate. My sixteenth birthday approaches. I've already logged sixty-eight hours of flight time. All logged as "dual received," most of it from flying with my instructor-rated father. I've never flown alone.

Sure, there was that time my dad sat in the passenger seat of a four-seat Cherokee and let me fly three landing patterns. He sat in the back, away from the controls. But he was still there, sitting in the back of November six-three-seven-seven Romeo. I wasn't alone. My father wanted me to know I was ready to solo, but didn't want to set the poor example of breaking regulations by letting me actually fly alone before I was legal.

Usually people solo with about eight to ten hours of flight instruction. I've been ready, but not legal, for a long time. I have flown cross-country all around the East Coast. That includes that ambulance flight to John F. Kennedy International Airport in New York. There have been hours of aerobatic training. I can loop, spin, and do snap rolls and hammerheads. At night with my dad, I've flown on instruments in scuddy weather. I've jumped all the required hurdles and more. I'm like an athlete who peaks three and a half years before the next Olympics. By the time I am sixteen, my sixty-eight hours are more than enough required to get a private pilot's license. But all my flight time has been dual instruction.

For me, age is my limitation, and it's driving me nuts. All I need to do is to jump the age barrier to fly by myself. Time is a major frustration. I'm close to neurosis. *Tick, tick, tick*. Chinese water torture.

But I wake on the morning of my sixteenth birthday and know the time is now. The day has been a long time coming.

A crowd gathers to watch me solo on the afternoon of my birthday, December 18, 1970, a Friday, and a week before the rest of the world will celebrate Christmas. Liberation at last. It looks like a party there behind the flight-line fence. People laugh, point, and yuck it up. Twenty or thirty people are here: Silas, Hubert, and most of the other airport regulars. My mother and sisters stand here. Kellen has flown in too.

"Wouldn't miss it! ho, Ho, HO!" he says.

Duff Green from the newspaper attends too, standing there

with a Nikon around his neck. But no one thinks to ask him to take a group picture.

My father and I climb into November five-one-seven-five X-ray, fire up, warm the engine, do the checks, taxi out, and take off. After two landings and a simulated engine failure, my dad tells me to stop at the taxiway.

This is a tandem-seat airplane, the two occupants in single file, each with a full set of controls. It's a Citabria 7ECA, a souped-up version of the Aeronca Champ in which I made my first memory when we did that loop.

I sit in the front seat with the engine running as Dad climbs out of the Citabria's back seat and shouts, "Make three more landings and then come on in. Have fun."

I taxi back out, check the mags and carb heat again, line up, and take off. All is routine except for the crowd watching me.

As an airshow, it's a pretty sorry performance. But I'm glad I don't muff up any of the three wheel-landings. I don't do any three-pointers, because there's something wrong with the Citabria's tailwheel, and it shimmies at higher speeds. Somebody needs to check the springs.

A lot of students, after their first solo flight, remark about how "the airplane leapt off the runway when the instructor got out." But I've flown so much by now, in so many airplanes, that the performance boost of having only one person in the airplane passes without notice. And I'm sure not scared or nervous. Just happy and satisfied that my time has arrived.

Finished, I taxi to the ramp and park the airplane beside the fuel pumps. As I pull the mixture to idle-cutoff and the little engine comes to a stop, I hear applause and cheers. Looking over, I grin at the crowd and see people hooting and waving. Kellen, in his blue bomber jacket, pumps his arms in the air. Still grinning, I climb out.

I'm pulling on my bomber jacket when my dad comes over with the scissors. "Don't put your jacket on," says Dad with a rare laugh. "I need to cut your shirttail!"

The *Orange Review* newspaper owner snaps a picture of my father clipping my shirttail, a post-first-solo ritual. Instructors sign students' shirttails and then tack them around the top of the airport operations office wall, like scalps.

We should treat everyone to a hamburger in the restaurant. They were good to come see the kid solo. But I'm too young and into myself to think of such a thing. My parents are too broke to think of such a thing. So the people in the party crowd express their best wishes and congratulations, and each member fades away along with the setting winter sun.

Alone, I push the airplane back to its hangar and bang the two heavy sliding doors closed. I did it. I soloed. I crossed this first major flying milestone. And if that forecast snow doesn't develop, I will fly again tomorrow.

*   *   *

All that winter, whenever the weather is good, I go up to fly by myself. Winter turns to spring. I continue to fly and work at the field. I spend many hours on the Allis Chalmers tractor trimming brush on the far edges of the runway, and putting up with high school. I still have to put up with the Witnesses too.

While wanting to pay Jehovah some homage, my father continues to celebrate once a year at the Witness's Memorial service. It always falls around Easter. I guess Dad hopes God will give him enough credit to clear the hurdle at Armageddon.

Between the shards of his religious practice, he worships the bottle.

I had thought the airport and the liquor would wash away all of his religious fervor. That would have been a benefit to booze. But, no. Unlike in Alaska, where he gave up booze for God, here in Virginia we're under the influence of both of his addictions. This year, he insists his entire family attend the hollow Witness Memorial festivity.

Some celebration. No dancing, no party, and again no food except unleavened bread and Manischewitz wine. None of us earthlings even eat the dry crackers or lousy wine —the "feast," it's called. A Jehovah's Witness celebration is an invitation to a symphony with no orchestra.

I'm in my coat and tie, my sisters all clean and dressed up, and we are all seated in a row. My mother looks fresh and refreshed with so many people nearby. I sit next to my father. He wears a white shirt and tie, sitting up straight in his dark-brown corduroy sports jacket. On his lap sits his green Witness Bible, his *New World Translation of the Holy Scriptures*, ready for action. He's a biblical Matt Dillon. One can never tell when you might have to whip out a scripture. Really let somebody have it.

My friends from school look forward to Easter with its big dinners, candy, and fun. Not me. I sit and wonder how the Witnesses arrived at this poor excuse for a celebration.

Protocol at the annual Memorial restricts consumption of the "feast" to the anointed ones. Only 144,000 human beings will take true communion or go to heaven. Ever. This lucky few will sit at the right hand of Jesus, becoming the Lamb's bride. It's another wacky Witness belief spawned from a literal interpretation of scripture.

From the stage, the ministerial overseer —he'd be the preacher in any other church— drones about what it takes for admission to heaven. He tells us that each of the 144,000 people must have lived after Jesus' crucifixion. This means that even Abraham, Moses, and David didn't make the cut. Nor did the perfect, upright, and long suffering Job.

Today's remaining living members of this little flock, this Israel of God, this bride of Christ, this New Jerusalem of anointed ones, are called the Remnant. The speech would have been much better if the speaker had cut the in-speak. Oh, to bring the blessing of brevity to church. It amazes me the Witnesses have so many names for things. Does their message have such poor coverage that it takes many coats of words to shellac the followers?

The ministerial overseer says membership in the 144,000 closed in 1935. Provided with a special revelation —I suppose it was like when Mary received the surprising news that she was pregnant without having sex, a story I hoped would serve me, as it served Joseph, if I ever found myself in a similar situation— each anointed one received a "positive assurance of adoption" by Christ.

Brides, adoptions, countries, cities, leftovers —Jesus! The speaker uses so many words. Has he exhausted the dictionary?

Tonight in the stuffy Kingdom Hall, I see Ed a few rows over. He's an old guy, famous in this congregation for being the only one destined for heaven, the only one of the Remnant in attendance. Ed is one of the Lamb's brides.

Isn't our family lucky? We've known three people in that august group. Of the roughly one hundred billion people who ever lived after Jesus, we've known three of the 144,000 who will go to heaven. In Alaska, we had two of these anointed ones in our congregation. In Virginia, there is one: good old Ed.

Ed was alive and well before 1935. That gave him some bon-afides. *But wait a minute*, I think. *He had a wife.* Revelations says members of 144,000 "have not defiled themselves with women, for they are virgins." I ask my father about this after tonight's soirée.

"Don't try to figure it out, Son. Quit quibbling," says Dad.

"Hmm," I say. "Do we get to pick and choose which Biblical reference to believe? And why is some stuff taken literally and some not?"

"You're too smart to learn," he says.

"Don't look behind the curtain," I mumble.

Maybe I am too smart to learn. Maybe it is better to be passive like stupid sniveling woolies. After all, the Bible tends to favor sheep. Ed is a nice old guy. He seems good and kind. And tonight, by whatever technicalities the Witnesses wish to use, he is this congregation's celebrity. The only Jehovah's Witness in Orange, Virginia, who chows down at the Memorial.

Now a teenager, I weave sarcasm like a Tabriz rug maker works with wool. It's gotten so bad that Billy Graves, the Navy officer now back from Viet Nam, a pilot friend working on getting his commercial ratings, reins me in. "If you don't watch it, somebody's going to punch you in the mouth," he says.

Just ten years older than me, Bill's saying it just once works better than a hundred scoldings from parents. After that I throttled way back on sarcasm, but didn't stop. But I never push it to blasphemy. I want to hedge my bets.

But I can't stop baiting my father.

"Okay, what's going on here?" I ask him.

Most of the time we grab our meals at the airport. Tonight, the day after the Memorial, we share a rare dinner at our rented farmhouse on Mt. Sharon. Spaghetti with meat sauce.

"How come, every year, there are always more people in the anointed class, in the Remnant, than the year before? Every year, the Organization reports more and more people 'join the feast.' Shouldn't the Remnant be dying off instead of spawning? Can you explain that one?" I wipe sauce from my chin. "Every year, more and more people chomp on the crackers and sip the wine. How do the geniuses at the Watchtower Society explain that math?"

"You refuse to read and study the books," says my father. By books, he means the Witnesses' own literature. "If you weren't so damned bumptious, forget what you think you know, and just took the time to learn, you'd know," he says.

Not happy with that nonanswer, I ask, "If I studied, would I find out why the Witnesses have missed so many end-of-the-world forecasts like they did in 1914? I guess I'm just not humble enough to see the Truth, right?"

I'm surprised he doesn't slug me.

Witness theology is chock full of revised prophecy. It's easy to point out things like that. My father thinks I'm badgering him and just being a wise-ass teenager.

"You're too smart to learn. And you're headed for a fall. Please pass the Tabasco," he says.

CHAPTER TWENTY FOUR

One thing I learn at the airport is to never leave teenagers in charge for very long. How many times at the Kingdom Hall had I heard about teenagers' failings? Teenagers rush to the hellish world of petting, naturally gravitate toward the rampages of smoking, swearing, drinking, and —God forbid— drugs. Unwatched, they become delinquents in mere minutes due to poor associations. Who knows? Maybe the Witnesses' predictions have merit. This summer, I learn that some juvenile delinquents —horrible influences— are sixty years old.

After leaving Alaska, my father's attendance at Jehovah's Witnesses' meetings has gone way down. He goes to the memorial "celebration" but few of the regular meetings scheduled three nights of the week. He's become a truant. A delinquent Witness himself. Working hard at the airport is his excuse. But I've thrown many beer cans away. I've found a lot of empty vodka bottles. I suspect alcohol might blunt his religious zeal. I suspect drinking makes him feel guilty too. Could this be why he's gotten meaner?

His drinking doesn't appear to affect his ability to work, though. Not on the surface anyway. Not that I can tell. And I don't suspect he drinks when flying or when giving me flying lessons. I can't —or don't want to— believe he drinks when he flies.

But the bottle of vodka he keeps hidden under the truck seat might explain certain goofy business decisions. Does alcohol make him forget to pay his taxes? Why doesn't my mother remind him? What's her excuse? She doesn't drink much at all. Is she in denial about the cash flow? Or does she not want to get yelled at?

The financial blundering doesn't affect me at the airport —yet. I get to work here, and I still get to fly. Still, I hate it when Dad drinks. His opinions and his hatred of the sharks, the World, and The Man gets bigger. He becomes more critical of my mother and me. His belligerent streak grows stronger with each sip and, when we're at home together, I'm glad when he falls asleep on the couch. I always hope sleep comes before he gets nasty.

This weekend, my parents leave to attend a conclave of Witnesses in Roanoke. I think Dad goes to make up lost ground with God. My mother goes because she enjoys being with people. The convention can pass as a party.

My parents leave my older sister and me in charge of the airport and our two little sisters, our two souvenirs of our time in the frozen north.

My sister takes excellent care of the little girls. She's cared for them like an extra mother since they were born. In Alaska, when each was learning to speak, they both called my mother and Debs "Mama."

I'm a lousy babysitter but do a great job with the airport. It turns out not always safe, but good.

With my parents gone, Kellen sits on his usual stool at the lunch counter. For hours, we've discussed current aviation events, and Kellen has pestered the girls. Then he grows nostalgic.

"Back in the outfit, we'd sometimes drop toilet paper. We'd see how many times we could cut a roll with the airplanes. And that was in UC-78s! Bamboo Bombers! ho, Ho, HO! You should've heard those wooden wings groan! ho, Ho, HO!"

"Sounds like fun," I say. "What was your best number? How many cuts did you get? How many times could you slice a roll?"

"Hmm," said Kellen. "So there I was at thirty thousand feet with nothing on the clock but the maker's name . . ."

"How about balloons instead of toilet paper?" I ask. This summer, we staged a small airshow at our airport. The gas company has yet to retrieve the helium bottle we'd rented to fill balloons we gave to children.

"Sure. Balloons would work," says Kellen. "Harder to see, but more of a challenge! What do you say? Ho, Ho, HO! Let's try it!"

I take the first turn. In our Piper Colt —a good trainer, but a sorry excuse for an airplane— I take off and climb to about a thousand feet. "Okay," I say over the Colt's transceiver, a device referred to as a "coffee grinder," an old Narco Superhomer that sometimes imitates a real radio. "Let it go!"

From the air, I see the dots of Kellen and all the kids: my siblings and the waitresses.

"It's away!" says someone over UNICOM. I can't see the balloon Kellen releases.

"Nope, can't see it," I say.

"Okay. There goes another one! It's red!"

They tell me each time he lets one loose, but they're hard to see. Kellen must have launched five or six before I see one approaching my altitude. While seeing one is hard, hitting it even more difficult.

I take several passes before success. A balloon meets the Colt's propeller with a satisfying *Oomph*. "Got it," I say.

Kellen says on the radio, "We heard the pop down here!" He's lying. "Outstanding work. Okay, my turn. Come on down!"

I land, man the helium tank, and Kellen takes off in his Mooney. "Don't let it go until I say so," he radios.

A single runway parallels a two-lane highway at our airport. The paved airplane parking and fueling area, called "the ramp," lies between the main hangar and the row of T-hangars. The ramp and hangars stand between the runway and the highway. A row of houses lines the far side of the road, maybe two hundred feet from the ramp.

Orange County Airport: Kellen flew down the taxiway
between the two buildings to break the balloon.

I'd done my balloon-busting attempts at close to a thousand
feet while running inline down the runway, staying roughly in
the traffic pattern.

Not Kellen. Right after takeoff, he immediately turns right
and does a two-hundred-seventy degree turn to head back in our
direction. He never gets over two or three hundred feet above the
ground. That's not much at one hundred sixty miles per hour.
"Now? Let it go?" we radio.

"Nope, not yet. Wait," says Kellen. The light wind blows north, which will take a balloon out across the runway.

The Mooney begins a strafing run toward the ramp, way out over the pasture, perpendicular to the runway and the road. In a flash, Kellen crosses the runway and flies down the short taxiway at about a hundred feet. Man, that's loud. Kellen races in, and the airplane gets louder and ever lower. It gets bigger each moment. I didn't know a Mooney was so big!

I stand by the helium bottle in the middle of the ramp, holding a red balloon. I wait for Kellen's word over the UNICOM speaker mounted to the hangar. It's turned up to full volume,

To my surprise, the Mooney gets even lower. Is the prop going to hit the ground? Bigger and bigger, it fills my field of vision. The girls on the ramp scatter, taking cover. They look like Cary Grant in that crop duster scene in the movie *North by Northwest*.

Kellen says, "Now!"

Time stops. Everything happens in a single, eternal moment.

I release the balloon.

The Mooney hits it.

Pop!

The slipstream blows, and I smell the exhaust.

Kellen pulls up and banks hard left as I spin around on my heels to follow his flight. He misses the trees beside the road, but the leaves flutter. He misses the houses. The Mooney shrinks in size and sound as it roars off to the south.

Wow! You can't beat those World War II guys.

And that's it. It's a perfect moment. Perfectly reckless. Perfectly illegal. Perfectly irresponsible. Perfectly deplorable. And we get away with it. We never hear a peep. No neighbors, no police, no county airport commissioner. No parent. Nobody says a word.

But for those of us who are there, Kellen smashing the balloon is the stuff of legend. While my parents are away hearing stories of the miracles of God, we have witnessed the parting of the Red Sea.

CHAPTER TWENTY FIVE

For the first time, I see Bob's slick, sporty Beechcraft Baron. It's flying low over the village of Hatteras, a nice throaty roar coming from the two Continental engines. From outside the little tackle shop set among weathered tourist shops off the highway, we see Bob fly in. His Baron tracks at about five hundred feet and going fast. My guess is two hundred miles an hour.

A sweeping left turn takes him toward Billy Mitchell Airport. Bob —the same Bob from the Pohick days— is flying home after completing an airline trip. He's based at Washington National, about two hundred miles north of Cape Hatteras. The buzz job is our signal to fetch him. Swinger and I hop in the car and drive to the unattended airport north of the village. Swinger is not her real name. It is, though, what everyone calls her.

When we pull into the sand-covered parking lot, Bob is under the Baron's wing, running a rope through the tie-down ring. I wait for the god incarnate to stand up. When he does, the late afternoon light catches his blond flat-top. Looking tall and fit, he's wearing blue slacks and a blue-and-white print shirt. His sunglasses make him look even more like a movie star.

A cigarette hangs from the corner of his mouth. It twitches up and down as he talks. "Hey, how're you doing?" he says with a crooked smile. He walks over to give Swinger a hug and kiss on the lips in the middle of a cloud of smoke, his arrogant swagger the same I remember. I would walk like that too, if I were an airline captain.

"Hi," I say, feeling way younger than sixteen. "I'll grab the other side."

I go over to his right wing and tie it down. I love twin-engine airplanes, and this Baron is a stunner. It looks like a stunner to me, anyway. Even if it is an older model with somewhat faded and chipped paint, it looks wonderful, a fitting match for Hatteras' weathered buildings. I can't believe the guy who owns it is our old family friend. We are among the blessed.

Bob looms large in my mind, just as he did when I was three years old. He's been a hero, someone to aspire to, as long as I can remember. Now that I'm flying, and unsure about my prospects, Bob gives me hope. He is a harbinger of my unreal future as I peer at him through my glasses. Even if an airline job will never be mine, Bob stands as a signal for the possible. He is not an idol, not a dream, and not a character in a book. He's a flesh-and-blood human who achieved greatness.

His A55 model is white with blue trim, a smaller and older Baron —and stellar. It's more than twice as big as my Piper Colt, my flying milk stool. Short-coupled and squat with a tiny engine up front, the Colt is also white with blue trim, but in a different category. It's a Ford Falcon next to Bob's Ferrari.

The Colt is fabric-covered and painted with dope, much like my old model airplanes. When I tap, my fingers make a thumping sound on the Dacron. Dad owns the airplane and leases it out —twelve dollars an hour wet, that is, with gas included— but I consider it mine.

"That's yours, huh?" Bob asks when he sees the Colt parked next to him.

"Yep," I say, embarrassed to meet his eyes.

"Nice little airplane." He patronizes. Bob locks his airplane and pulls a cover over the windows. He doesn't want the blowing sand to ruin the plexiglass.

"Do you mind signing my logbook while we're here?" It's like asking the pope for a blessing.

"Sure," Bob says. He sets my black logbook on the wing of the Baron. Does he get any pleasure from signing the flying logbook of the kid he's known since a baby?

He has signed the page and put his certificate number down with the letters ATP behind them. Airline Transport Pilot. I can't keep from smiling. That's the most impressive signature I've ever had —probably ever will have— in my logbook.

The smell of stale cigarettes and fresh tobacco smoke fills the car as the three of us get in for the drive back to the tackle shop.

"How was your ride down?" Bob asks. He doesn't say "flight" down.

"It was fine, cloudy," I say, wondering why all my words sound stupid when I talk to Bob. "Takes a while to fly two hundred miles in one of those." I try to laugh as I raise my chin toward the Piper Colt, trying to be a little dismissive.

"Yeah, when I came down just now, the thunderstorms were popping pretty good," says Bob. "From back over the Chesapeake, looked pretty bad to the west, out toward your place. Are you planning to head back this evening?"

I nod. I'd come down to Hatteras to log some cross-country flight time. I thought it would be fun to see both the ocean and Bob. He's sitting in the car's front passenger seat, his left hand on Swinger's shoulder. He holds his cigarette out the open window with his right. The tip glows red in the breeze. I'm in the back seat.

"Why don't you just stick around tonight? Let those storms settle down."

"Okay," I say. If Bob thinks I should, that's the right decision, although I haven't planned on an overnight. I figure I'll sleep on Bob's couch.

"We'll see about a room," he says. "Swinger, check with Dave across the street and see if he has something at the motel."

A motel? That's nice of Bob. Who knows how much money he makes as an airline captain on a 727 —probably loads. An apartment in Alexandria, a Beechcraft Baron, a tackle shop, and an apartment in Hatteras. My parents always talk about airline pilots being richer than Rockefeller. One night at a motel? He won't miss that money.

We arrive at Bob and Swinger's shop, called Fish 'N Stuff. It smells of fishing line, cigarettes, and something sweet like perfume. Swinger, Bob's second wife, a petite, good-looking woman with straight posture and curly, longish, light-brown hair given to blonde, runs the gift shop part of the store. She's packed it with knick knacks made of seashells, ceramic fishermen with clocks in their bellies, and books about the Outer Banks. Her side of the building makes the shop smell sweet. Sickly sweet. The smelly stuff is called *pot-pour-ee*. That's an odd name, I think. The light machine oil on the fishing reels in the next aisle smells a lot better.

As I wander around the store, Swinger gets on the phone with Dave at the motel. Bob appears with a drink in a party glass covered with palm trees. A topless hula girl sways her hips between two layers of plastic. A fresh cigarette perches between Bob's lips. I like how he can talk and smoke at the same time.

Swinger hangs up. "Dave's got a room."

"How much is it going to cost Russ?" His cigarette wiggles up and down as he talks.

"Eight dollars," Swinger says. "Dave gave me a deal."

What? It feels like a punch to the gut. I'm on the hook for eight dollars? That's a lot of money. I try to keep the shock off my face as I calculate the damage to my savings. I have twenty dollars on me —a big hunk of my entire fortune— which equals two full tanks of gas for the Colt.

I had stopped on the way down to fuel up, so I am okay to fly home tomorrow. But still, eight bucks will set me back. I worked hard washing airplanes to save up that money. Every ten dollars means fuel for three hours of flying —gas money that's like gold to me.

I know I shouldn't have assumed Bob would pick up the tab. But still.

"Hey, Russ, why don't you go on over," Bob says, looking at Swinger. "Go and get comfortable. Come back at six and we'll have a drink and dinner."

The only thing I'd brought was my flight bag. I pick it up and walk across the street to the small, ragged motel. Dave, wearing faded blue jeans and an old Hawaiian shirt, his cigarette burning like incense in an ashtray, wants his money at check-in. That's okay —might as well get the pain over with.

Dave gives me my key on an enormous ring, and points me to my room down the sidewalk. I open the door, which takes a bit of finagling because the key is loose in the lock, click the door shut behind me, and stretch out on the bed. All I have in my flight bag is my logbook, a little E6B circular slide-rule aviation computer, scrap paper, pencils and pens, and navigation charts.

I get up to turn on the air conditioner. It's rusty, noisy, smells like mold, and rattles. I flip on the TV. The signal is weak, and the black-and-white picture is scratchy. Fine-tuning doesn't help. I splash water on my face from the sink that wobbles on two loose bolts that barely hold it to the wall, then flop back down on the bed. I take out my logbook and turn to Bob's signature. ATP. Wow. That's an awesome autograph.

But Bob, a god to me and, according to my parents, richer than Croesus, didn't pay for the motel. Are airline pilots subject to material concerns? Could money be real to airline pilots?

After brushing my teeth with my index finger and water, I arrive at Bob's apartment behind the tackle shop right at six o'clock. Swinger is cooking steaks in the kitchen, which is in a nook of the living room. Even in casual pants and little makeup, she looks like a hostess in one of her company's advertisements: "Everyone gets warmth, friendliness, and extra care. And someone may get a wife." Swinger stands at the stove with perfect posture and a smile.

I find Bob halfway reclined in his La-Z-Boy chair, an end table on each side. One table holds his ashtray and a pack of Marlboros, the other a lamp and a coaster for his drink.

"Hey, Swinger, how 'bout another 7&7?" He laughs and nods toward the kitchen like *all I gotta do is command.*

Now in a proper glass, the fresh Seagram's 7 Crown and 7-Up sweats, wet and inviting, drops rolling down the side. Swinger brings me a glass of sweet tea.

Movie-star handsome, like Tab Hunter, but older and more worn, Bob always wears an expression like he's up to something, as if he's right on the edge of mischief. It makes being with him feel exciting.

I sit on the couch, and we talk about airplanes. "What's it like to fly the 727?" I ask. What a lame question.

He takes a long drag and says, "Oh, you know. Boeing makes a good airplane. Always has. The 727 is built well. Like the rest of them." He pauses like he's thinking about how to answer some stupid news reporter's question. "You know, it's a little 'special' to land. But you deal with that, you know? Just fly the airplane . . ."

Swinger walks in, bringing Bob another drink, his third that I've counted, and as she passes in front of the La-Z-Boy, he reaches out and grabs her by the crotch.

"Oh, Bob!" she says, only sort of upset, looking back and forth in my direction. Her expression says, *There's a kid in the room!*

He laughs and lets go.

Swinger sets the drink on the table and gives Bob a little swat. Bob picks up what he had been saying about the landing qualities of the 727, but my mind sticks on two seconds ago. I've never seen that before. My parents sure don't act like that. It's shocking, but it's like the stories I've always heard about pilots and stewardesses.

My mom talks like the whole bunch of them are sex-crazed maniacs. I've never figured out if her words are condemnation or envy. And I never know whether to believe my mother when it comes to carnal affairs. Mom once read a skydiving article where a jumper said, "Free fall is like sex." Since then, she's believed skydivers have orgasms on the way down.

But where there's smoke, there's fire. Nobody's said how Swinger got her nickname. She's named Susan, or Sally, or something like that. She got the nickname at the airline. My mother said it rhymes with her maiden name —Winger, Singer, something like that, I guess. I wonder if the rhyme is all there is to it.

I'm still kind of stunned and thrilled by Bob's maneuver when Swinger calls out that dinner is ready. Bob brings his glass, Swinger refills it, and we sit down at the table. In front of me is a plate with a steak and a bowl with iceberg lettuce. It's a lettuce head cut in half —not my idea of a salad. A bottle of French dressing sits like a centerpiece in the middle of the table. How the hell I am supposed to eat half a head of lettuce? I decide to wait and see what Bob and Swinger do with their heads of lettuce, and I cut into my steak.

"Umm, good," I say.

Bob asks about my parents, "How's that restaurant coming

along? That's tough work. But your mom is a pretty good cook."
He tells the story of the time he came to visit us in Fairbanks. "I
rented an airplane to see the country, a little 172." He takes a long
pull from his 7&7. "But I came back after about fifteen minutes
in the air. I told your dad, 'I gotta buy some survival equipment.'
Jesus Christ! If you went down out there —even just a few miles
out of town— damn! You'd be out there for weeks. Maybe you'd
never be found.

"I bought a tent, a sleeping bag, an axe, matches, food, and
water jugs before I went back out again. For an hour ride!" Bob
laughs. "That hardware store had everything I needed. Damn!
I told 'em what I was doing, and they fixed me right up. Knew
right off what I needed. Expensive for a little sightseeing —but,
Christ! Worth every penny.

"Man, there's a whole lot of nothing out there flying in
Alaska," he says. "That's some serious stuff. Big-league flying." He
talks about my dad's bush-flying days in Alaska and how dangerous it was. I feel pride hearing Bob talk about my father that way.

Swinger asks about my plans for when I grow up. I hedge.
I'm looking at her through glasses. If I say I want to be an airline
pilot, they'd both know I was an unrealistic punk and might as
well be wishing for a leprechaun to show up with a pot of gold.
Poor kid.

"Oh, I dunno. I will probably fly for a company. Or maybe
I'll run the airport."

"Sky's the limit!" says Bob, even though it's not.

Around the table, we all know where the top of the aviation
hill lies.

"Who'd you fly with this trip?" Swinger asks Bob.

"The other two pilots said they didn't know you. But I did fly with Sarah —you know whom I'm talking about, right? Dark-haired girl, dimples. What's her last name? Anyway, she said to make sure to say hello."

The end of Bob's drink —his fourth— makes him louder and more profane. "Damn" becomes "goddamn." Instead of using his swear words for emphasis, he's using them now as filler, punctuation, and adjectives.

"Well, shit, I wonder if I'll get up to Orange County this year. Be good to try your folks' restaurant. Jesus Christ! Wouldn't you like to try it, Swinger? Hard to do everything you want. Not enough friggin' time. Please pass the goddamn butter. But there's so much shit to do." He inserts a word I've never heard an adult use.

Hearing an adult say it is shocking. I first heard that taboo word six years ago. After a service at the Kingdom Hall in Fairbanks, one of the Witness boys said it while we were playing.

"What's that mean?" nine-year-old me asked.

"It's got something to do with girls," another kid answered.

In Alaska, the neighbor boys and I kept our *Playboy* magazines in a locker under our treehouse. After adding to my vocabulary at the Kingdom Hall, I thought it was cool and sophisticated to pull out a centerfold and say to the guys, "Nice fuckers."

Until I got to middle school, I thought fuckers were breasts.

I only go to the Kingdom Hall once a year now for the Passover "celebration," but the teachings linger. The Witnesses would say I am definitely among the World here at Bob's place. Christ! I might be in Gehenna. Bob is like an ambassador for Babylon the Great. It feels I'm a world apart from my home.

But my parents approved this trip. They know how Bob is. After several years with the Witnesses, my parents are supposedly different people now than they were back in the Pohick days. They —no, not they, it's only my dad— profess to be apart from the current "system of things" and the corrupt World of Christendom. So why is he okay with this? A transient lapse of judgment, maybe?

Me? I'm loving it.

The pauses in the conversation become longer. Maybe I'm imagining it, but I get the feeling Bob and Swinger want to be alone. I can't think of much to ask Bob that doesn't sound like babbling from some goofy teenager. How's it feel to grab your wife by the crotch, Bob? So, Bob, how's business going? I noticed there weren't any customers in your tackle shop. Are you glad to have that airline job? Are airline crews really sex-crazed maniacs?

I want to please Bob. I don't want to do or say anything that will make him uncomfortable. And what can I say to a god? Sixteen-year-old me is not much of a conversationalist here in Hatteras. I find myself saying lots of I don't knows, maybes, and yeahs. Talkative around my friends, here with Bob and Swinger, I sound like a grunting troglodyte —those mumbling, filthy, poverty-stricken trolls from TV's *The Time Tunnel*.

Bob in Hatteras (1970)

It doesn't take me long to finish my steak, and I never do figure out how to eat my head of lettuce. Swinger poured oil and vinegar on hers and ate it with a knife and fork. But I couldn't do it. It was just too weird.

At the next long pause, I push back from the table and thank them for dinner. "Sure was good," I say. Swinger glances at my unfinished salad, but says nothing.

Bob tells me either he or Swinger will come by at nine in the morning to take me back to the airport. He gets up and goes over to the liquor bottle for a refill. "Nine work for you?"

I nod yes.

I walk back across the street to my first night alone in a motel. It's maybe only the second or third night I've ever been in a motel. I sit on my bed, still coming out of the fog of cigarette smoke and alcohol fumes. I replay Bob's grabbing Swinger. Holy smokes. I lie back on the bed and stare up at the ceiling.

Bob is doing something right. He's got a cool tackle shop

and pretty wife. He flies a 727 for a living and commutes in a Beechcraft Baron. My folks can't scrape two cents together. Even among the booze, cigarettes, cursing, and sex, I felt safe with Bob. I enjoyed being with him. He's an airline captain. He takes care of people. But his behavior seems extreme. The smoking and drinking don't look healthy to me. I'm not sure about the grabbing.

I get up and open the window. The falling salty sea air spreads a damp film on my skin. I can hear the bass sound of waves from the Atlantic beach to the east and lapping water from Pamlico Sound right next to the motel.

I think about Bob's swagger and how wonderful and arrogant it looks. I remember the many times my father has called me arrogant. Hearing Dad say it sounds like a curse.

When directed at me, the word always seems to precede something contemptuous like "SOB" or "jerk." Or, worse, "worthless." "You're heading for a fall," usually follows.

But arrogance looks great on Bob. I wonder if I'll walk like him when I become an airline pilot. I bet it will feel great.

I wipe the mist from my glasses.

Hold on a minute. Back to earth. You will not be an airline pilot.

CHAPTER TWENTY SIX

In the morning, Swinger picks me up and takes me back to my tiny, slow, ugly Piper Colt. She gives me a smile and a wave as she leaves me beside the tied-down airplane dripping with morning dew. This morning, the storms are gone, but they've left behind a lowering cloud ceiling. By the time I get to the James River, I can't fly more than two thousand feet above the ground without touching the clouds. That would be illegal for a visual-rules-only pilot like me. So I stay clear below the clouds. Here I am, still legal, but getting concerned. I work out a plan to turn around if the weather gets worse.

The lower James River has a lot of military facilities around. So I constantly check to make sure I am out of any official military air operations areas. With the clouds a few hundred feet above me, a couple of miles of visibility in front, and at only 105 miles an hour, I figure I am okay.

Again —as has happened more than a few times now with airplanes— time collapses as everything happens at once. A dark-gray shape is rushing up on the right side of my Colt. I recognize it as another airplane. A fighter. An F-4 Phantom II. He breaks hard right to miss me. I break left. I hear the roar of engines as he passes my right wing. One normally doesn't hear other airplanes while flying. He is close. I can see his letters and numbers. Navy. I see them, the pilot in the front and the weapons systems officer —the wizzo— in the back seat.

Did he see me on radar? Had he known I was there? Was he just trying to scare me? Or did I surprise him as much as he did me? Thinking about it in the moments after the near miss, my leg shakes from adrenaline.

I will not be talking about this one. What would be the point? I sure don't want my parents having second thoughts about letting their teenager take off to fly to another state. Maybe I can learn from this, though. What is the lesson here? Get a better radio? Grow eyes in the back of my head?

Lessons and experience. Those are my flying goals while I spend what seems like endless time on the way to getting my private pilot license. I grind away, burning fuel to keep the wind blowing over the wings, accumulating the minutes that turn into flying hours. The Colt isn't much of an airplane, but it's the one that is most available. Cheapest too. So even though the Colt is like a girlfriend you don't want to show off, we do have some good —and even educational— times together.

Bored one afternoon after school, I take off with a pack of Pall Malls I'd sold to myself from our gift display. It's bad enough to want to smoke. I'm not adding stealing to the list of sins. My parents profess never to have smoked and preach of cigarettes' evils. "Less-tar cigarettes?" says Dad. "How 'bout 'no-tar' cigarettes? Just stay away from 'em." So why did I find a pack of cigarettes in his toolbox?

My folks don't want me smoking, and I know it. But Bob sure

looked good when he smoked. Maybe I'll take up smoking and look good too.

Aloft in the Colt, I find the solitude needed to experiment. Nobody can see me here. I crack open the side window and puff away, letting the ashes and the butts flick away in the slipstream. I smoke about seven or eight cigarettes before I swoon and my throat burns. I decide cigarettes are not for me. Before I reenter the traffic pattern, I chuck the remaining cigarettes out the window.

*   *   *

I've been waiting for my birthday in December to be old enough for a private pilot's license. So on my birthday, with more than enough hours in the logbook —I have enough flight time to qualify for a commercial pilot's license— and with the written exam passed, I fly to Manassas and take the private pilot inflight check ride.

Pleased to have a license and able to take passengers, it seems an anticlimax after over two hundred hours of flying experience. It'll be another full year before I will be old enough, eighteen, for what feels like my most important prize, a commercial ticket —the permit needed to be a working pilot.

Meanwhile, business at the airport restaurant stays busy. But the taxes don't get paid, and my parents argue more often about money. I'm not sure the airport business will last much longer. But what can I do about it? I'm not in charge. All I can do is keep flying toward my goals. That's in my control. So while I wait for my commercial license, I hatch another plan to pole vault ahead.

The Federal Aviation Regulations require that an applicant for an FAA flight instructor certificate must have the required flight experience for a commercial license. The wording says nothing about age. Is there something I'm missing? Will the FAA license a seventeen-year-old as a flight instructor? A certificated flight instructor? I've already taken the written examinations for both the CFI and commercial. So over a snack of a loaded burger and a large order of fries, and with a copy of the Federal Aviation Regulations open on the restaurant counter, I talk it over with Kellen. It's Friday, and he's eating a big sirloin.

"You know, I don't see anything in the regs that says you can't be an instructor at seventeen. Doesn't say anything about age, does it? ho, Ho, HO! Give it a try! All they can do is kick you out!"

My father, who agrees that it can't hurt to try, gives me the required recommendation for CFI. My father and I aren't spending much time together now. I don't need more lessons from him in the air. The CFI endorsement is the last one I'll need from him. I can't trust him with my feelings anymore, and find his company on the ground almost intolerable.

My mother? I feel like she's been doing a walk-on role in my life since she caved on the Jehovah's Witness thing in Fairbanks. Since she let Christmas disappear.

I make an appointment to take my oral exam and inflight CFI check ride with the FAA General Aviation District Office in Richmond. I make the appointment via the telephone, and the secretary doesn't ask how old I am.

In two weeks, I am sitting in the office with the FAA man.

"Let's get to the oral exam, and then we'll do the paperwork," he says. That's weird. That's a break from the usual order of things. "If all goes well, we'll go up for the check ride."

For the next hour, we cover the fundamentals of instruction and talk about how I would teach various maneuvers. "Well, that went okay," he says. "Before we go out to the airplane, let me see your logbook, medical certificate, and license."

I hand over the documents.

"Hmm, you only have a private license? Why are you getting a CFI now?" Before I can answer he says, "Hey, wait a minute. How old are you?"

"I'm seventeen."

"Well, you know you have to be eighteen to get a CFI, don't you? You're too young. Wish I'd known that earlier. Wouldn't have wasted half the afternoon." He's staring, and I wish something would take his attention off me. I feel like when Mrs. Morrow said she knew about "you people."

"Um, I'm not sure the regulation says that," I say in the most humble and beseeching voice possible. "Can we take a look together? I'm sure I misread it." I've already learned to defer to government inspectors. Let them have the benefit of "teaching you something" to lube up their egos.

"You have misread it. It says you have to be at least eighteen," he says, irritated, as he pulls down a copy of the Federal Aviation Regulations. I haven't waxed on the subservient grease thick enough. He's pissed that this kid is taking up his valuable time.

I try to shrink in deference, keep my mouth shut, and try not to piss him off further. The GADO office holds the power to issue licenses. Each man there —if he wants to— can make a check ride hell. Every examiner has the power to push an applicant beyond his limits and fail him on any check ride. Even at seventeen, I know humble rapport with the Fed is important. But my demurring is not an act. Maybe I am wrong and have misinterpreted the regs.

The GADO man reads to himself. "Hmm," he says. "Okay, let's see if we can show you what it says and what it means."

We go over the requirements for a CFI word by word. We go over them several times. "Hey, Jerry," he yells to a man in the next office. "Can you come in here for a minute?"

For the next fifteen minutes, my examiner, Jerry, and I go over the verbiage. We find nothing about an age requirement. Nor is there a requirement to have a commercial license before getting a CFI. It just says one needs to meet the flight time criteria for a commercial license before applying for a CFI.

"You know, I think you might be right," says my examiner, shaking his head like he can't believe it. He reads out loud: "'An applicant must have the required flight experience commensurate with a commercial pilot's license.' Doesn't say a thing about age. Young man, I think you've found an unintentional loophole. Do you agree, Jerry?"

"Yup," says Jerry.

"How are you going to use the CFI if you get one?" asks Jerry. "I mean, you're seventeen and don't have a commercial license."

"Well, until I do get my commercial ticket in December, on or right after my birthday, I won't be able to charge for any lessons I might give. It seems to me that the regs say that a private pilot can have a valid CFI certificate and give lessons as long as he doesn't receive compensation. Doesn't get paid." Time for more grease, "Is that right, sir?"

"I think you're right. But I'm going to have to run this by the folks in Oak City," he says, meaning the FAA headquarters in Oklahoma City. "No sense in you making two trips, though. The oral exam is already out of the way. I'll make the call to Oak City now, and let them mull it over. Let's go do the check ride. If they approve it, you'll be the youngest CFI in the country."

The check ride goes fine. While we were out, the FAA in Oak City had "mulled it over" and did not return a negative response. The examiner writes out a temporary CFI endorsement. "We'll send this to Oak City 'on review.' Just because we didn't hear a 'no' doesn't mean a higher-up might not shoot it down. Don't be surprised if they revoke it," he says.

What's that thing about possession being nine-tenths of the law? I put the temporary license in my wallet before he has second thoughts.

I catch myself smiling a few times while flying home in the Cherokee 140. On the way, I think I had better hurry and take the tests to get an FAA ground instructor certificate. I don't know how I'd use it, but I'd better get it before they close that door. Now that they've found the loophole, they might close it. The ground instructor certificate requires a written test only, so I won't have to face an examiner again.

A few weeks later, the FAA sends my permanent CFI certificate. Soon after that, the ground instructor license arrives.

Some months later, I'm sitting in our airport's office. I've done the fuel log for the day and am working on inserting the revisions to the book of aviation regulations. Under the CFI criteria, I read that the government has amended the rule. A person now has to be eighteen to get any aviation instructor's certificate.

CHAPTER TWENTY SEVEN

"Is Russ Roberts in your class, Mrs. Coleman?" asks a hall monitor, sent from the office. This is Geometry, the sleepy class after lunch. "Mr. Teed wants to see him as soon as possible."

I've never heard of Mr. Teed. But Mrs. Coleman thinks "as soon as possible" means now. In her gravelly voice, carefully pronouncing each individual syllable as always, she says, "You'd better go now. Make sure you get the assignment from the blackboard."

I disappointed Mrs. Coleman when I didn't get tapped for the National Honor Society. She's the group's adviser and can't believe that my grades are so average. "There's no reason you couldn't be in the Society, except that you just don't care about making your grades better. I can't believe you don't apply yourself in school."

I couldn't care less about the National Honor Society, or grades, but I care very much about her disappointment.

I knock on Teed's classroom door.

"Yeah, hey, I'm back here! Back in the storage room."

"Hello? Mr. Teed?"

"Is that Russ Roberts? Come on back!" The storage room is a narrow anteroom between classrooms that's loaded floor to ceiling with books, beakers, test tubes, boxes, and junk. Mr. Teed sits on a wooden chair at the far end of the room by an open window. He's smoking and holds a pack of Luckies. He waves the cigarette in the air as if trying to push the smoke away. "Yeah, I know. I should quit. But not today." His smoke escapes from the open window and he flicks a bit of tobacco from the end of his tongue. "I hear you're a flight instructor. That right?"

"That's right. I got my ticket earlier this year." It's 1971.

"You're a junior, right? That's somethin'. A kid gettin' a pilot's license is one thing. But you're a licensed instructor! How old are you?"

"Seventeen."

"Goddamn! Imagine that!" Mr. Teed shakes his head.

It doesn't seem like that big of a deal to me. It's what I wanted to do. "I'm trying to get all my licenses as soon as possible," I say. "Knock the pins down as quickly as I can."

"Yeah. Well, I been hearing about you in the teachers' lounge."

That's weird. I thought I was invisible at school.

"And it's a damn good thing I did hear about you, 'cause I got a hell of a problem! I'm up to my goddamn ass in alligators!" He takes a long drag from what remains of a Lucky Strike and lights another. For a teacher, this guy is kind of unusual.

"Before I ask you to help, let me tell you about me," he says. "I'm a retired Navy chief. Got out of the service and finished my degree. Spent some time retired. I helped build the golf course over in Greene County. You heard about it? Greene Hills Club?"

I shake my head.

"Well, hell, it don't matter." He takes a long drag, laughs. He picks more tobacco from his tongue using the fingers of his right hand that are not holding the cigarette. I watch the lit end wobble close to his cheek. "Now I got a place to play right out my front door!

"Well, lemme tell you. After the golf course deal, I got bored. Kinda broke too! Ha, ha! So, I got my teaching certificate and got this job starting this year. Teachin' science. You know, general science. Geology. Stuff like that. I was okay with that crap, since I was a science major. Science is what I wanted to teach."

He finishes the second Lucky and fires up another one, being careful to make sure the smoke goes out the window.

"Well, listen to this. I came in this summer and got my assignments for the term. And guess what? They gave me an extra class. Aerospace. The teacher they had for it quit. Hell, man, I don't know shit from Shinola about aerospace. Don't get me wrong. I love airplanes and all that. Space program too. But I'm outta' my depth thinkin' about tryin' to teach it.

"I'm an old hard-hat diver. What did I learn about airplanes from a hundred feet under water? Let me tell you, kid, that's some job," he says. "My last job in the Navy was doing deep-dive welding out of Pearl. That'll make you old quick! Look at me. I'm only twenty-nine!" He laughs at his own joke, and coughs, smoke coming out of his mouth and nose like a spent steam engine.

Mr. Teed doesn't look very tall under his sailor's buzz cut, sitting there on a wooden chair as he smokes near the window. He has glasses and wears a worn gray cardigan sweater. Adults all look old to me, but this guy looks especially elderly. If I had to guess, I'd say Mr. Teed is almost fifty.

"Here's where you come in. I'd like to make a deal with you. Can you come in and help me teach the aerospace class? You can come up with whatever you want to teach the kids —hell, you're an instructor! I've got fourteen students in the class. I've just had 'em reading this aerospace textbook." He tosses me the book. "When I couldn't do anything more than ask them the questions at the end of the chapters, I knew I was in real trouble. They'd ask me a question. I'd just stare at them like a dumb shit. That ain't no damn good."

I wonder if all the people of the World —those who don't hang out at the Kingdom Hall or the Orange County Airport— smoke so much and, the expression being timely in present company, swear like sailors.

Teed looks at me over the top of his glasses. Taking a long drag, he says, "Whaddya think?

"When's the class?" I ask.

"It's the period just before lunch. What do you have then?"

"English." I name the teacher.

"Yeah, good guy. I've met him." He coughs again. This time it's more of a long fit. "Jesus Christ, gotta quit!" He wipes his mouth on a handkerchief. "Look, if you can help me, I'll talk to your teacher. Maybe I can 'borrow' you and get him to pencil whip a good grade and credit for English. You do okay in English, don't you? No problems, right?"

"Yeah, I do okay. And this year we're doing English literature. Stuff like Chaucer. I saw he wrote *A Treatise on the Astrolabe*, something I think I might be able to live without. Not much call for knowing how to use an astrolabe these days." We laugh.

"Yeah, I think I'd like to work with you. I've got my ground instructor license too, but I've never done a formal ground school class. Might be fun. It's got to be better than Beowulf."

"Great. Yeah. Lemme' talk to your English teacher. Meanwhile, what should the kids do this week?"

"Is there a section in the textbook on aviation history? I think they should know about everybody from Daedalus to Neil Armstrong." The flight of Apollo 11 is already two years in the past. "You know, give them a little background on how we got from nowhere to here. I'd spend the week with that." It is Monday. "And then we could run them through a private pilot ground school program. We can get that ginned up while you're doing the aviation history bit. The ground school will take the whole term. Maybe we could get them to take the private pilot written exam at the end. Show them a good movie about airplanes and rockets once in a while. Let them read a little Richard Bach for variety. *Jonathan Livingston Seagull* and *Stranger to the Ground*. Maybe some Ernie Gann. Have you read *Fate Is the Hunter*?"

He shakes his head no.

"You'll like it," I say. "Yeah, I think that program will work. What do you think?"

"Great. Sounds good to me. You don't smoke, do you?"

I shake my head. I gave up smoking that day in the Colt.

"Have a Coke then." He reaches into a small ice chest and pulls out a dripping six-and-a-half-ounce bottle. He pops the lid with an opener tied to the wall with manila twine and hands me the bottle. "Stop by after school, and we'll iron it all out."

"Well, I'm driving a school bus. I won't be finished until about a quarter to five. I can come back then if you want."

"Great! See you before five."

When I get back to the high school after my bus run, Mr. Teed says, "I talked to your English teacher. He wasn't too happy about pencil whipping your credit and grade, but I appealed to him on humanitarian grounds. Jesus H. Christ! You might have to write some papers and agree to read some stuff, but . . ." Teed blows out some smoke. "Told him if I didn't get your help I might be canned. So it looks like we're set. Let's get started."

After that first week, I spend my study halls in the storage room poring over the private pilot syllabus with Mr. Teed.

"For Chrissakes, call me George. We're equals here," says Mr. Teed.

It's hard calling a teacher by his first name, so sometimes I call him "Chief." He likes that, and it dredges up a lot of good Navy stories. Besides, I don't feel like equals. I'm just a kid at school. It doesn't feel like anything I've done has made me equal with a teacher. I'm just catching the occasional ride as events sweep past.

But never mind that. The aerospace students seem to enjoy the class we develop. Most of them do good work and take part in class discussions. They seem to like it when George slips off into a Navy story. I like that too. And in class, there's no "shit" or "goddamn." He cleans his stories up for the classroom.

"Flying on instruments seems like it would be a lot like hard-hat diving," says Mr. Teed, creating a neat segue. "Back at Pearl, a lot of days you couldn't see the end of your arm."

A lot of his stories start with "Back at Pearl."

"The day I'm talking about was like that," George continues. "Like flying on instruments would be. Nothing but goop. The guys up top had to let me down slowly, talking to me all the time. Kind of like an air traffic controller, I guess, as they let out the line inch by inch. I talked back, letting 'em know what was going on and not letting anything snag. Then it all went to hell in a hand basket!

"All of the sudden, a piece of metal from the ship I was working on fell on top of the comm line, snapped it, and knocked me as—"

I can tell he's about to say "ass over teakettle," because it's one of his favorite expressions.

" . . . Knocked me over, tangling the air hose. I was gasping like a goldfish dropped on the floor. Jesus!

"You haven't lived boys" —there are no girls in the class— "until you've been down in the murk and the muck with a fifty-pound helmet on your head, a burning welding torch in your hand, and your feet sticking up in the god . . . sticking up in the air."

Away from the high school, George comes to the airport on some of his days off. The pilots get to know him, take him for rides, and enjoy the company of the smoking, profane Navy veteran. I give him a couple of flight lessons.

About mid-year, George switches to unfiltered Camels. "They're a little lighter," he says. "Been smokin' damned Luckies for forty years. Shit! Surprised I'm not dead yet." When we're in the storage room doing lesson planning, no matter the temperature, the window stays open anytime the Camels burn. The window is always open, since the Chief never stops puffing.

When spring arrives, George and I decide the class has been doing a good job. We organize a field trip to the big Transportation Department airshow at Dulles International Airport outside Washington. The once-in-a-lifetime airshow runs an entire week. We think Tuesday will be the best day to go. We figure the crowd will be lighter after the weekend.

"Hell, I can't go," says George. "Son of a bitch. I gotta teach those other science classes. So you take 'em up there. Okay, Russ? You're a licensed school bus driver, right? It seems like it oughta be legal for you to look out for the boys. I'll call the school bus garage and tell 'em you need a bus.

"Take a bunch of pictures up there. Damn, I wish I could go."

It turns out we don't need a school bus. Not all the kids could go on the trip. So, at six o'clock Tuesday morning, with parental permission slips in hand, I load five students in the VW microbus —the same bus my family used to travel from Alaska— and drive seventy-five miles to spend the whole day at the airshow.

With superb weather, we do get a lot of good pictures. The students explore the new C-5 Galaxy cargo aircraft, the new 747, DC-10, and L-1011. We don't see the Concorde. I had expected it to be there, but when we arrive, I learn that they've banned it from the show for being too noisy.

A lot of other stuff besides airplanes is here. It's a transportation exposition. We see high-speed-train mockups, plans for underground tube railroads, pictures of flying cars, and lots of other things. But nothing shines near as bright as the airplanes out on the flight line.

We're leaving the show when we watch a hang glider demonstration out over the runway.

It looks to me like the pilot is climbing at an acute angle of attack. When the pilot cuts loose from the automobile-pulled tow line, the glider pitches up and goes inverted. The twenty-six-year-old pilot falls in his harness into the folds of the flapping Rogallo wing. We see him kick and kick. His arms flail as he tries to right the buffeting cloth wing. But no amount of kicking changes the flight profile, and the glider and pilot flutter to the ground from five hundred feet, not like a leaf so much as a wet towel.

Why did he show off like that? I'm reminded of my dad "flying on the ragged edge" and the resulting wrecked Luscombe. As the sirens wail, the red lights flash, and the crowd watches in fascination, I wonder why the guy didn't just climb out at a normal rate. The crowd wouldn't have known the difference. They wouldn't know a super steep climb from a regular one. It's a real bummer and the first time I —or any of the students— have seen anyone die.

You don't have to operate on the ragged edge. Especially not to impress people. On the ride home, talking to the students, I concentrate on the reason the accident happened, not the fact that a guy only a little older than us got snuffed.

I don't know if the accident puts any of the guys off flying or not.

After the airshow, we have only a few days left of aerospace class. All the students pass the high school course as we designed it. The final exam is a practice test I copy from the Acme School of Aeronautics' *Private Pilot FAA Exams Made Easy* booklet. We send some higher-scoring students to the FAA in Richmond to take the official FAA private pilot written examination. They all pass. Several boys tell George and me aerospace is their favorite class ever.

CHAPTER TWENTY EIGHT

During the spring of 1972, just as I'm ending my junior year in high school and about the time we're wrapping up Aerospace class, big changes occur. The IRS visits the airport. So do people from the Virginia Department of Taxation. All want money. They want money now. The bank wants money, and creditors want money. My parents file for bankruptcy, and we leave the airport.

During the summer, before my senior high school year, I listen to George Carlin's comedy album *FM & AM*. Without my work at the airport, I have a lot of time on my hands. I know the cut "Son of WINO" by heart. And you know what? I think I could be a radio announcer too. Funny and bright, I'd be just like George Carlin.

Flying hadn't turned me into a heartthrob like I hoped; neither had driving the cheerleader's school bus to away games. My dating life was still dust. But I bet radio would change that. I could be a fun and bright-sounding beacon of sex appeal on the air.

I show up unannounced at our local radio station to look for work.

Arch Harrison, the owner and manager of WJMA Radio, tells me, "I always wanted to take people from scratch. Start with people with absolutely no background in radio. I'd like to teach them the right way to broadcast. My wife, Marion, and I were talking about it just the other day. And here you stand, in your tie and sports jacket, asking for that very thing."

There's a glitch.

Arch says, "Your parents . . . What a disaster . . . Bankruptcy . . . a shame. Yes, a real shame. They pulled up stakes owing a lot of money to folks in town. Including me." He stands looking at me.

My hand is halfway to the doorknob to let myself out.

"But you know, I will not hold the 'sins of the father' against the son. That doesn't seem fair, even though one is subject to inheritance."

I'm not quite sure what he means by that last bit.

"Well, shoot. You can fly an airplane. I think you'll be able to fly a control room too."

I nod, my corduroy jacket too warm in the June heat.

Over the next months, Arch teaches me the radio ropes. Jean Love, a fifty-year-old high school art teacher and member of Arch's church, is another member of what we call the "Ace Announcing Academy." She's learning the ropes too.

The airport is dead now. But I do not lose all hope in a decent future. There's the allure of a budding radio career. It turns out I'm not George Carlin, but I've found I love radio. Couldn't broadcasting be a new avenue? People don't care about glasses in the radio business. If I can't fly for the airlines, I could travel the air waves instead.

With school ahead, maybe I could do part-time broadcasting to make money. My folks are bankrupt and, even when at the peak of their earnings, never paid for things like braces. Money from them for college? Fat chance. Besides, "Armageddon is coming," they constantly remind me, so who needs college? It's clear that all college expenses will be on my dime.

The end of our time at the Orange County Airport is the end of an era. A major chapter in my life comes to a close. I graduate from high·school in June and enter college in the fall.

For a while, without the airport, I'm a little lost as time wears on. I'm enjoying working in radio, but feel that I'm cheating on my first love, flying.

*   *   *

During the next few years, I never wholly leave aviation. My life is much like so many others entering adulthood; I question my path, try to find my way while juggling school, work, and money. I continue flight instructing, pick up charter flights, and put hours in my logbook. I add a multiengine rating to my pilot's license. The next license goal is an airline transport pilot's license —the license required to command airliners— but I must wait for that one until I'm twenty three —the minimum age.

For the next six years, I watch the contrails of airliners fly overhead.

PART THREE

CHAPTER TWENTY NINE

"I'd like to fly to Parkersburg for my long cross-country," says Christy. "My folks are having a family reunion."

Christy is one of my students. It's 1979 and I'm instructing part-time now out of the Gordonsville Airport. It's in central Virginia, just a few miles south of Orange County Airport. I'm flying a lot of airplanes, but haven't moved too far from the nest.

I'm flight instructing, still working in radio, and am putting the finishing touches on writing a flight operations manual that is the last step in getting an FAA approved Part 135 air carrier certificate. This will allow me to sell charter flights.

I'm cobbling jobs together, hoping to craft a living.

After getting married to Judy two years ago, we are having a new log house built on a nearby hill, in hopes of crafting a life.

Today, I consider my student's request. When I think of West Virginia and summer, two things pop to mind: mountains and thunderstorms, both significant challenges for any pilot. And Christy is a student pilot, a wet-behind-the-ears rookie. Still, I don't want to give her request an automatic "no." I like to keep my students motivated by pushing to expand their personal envelope. Ignoring my conflicting feeling, the one that thinks she should stay on the normal training program, I think a flight to West Virginia might be an opportunity for Christy to push and learn.

"Well, you're doing really well. I've told you that. But we'll have to play that one by ear," I say. "Let's have you take a long cross-country here in the flatlands first. You can do that this weekend, right?"

She nods.

"We'll really have to go over your route to Parkersburg ahead of time. I'll want you to know it front, back, and sideways. On the day you're planning to go to your family reunion, we'll have to look at the weather —make sure it's good. If you do go —and you may not— you've got to leave early, before any storms start to pop. That's important this time of year."

She is happy and agrees. "Sounds good!"

Christy and I are both twenty-four. She works as a radiologist in a hospital in Charlottesville. She is serious about her flying, but effervescent in her personality. Eager to learn, interested in the world, and grateful for the opportunity to fly, she seems an ideal student. I know that arriving in West Virginia in an airplane she flew will make a big splash with her family. Who wouldn't want to show off a little?

Christy's standard solo cross-country flight that weekend gives me no cause for worry. After debriefing that flight, we study the Cincinnati region aeronautical charts for her potential two-hundred-mile trip to Parkersburg. For pilots flying under visual rules, the colorful topographical maps show things like railroads, towns, roads, and radio-navigation aids. The idea is pilots can see visual landmarks depicted on the map, look outside to find those landmarks in the real world, and get their bearings.

Studying the chart for Christy's route, we see wave after wave

of mountain ranges. She'll be flying over every range of the Appa-
lachian Mountains, all the way to the banks of the Ohio River.
Elevation shouldn't be a big issue. In her Cessna 150, she'll be
cruising at sixty-five hundred feet, in good weather, well clear
of the ancient mountains. But clearing them doesn't mean dis-
counting them. In a jet, one wouldn't give those mountains a
second thought. But in a puny Cessna 150, it's a different story.

I am concerned about her options in an emergency. The moun-
tainous terrain offers limited spots to land. Around Gordonsville,
we have lots of pastures, fields, and many small airports. What
if, in West Virginia, the airport Christy needs is beyond the next
mountain range? What if she can't climb to clear the mountains
because of clouds, engine trouble, or whatever? And we must add
to the mix the possibility of thunderstorms. If storms develop in
her path, she must divert around them. By diverting, she'd burn
more fuel and increase the chance of going off course down some
mountain valley.

This afternoon, in the safe airport office, she plots her flight
with me, and we go over it mile by mile. I talk to her about the
challenges and the things to watch out for. Despite the risks, I
lean toward letting her go. She's doing better than the average
student. She's smart and has shown excellent reasoning skills. She
doesn't miss a beat giving me the right answers to my quizzes.
We're the same age, she's nice, smart, and it's a pleasure working
with her.

But I can still tell her no. I've given myself an out with the
weather. Everything hinges on the forecast for the two days of
her trip.

The day before the flight, a Friday, we talk on the phone. "The weather tomorrow is looking great," I tell her. "But remember. Thunderstorms in West Virginia pop like popcorn in the afternoon. Because of what? Prevailing winds, the mountain updrafts, and humidity. We've talked about that, right?"

"Right!" she says.

"It's a thunderstorm factory over there. But like we've talked about, if you go in the morning before the convection starts, you'll be alright."

"Early is the ticket," she says.

"That's right. I'll say it again. If you're up and gone early —before storm activity— we eliminate one of the major challenges of the trip," I say.

"Right!"

Things still look good the next morning, the morning of the flight. The air is drier than normal and the sky sparkles on this Saturday. There's little normal haze of summer, humidity is low, and we have plenty of visibility. I feel good —or at least okay— about Christy's trip.

I go to the airport to see her off, feeling nervous, like I imagine a dad would be before sending his child off on a two-wheeler for the first time. I'm letting go, giving up control. This is a challenging trip for someone of her experience, but she can do it. Challenge is one of flying's pillars. A joy. Without challenge there would be few "hangar stories" told.

"Know your airplane's limitations and your own." Every student pilot hears this. Test pilots push aircraft operating envelopes, push aircraft into unknown territory.

Learning to fly is all about pushing one's personal envelope, expanding one's own limitations. Student pilots don't press an airplane's envelope. They grow into their own. Today, we're pushing Christy's personal limits faster than the average. She's shown the aptitude. She's eager. And I like her too. I like the way she sparkles. But has my liking biased my judgment? Boy, I hope not.

Since she's staying the night after her family reunion and returning the next day, we dissect the forecast for Sunday too. It looks much the same as today.

"If you guys are partying," I caution, "go easy on the alcohol. I want you to be sharp for the trip home."

Christy nods with a serious expression.

"I want you to get out to the field early tomorrow, and call me —call the airport or my house— so we can talk over the weather just before you take off. We want to make sure it's okay just before you go. Whatever you do, get out of there early." I make eye contact. "The earlier the better."

In her cheerful, unburdened way, she says, "Super-duper. Got it. I don't want to get wrapped up in the hurly-burly." She likes to rhyme and calls animals critters. The rhyming gets to me a bit, but I like the way her words are honey-glazed, in a soft West Virginia accent.

Realizing I've been very serious, I smile, "Go and have a good trip. Call me when you get to Parkersburg."

She climbs into the little black-and-white Cessna 150, her training machine and the only airplane she's ever flown. It's not a powerful airplane. It would be better to have a more capable machine in the mountains. It's old too, with only one ancient radio. But it's the only training airplane we have. It will get her there.

She looks confident in the cockpit, and that gives me pause. There's no sign of concern from her. She only has a few hours of flight time. Is ignorance bliss? She may not have enough experience to worry. She fires up the little engine, and I see her running through her checklist.

She has thirty-two hours in the air and three solo cross-country flights under her belt: two short cross-countries and one a bit longer. Technically, she's ready for a more challenging long cross-country solo flight. But in flying, against the backdrop of collective experience, Christy is still a greenhorn.

Pessimists make the best pilots —always wondering what will go wrong next. It's difficult making Christy a pessimist, but I painted enough worst-case scenarios for her that she should feel some measure of caution. That's my hope.

A couple hours later, right on schedule, Christy telephones from Parkersburg. "Eight-seven-four-three Sierra, on the ground in Parkersburg," she says like she's speaking on the airplane's radio. She laughs. "Everything went good, all safe. Hunky-dory," she says.

"Airplane tied down?" I ask.

"Yep, airplane's good. Double half-hitches. Tied down, locked, and put to bed for the night," she replies, sounding perky and proud.

"Great. That's good. Call me first thing in the morning before you leave for the airport, then call me from the airport when you're ready to take off. Thunderstorms will start to pop in the afternoon."

"Yep. Thunderstorms. I'll call you," Christy agrees. "Nighty-night!"

The next morning, her first call comes later than I expect. It's nine o'clock, about the time I'd want her to be taking off, not leaving her family's house. I've already called the flight service station in Leesburg to check the weather. A few cells —cumulus clouds that are, or soon could be, thunderstorms— are forming down south, around Tennessee. Even though it's later than I'd hoped, she'll still be fine if she gets out soon.

When I get Christy's second call, from the airport in Parkersburg, it's almost eleven thirty. I'm surprised and irritated. "This is later than I expected," I say in understatement, my voice disapproving.

"Well, my brother was late picking me up, and then he had to stop to get some things from the store," she says, sounding sheepish.

I'm almost angry and think about telling her to go back to the house. But I don't. "Man, for my comfort level, you're cutting it close. When are you going to be airborne?"

I should tell her to go back to the house.

"I've already pre-flighted the plane. I can take off in a few minutes," she says in a business-like way designed to please me.

"Okay, well, don't rush —but don't dawdle, either. Get out of Dodge, and I'll see you in a couple of hours." I look at my watch again and figure she'll land in Gordonsville about two o'clock.

When I leave my house to drive to the airport, I'm hit with a blast of moist air. During the morning, it's gotten humid. It's much more humid today than yesterday. Today there is no doubt it's summer in Virginia. A light breeze comes out of the northwest. But there's no refreshment. There's plenty of fuel for West Virginia's air mass thunderstorm factory today.

I'm at the Gordonsville, Virginia airport at 1:00 p.m., alone in the office taking care of some paperwork. My old home field, the Orange County Airport, ten miles northeast, has yet to recover the flying business lost after my parents' bankruptcy. So I'm doing most of my flight instructing out of Gordonsville Municipal Airport these days.

At 2:00 p.m., still finding chores, I listen for Christy's call on UNICOM. At 2:20 p.m. I lean back in my creaking chair and exhale hard, looking out the window over Merry Mountain, toward the northwest. No airplane. Silly to expect to see one. She'd call on the radio well before she came into view.

Maybe it took her more than just a few minutes to depart. I refocus my attention on the paperwork. When I check the clock again, it's 2:32 p.m. I pick up the radio microphone. "Cessna eight-seven-four-three Sierra, Gordonsville." I try several more times over the next few minutes. No answer to any of my calls.

I pick up the phone and call the FAA Flight Service Station that serves the Parkersburg area. Though not required by regulation, filing a flight plan is a good idea for any pilot on a visual cross-country flight. As her instructor, I required Christy to file a flight plan with them before she left. "What time did she report off?" I ask.

"November eight-seven-four-three Sierra activated their flight plan airborne at 12:15 p.m.," says the FSS man.

She should be here by now.

A knot forms in my stomach. I sent her off with what I thought was enough information. But was it? My job, as her instructor, was to cram her brain, make sure she's been studying, quiz her on her knowledge. Today, she's the pilot-in-command. But as a student pilot, she's still under my supervision. She's a PIC with training wheels. Her being late is my problem. I feel a little sick. I want to fix this situation and fix it now, to reach across the miles and control her and her little airplane like a radio-controlled model. But once launched, a student is —however much we might wish otherwise— uncontrolled by the instructor. What to do?

I need to talk to her. Her single VHF radio operates via line of sight, so if she's not within range of our airport, the only way I might talk with her is with a very tall antenna way up in the air. By getting high enough in my airplane, I might reach her on the radio. Then I can help her figure out where she is and help get her safely to the ground. I grab the keys to my flying club's Piper Cherokee and head out to the ramp.

I do a quick pre-flight, warm up, and take off in the Cherokee on a heading to the northwest. I'm aiming to get as close as I can to Christy's planned inbound course. If she's not too far off, and generally inbound to Gordonsville, I should reach her right away.

Once airborne, I transmit on 122.8 MHz, the common UNICOM frequency that Christy would use on her way into the airport. "Cessna eight-seven-four-three Sierra, this is Cherokee two-zero-five. Do you read?" A pause now. And nothing. I check my chart and confirm the heading for Parkersburg. As Gordonsville disappears behind me, I call over the radio again. And again. No one answers.

I'm angry. She pushed it by getting to the airport late. She is the pilot-in-command — her brother shouldn't be in charge. *You're the pilot*, I tell her in my head. *You don't monkey around waiting on others. You tell your brother, "No, we can't stop at the store. I've got to get to the airport."* Why hadn't she been more assertive? She pushed me out of my comfort zone, but she wouldn't push her brother. Why hadn't I been more assertive? Did I want to look gung ho in front of a girl? Why did I let her push me? Where was my judgment as her instructor? I should have told her that she'd blown it. *Go back to the house, wait another day, no matter how inconvenient. You have to be at work tomorrow? Tough. That's flying.*

I call again. Nothing. I call the flight service station by radio. "How's the weather between Montebello and Clarksburg?" I ask, using two navigation aids close to Christy's flight plan.

"A few cells are beginning to pop up in that area," the operator says.

"Has Cessna eight-seven-four-three Sierra made a position report?"

"Negative. No report," he answers.

The knot in my stomach moves to my throat. My breath is shallow. I lost my student. This is a first for me, and I deny the possibility. This can't happen. Before, I've always felt in reasonable control with students, that all was well in hand. I don't send pilots out unless they're ready. That's been a point of pride with me. Every one of my students — there have been many dozens now — have passed the private pilot check ride on the first try. Nobody has gotten into trouble. Nobody has gotten lost. For each test, and each hurdle along the way, I wanted them beyond ready. And they have been. Until now.

CHAPTER THIRTY

Only a few miles into West Virginia, I see three large thunderstorm clouds, fat and puffy in the classic anvil shape, white where the sun hits them and gray in the shadows. In their depths, some cloud is almost black. This far away, they look like week-old bruises. But the bruising is not a mark of healing. Today, we head toward increasing pain, toward the thunderstorms. I check the time: 3:01 p.m. Christy has only an hour of fuel left on board, if she's still flying.

That Christy is lost or worse drills into my soul, hollowing out my core. Physical feeling leaves my body, leaving only emotion. God, I've let her down. I didn't impress on her the importance of leaving early. I didn't tell her no.

I grit my teeth, fending off despair, steering the Cherokee toward the Allegheny Mountains. I see bigger storm clouds now, large and menacing, seeming to lie in wait to swallow little airplanes with student pilots. I call again for Christy. Nothing.

I'm hoping that Christy is diverting around the clouds, navigating this minefield of giants, and keeping her wits about her. For years, I've bordered on agnosticism. Even dipping into atheism. Now, though, I'd welcome some divine help. So far, I've been projecting my will into her Cessna like some ineffective guardian angel, foolishly transmitting to her mind, trying to coach her around each cloud and willing her to get back on track. The whole effort is like pushing on smoke.

Onward to the northwest go the Cherokee and I. The clouds, more than the natural horizon or the mountains, limit my line of sight. I fly on as an admonition beats in my head over and over again: I should not have let her out here. I should have kept her on the prescribed program like everyone else, made no exceptions. Easy cross-country flights over flat ground. That's what works. Save the mountains for later, when experience and a pilot's license builds more foundation.

I check the clock again: 3:10 p.m. Only fifty minutes of fuel left.

I call the Clarksburg Flight Service Station in West Virginia.

"No, sir. We haven't heard from that aircraft," says the FAA man. Hollow desperation spreads from my core into my arms and legs. I don't feel my body at all now, as I switch my radio frequency back to 122.8 MHz.

"Cessna eight-seven-four-three Sierra, Cherokee nine-five-two-zero-five, are you on frequency?" No answer. I wait and call again. I feel as though the thunderclouds I see outside have entered my hollow body, filling me with a building and menacing chaos. The radio crackles, and I freeze. I want nothing to interfere with reception.

"This is Cessna four-three Sierra," says a voice, broken and faint, on the radio.

I pause a beat.

"Cessna four-three Sierra, this is Russ in Cherokee two-zero-five. What's your position?"

There's no immediate answer. Have I imagined her call? I say, with more urgency, "Four-three Sierra, where are you?"

"I don't know exactly," she answers, and now the voice comes through more clearly. At least she's still alive. A wave of relief blasts through my body, blowing out the storm clouds and returning feeling to my limbs. Then, immediately, tension rushes in like a secondary tornado. Search has become rescue. I need her safe and on the ground.

I glance at my clock: 3:20 p.m. She has only forty more minutes of fuel, assuming everything is working normally. Assuming she'd filled the tanks all the way to the top in Parkersburg. Assuming she hasn't been running the little engine full rich and wide open.

I still don't know where she is, or how far from an airport she might be. I hope to help her out of this mess by getting my airplane close enough to hers so she hears my signal, my voice, with strength and without crackles. So far, she's sounded calm on the radio. I hope she stays that way.

I feel new energy. But not good energy. Different energy. I go into instructor mode.

"Okay, the first thing we need to do is determine your position." My voice tries to project the confidence I want her to feel. That's the intention, anyway. Not wanting to risk losing her, I don't suggest we switch to the proper, and less busy, MULTI-COM frequency. We stay on UNICOM. "You're going to get radials —lines— from two VOR stations. Tune into what you think is the closest VOR. Then line up the needle and tell me what it says."

"Okay," she replies. I wait for a minute, but it feels like ten. No, twenty. I wonder if I'm flying closer to her. I want a giant mechanical arm to reach out, pluck her out of the sky, and place her safely on the earth.

"Ah . . . no," Christy says. "It just went off. It says 'off.'"

It went off? I know what's wrong.

"Remember, four-three Sierra, your radio can transmit or receive —it can't do both at the same time. Remember? So, before you key the mic, before you talk, you have to read the VOR needle. Look at the number where the needle lines up and remember that number. Write it down. When you key the mic to talk to me, the VOR part of your radio will say 'off' whenever you transmit. We went over that, remember?"

More time passes. Time we don't have to spare. "It says two-forty," Christy finally says.

"Okay, and what station —what VOR frequency— are you on?"

"I'm on one-sixteen point two."

"Does it say 'to' or 'from'?"

"From."

My chart confirms what I already know. Over the years, I've learned all the frequencies of my region's VORs. I didn't even try. It happened like a baby learns to speak.

"That's Clarksburg VOR. So you're on the two-four-zero degree radial off of Clarksburg," I say. "Now we have to get another radial so we can get a fix —find out exactly where you are. So far, we know you're southwest of Clarksburg. Find Clarksburg on your chart." I look at my chart again. At least she's west of the highest mountains. "Now I want you to tune in Elkins VOR and tell me that radial. It's on one-fourteen point two."

She comes back in another couple of minutes. "I can't find it," she says, still sounding remarkably calm.

What does she mean she can't find it? Is she out of range of Elkins?

My clock says 3:30 p.m. About thirty minutes of fuel in the Cessna. Quick now. Develop a plan. All we know is she's within range of Clarksburg VOR, to the southwest, in the hills, surrounded by thunderstorms in three quadrants. She doesn't have enough fuel to cover a distance greater than fifty or so miles. And that's to dry tanks. At the end of fifty miles, her engine will quit and the airplane will glide to a landing in a field, if she's lucky, and a crash if not.

With no fuel, there will be no fire. If she crashes there will be a muffled thump and sickening crunch. A pile of mangled black-and-white aluminum will remain, mixed with the unspeakable remains of a once-beautiful person. We need to get her to an airport before then. To a landing and the surety of life.

"Tune into Clarksburg approach control, and we'll see if they can get you on radar." I give her the frequency.

This is a quick way to find her position, but I still don't like handing her over to Clarksburg. By changing frequencies, we run the risk she'll tune in the wrong one. If that happens, I can't talk to her again. My stomach clenches.

"If you don't get Clarksburg on the radio right away," I say, keeping my voice calm, "come right back to one-twenty-two-point-eight and we'll talk again." I'm not sure she hears me. I should have said that last part first.

I give her a beat to come back, then tune my radio to Clarksburg. I immediately hear her voice. Whew, we didn't lose her a second time.

"Clarksburg, this is Cessna eight-seven-four-three Sierra. I don't know where I am. Can you help me find out?"

"Affirmative, stand by," Clarksburg replies.

I get on the radio, "Clarksburg, this is Cherokee nine-five-two-zero-five. Four-three Sierra is my student. She should be on the Clarksburg two-four-zero degree radial. Standing by to assist."

Clarksburg approach tells Christy to squawk ident two-three-four-five with her transponder, which will make a signal bloom on their radar. I sigh, my knee jiggling. I know that her Cessna doesn't have a transponder. Christy remembers this about her airplane too, and says so. The controller goes to his backup plan.

"Roger, we do have a primary target forty-seven miles southwest of Clarksburg," they say. That means they see an airplane, which might be hers, on radar. "Turn west to two-seven-zero degrees for identification."

I hope she turns to two-seven-zero degrees. I have no way of knowing what she's doing.

"Four-three Sierra, key your mic. Press your transmit button for five seconds," Clarksburg says. "No need to talk."

I hear a signal with no voice.

"Okay, good," says Clarksburg. "Turn left to one-eight-zero degrees." A pause. "Okay, key your mic again."

They want to confirm it's her airplane. By what they're asking, I assume they must be coordinating with the Clarksburg Flight Service Station, a facility with direction-finding equipment. By coordinating, they'll have her identified two ways, on primary radar and DF.

I glance at the clock: 3:35 p.m. This is beyond getting tight. I know that telling them about the fuel won't make this go faster, so I stay quiet.

"Roger, we have you identified on primary radar," Clarksburg says. "You are three-zero miles northeast of the Charleston, West Virginia, airport. Turn to two-three-five degrees if you want to head in that direction."

Wow, she's way south of where she's supposed to be —almost directly south of Parkersburg, the place she'd departed. She's made little easterly progress.

"Four-three Sierra, this is Russ. Turn to two-three-five degrees and go to Charleston now."

I quickly calculate in my head. It should take her eighteen minutes to reach the airport, and she's got twenty-five minutes of fuel left, in theory. She'll make it, I tell myself. She'll make it if she doesn't encounter any thunderheads in that thirty miles. And if she has as much fuel in the tanks as I calculate. Seven minutes reserve is next to fumes.

There are fields below. We train to use fields for emergency landings. I've taught Christy how to pick out a good one, check the wind direction, and make a good approach. But here, in the coal fields of West Virginia among the rolling hills, the fields are small and rocky. If she runs out of fuel, she might make a successful emergency approach and come to a stop, safely, before a ditch, fence, tree, or boulder smacks her. But then again, she might not. A landing in a field is a challenge for any pilot. But for a student? In the crags and hollows of West Virginia?

Christy hasn't answered.

"Cessna four-three Sierra, fly to Charleston, and I will meet you there. Steer two-three-five degrees. The Charleston VOR is on one-one-seven-point four," I say.

"Okay . . . ah, roger," she says.

Clarksburg gives her the Charleston approach control frequency. "Return to this frequency if you don't get them right away," they say.

From my map, I see that I'm about thirty minutes —about fifty-five miles— away from Charleston. I head in that direction too, and switch frequencies. Hearing Christy on the approach control frequency for Charleston, I stay quiet and continue heading their way.

"Four-three Sierra, we have you on radar fifteen miles northeast of Charleston," says the controller in Charleston after a few minutes. "Do you see the airport?"

"No, not yet," Christy replies.

I listen, holding my breath.

"Oh, yes, I see it!"

"Good. We'll keep you on this frequency. Eight-seven-four-three Sierra, you are cleared to land. Straight in. Runway two-three," Charleston says.

If approach control had suggested her entering a traffic pattern, or turned her away from a direct course for traffic avoidance,

I would have intervened and told them, and her, she was going straight in due to a fuel emergency. But she's cleared straight in, and that's as good as we can get.

She's not safe yet, but she's so close now. If she can just follow through —and if the fuel holds out. I continue to listen to the Charleston frequency. I've never seen a clock tick this slow.

Tick . . . tick . . . tick.

Is it stuck?

After a lifetime, I hear a call. "Cessna Four-three Sierra. Turn left and taxi to parking. Right under the Gulf sign."

She's on the ground. Landed safe. I slump in my seat, wiped out. A wave of nausea, stress release, I guess, passes through me, and I reach up to rub my eyes.

I feel like a water balloon beaten with a sledgehammer. Or run over by a train. Or both. I don't pump my hands with joy at her landing. I don't yell, "Yahoo!" Instead, after a sick feeling passes, no feeling remains at all. But my muscles still work machine like, going through the motions of heading toward a landing.

They chopped off a mountain to build the Charleston Airport. My granite is chopped off too. Confidence, strength, competence, all chiseled to dust. Nothing is left.

When I taxi off the runway, I see Christy standing under the wing of her airplane, looking the same as always in denim overalls and her hair in a bun. Hayley Mills at summer flying camp.

As I park the Cherokee next to her Cessna, she looks at me with the expression of a kid in trouble. She has arched eyebrows and a smile that says, "Don't yell at me."

She needn't worry. Today I wouldn't have the strength to shout, and besides, it's not my style.

I smile back. It's probably the smile of a decayed Halloween pumpkin, and I hold my hand up to wave through the cockpit window. This isn't her fault. Even though she was the pilot-in-command of her little airplane, she was still under my wing. She's barely fledged. I'm responsible for her. Today, I let her go too far, too fast. I hadn't listened to that voice from the beginning that said, "This may be too much." I should have listened.

I shut down my airplane and run the checklist. Christy walks over to the tip of my wing, safe and away from my propeller arc like I taught her. But it looks as if she's keeping a safe distance from me too. I pop the two right-hand door latches open, and warm, humid, smelly air fills the cabin. Is that burned coal? A paper plant? I realize that I'm wet with sweat. Is the stench me?

"Well, welcome to Charleston." There's an unwanted edge in my voice, but still, I try to smile. I'm relieved to see her alive.

"Yep, Charleston," she says, smiling, digging her hands in her overall pockets. "Who woulda thunk it?"

I climb out of the cockpit. My joints are welded together, but I keep from groaning when I say, "I'm interested to find out how you got here. What happened?"

"There were these thunderstorms, and I had to turn right off my course to go around them. But I was looking at my map," Christy says, her voice steady and chipper, as usual.

Standing on the ramp with her, I'm close to keeling over. It's rare to feel pure exhaustion. But this is it. I'm irritated that she's standing here, not more shaken. Hell, she's not shaken at all. This day nearly killed me. I feel ancient and spent, but she seems fresh as spring. I need a minute.

"Listen, I want a Coke," I say. "Grab your chart and let's go in and talk about this." I can tell that Christy doesn't understand how serious this was. That she could have died. I feel like finding a cave and hibernating. But as her teacher, I want her to learn from this. It must never happen again. It was my fault. But she can learn now, while it's fresh. This was way too close.

We sit down inside the airport lounge with our sweating bottles and spread her navigation chart on a table.

"When I turned away from the thunderstorm, I was looking at my map, and I saw this," Christy says, pointing at a river and a power plant on the chart. "See? The thunderstorm passed kind of behind me, so I turned back to east, heading so I'd get back on the line to Gordonsville." She points at the line she had drawn with a pink marker.

"Then I didn't recognize anything, so I thought I must have been north of where I was supposed to be. So I turned right to get back on my line," she says. "After that, I milled around, helter-skelter, trying to find something I recognized."

Looking at the chart, I think I know what happened. It's a common rookie mistake. "Is it possible you were looking at this?" I point to another power plant and river, in the same configuration as the ones she identified.

"I don't know," she says.

"It can happen," I say. "The same thing happened to me right after I first soloed. I spotted a tower, thinking it was the one I'd marked on my map. But it wasn't. I continued on, fat, dumb, and happy. Then I stumbled across a river that shouldn't have been there. Whoops. Lesson? What we think we see isn't necessarily the reality."

"Ah, maybe," Christy says, leaning over the map to contemplate her possible error.

"Count on it. Never look at one thing and think you know where you are. Or even two things. Ask questions. Does my heading make sense? Does what I'm seeing on the panel or out the window make sense? Always back yourself up with as much information as you can. And then try to get more. You could have called a ground station earlier and gotten a radar fix or a directional finder steer. But then, initially, you thought you had it nailed, right?"

She nods.

"You never want to let yourself wander around in the unknown. Don't guess," I say, being firm. "It finally dawned that things weren't lining up, because you didn't see anything that looked recognizable. Right?"

"Right. Got confusing, and I didn't want to run into those clouds," Christy says, with a tone of apology. She doesn't want to call them what they were. Thunderstorms.

"Well, when you can't figure out where you are, don't just keep wandering around thinking things will get better. That's magical thinking. Get help early. Use whatever resources you have. Tune your VORs. Get a fix. Find yourself."

I don't feel it polite or right to ask her what I think are obvious questions: How could you continue flying not knowing where you were? What the hell did you expect to happen?

No, those questions are not polite and not fair. Instead, I should direct any brain power questions back at myself. What was I thinking sending a rookie out across those mountains in summer? How dumb am I?

But I offer one more lesson by way of admonishment.

"By not getting up and going early, like we planned —well, the thunderstorms built up, didn't they? And winding up in Charleston is what happened," I say. "But it could have been a lot worse." I tip the bottle and finish the drink. "Do you know how much fuel you had left?"

"No," she shakes her head. "Ten gallons?"

"Seven minutes. You had seven minutes of fuel left. Not ten gallons. Not even one gallon. Holy smokes, that's nothing!" I let that sink in. I hope it does.

"Those thunderstorms had time to perk, didn't they? Just like we talked about. As a pilot, you must know when to say no. When you're the pilot-in-command, you can't make a decision based solely on other people's needs or what other people do or want," I say this more to myself than to Christy. "I made a mistake by not telling you to stay put in Parkersburg. Both of us could have done better. Remember this throughout your flying career: The pilot-in-command is the ultimate authority for a flight. The passengers are not in charge. The air traffic controllers are not in charge. No one but you is in charge. You are the general, the boss, the CEO."

An unease rolls through my body that I recognize as guilt. I'm guilty for allowing somebody to nudge me beyond my better instincts. And I am guilty for not teaching her what she needed to know.

I sit up straighter in my chair and drain my cola. "I don't know about you, but I'm done," I tell Christy. "We'll go back to Gordonsville in the morning when the weather's better. Before those thunderstorms start to pop again."

She seems surprised. "But I have work in the morning. Nine o'clock."

"We'll leave early, like you're supposed to most summer days out here. We'll take off no later than six. We'll avoid thunderstorms, and you'll be to work on time." I fold the navigation chart. I think Christy senses I'm done talking about it.

I feel like a shell. My own decisions had looted my confidence. Before today, I'd never felt such fear for someone else's wellbeing. For their life. It frightens me and leaves me empty.

I'm twenty-four, and today I'm an old man. As I hand the chart to her, I feel the need to find a cave and drink vodka straight out of the bottle. Forever.

CHAPTER THIRTY ONE

Bill transferred to his airline's Denver base and left Orange County. Before he moved away, I visited him at home on his mountain to get some last words of wisdom from my airline pilot mentor. Even though my family no longer runs the airport, Bill and I have kept in touch.

"You've got, what, two thousand hours? Some good multiengine time included. You've got that Part 135 certificate and are operating two Beech Barons. That's a good deal," says Bill. "You're still in your twenties, so you're not too old yet. No turbine time though. Turbine time would be good. But, you know what? It can't hurt. Send your applications to the airlines and see what happens. You'll need to go *sans beard* to any interview, though. You'll need to shave before you see them."

Is there a chance? What about my eyes? Bill only mentioned my beard. What about my glasses? The major airlines do not hire pilots with glasses. Maybe Bill's just be patronizing, playing along so as to not disappoint the kid. But then, most old pilots wear glasses. Everyone needed glasses after a particular age. Why discriminate against new hires?

But let's face it. They do. And in the current economic environment, today not even Steve Canyon or Captain Kirk could get hired. Not even after making two lunar landings. No one is getting hired. But even before the hiring pipeline last shut off, the only pilots hired by major carriers were perfect, with perfect vision, perfect teeth, and thousands of flight hours.

But I send the applications anyway. You can't win a lottery if you don't buy a ticket.

As expected, though, all I get back is form letters saying, "Thank you for your submission."

But the flying's okay here in Virginia for now. I'm enjoying it. I like my clients and flying friends. On free days, there's still a bit of instructing going on, like with Christy. Most of the time, I'm operating two Beechcraft Barons under my FAA Part 135 authorization.

Not only am I flying upscale-model Barons, much better than Bob's, there's also hope that soon I will have an airplane like the governor's. There's talk my best client, Stan Oginz, wants a Beechcraft King Air, a jet-powered turboprop. I don't have an airline job, but I'm having fun. And thanks to Stan and his wife, Flo, even though I'm getting a little old for it, I'm getting another shot at having parents too.

*   *   *

"You're a buck ninety-eight, Stanley. A buck ninety-eight," says Flo as we push her into the back seat of a Cessna 182.

She's used to the Baron, where she can step into the airplane's back seat with a nod toward elegance. Today though, Stan economizes and takes the single-engine Cessna rather than burn twice as much fuel in the Baron. This is a fun trip, not a business mission. Stan is making a point of frugality. His wife always gets first-class service. But not today. This is her first trip in Stan's "toy" airplane.

"What is this thing, Stanley? You gotta squeeze in like you're coming out of a piping bag! You're a buck ninety-eight, Stanley!"

Over the past couple of years, Flo and I have developed a routine. We're both aware it's a scam.

Every spring, we fly Flo's Russian lynx coat to New York. We take it to Bergdorf's cold-storage fur locker in New York for the summer. Then, as winter approaches, we fly back to fetch the coat.

The Russian lynx is a ticket for two New York fun trips every year. We spend two or three days each time; eating, shopping, and seeing shows. Today, Stan is pushing back. By cramming her into the 182, he's letting Flo know he's on to the racket.

Today, with Flo pushed and strapped in, I hand her the heavy Bergdorf's garment bag. She puts in on her lap. You can't be too careful with a Russian lynx.

Flo and Stan are great people, like family. I have been operating Stan's Beechcraft Baron about five hundred hours a year to support his factory. I also lease the airplane from him for my air-charter operation.

Flo looks and sounds like Anne Meara, the comedian. Redheaded, Irish Catholic New Yorkers, Meara and Flo each married "a nice Jewish fellow from the Lower East Side." Flo married Stan as World War II got started. Right after the wedding, Stan went to the Pacific with the Navy. Flo remained in Brooklyn, helping build super-secret Norden bombsights. They didn't see each other for two years.

Norden employed eighteen thousand New York workers. None of Flo's coworkers wanted to be the union shop treasurer. So they elected nineteen-year-old Flo. "Every month, all the guys and gals would pay me their dues. In cash," she told me. "I didn't know what to do with all that money. It just kept piling up."

Stanley Oginz (1980)

"What did you do with it? Put it in the bank?" I asked.

"I spent it!" she said. "Every penny of it! I gotta tell ya, I was the best-dressed gal at the bomb sight plant. And you know what? All that time, nobody ever checked on me! Never heard a word about it! It sure wasn't right, I know that. But at nineteen? I didn't know the first thing about nothin'! Ay, ay, ay! I coulda wound up in the slammer."

When Stan was twelve, his father abandoned the family. With the Great Depression under way, eighth-grader Stan dropped out of school to push carts in the Garment District.

"Every day, I pushed those carts. Winter? Summer? Didn't matter," said Stan. "That was hard work. But we needed the money. My father had left, and my mother was home with my kid brother." Stan pronounces them "fathta," "motha," and "brotha." "We needed every penny we could scrape together.

"I worked for my uncle too," Stan continued. "During Prohibition, he made beer. We'd pull his water truck up to fire hydrants in the city and pumped beer right into the basements of the speakeasies. Made quite a plumber out of me right off the bat!"

Stan and I flew many hours together. There was a lot of time to hear stories.

"After the war, I stayed in Japan. The Navy gave me an ocean-going tug. We'd run between Sasebo and Shanghai. MacArthur had me hauling a bunch of Chinese crap to help rebuild Japan. That went on for a year or so after V-J Day until they shipped me home —on a submarine.

"A bunch of years later, I went to a salvage auction in Norfolk. Bid on a bunch of stuff for scrap value. I wound up buying an amphibious tank and —I kid you not— a submarine," said Stan. "When I went to get it, I found out that, not only did it still run, it was the same sub I shipped home on!"

"What did you do with it?" I asked.

"We ran it around the Chesapeake Bay for a while. You should've seen it, Russ. Motoring around in a damn sub. I wanted to see if we could get it to submerge, but the Navy wouldn't let me. Said they'd throw me in jail if I tried. So I had it cut up for scrap. We made a few bucks on it.

"But I kept the tank for a while before we cut it up. I'd take the kids around the farm. We'd fire up that big diesel DD Sherman, and off we'd go. We'd drive it right into the pond. That tank's big old snorkel would just gurgle away as we drove the tank along the pond's bottom. All that mud and it never got stuck. What would we have done if we'd gotten stuck at the bottom of the pond? Sheesh! That was some fun. You should've heard the kids scream and laugh. We took pictures. I've got the film somewhere." He called it "fill-em."

Over the years, Stan bought and sold not only amphibious tanks and submarines, but also commercial real estate and businesses. He became a turnaround expert. "You just gotta take a hard look at businesses other people have run into the ground. See what happened, what went wrong. In a lotta cases, there's value there."

I love Stan. Flo too. They've taken me in like an extra son. Every time I'm with Stan, it's like a business course with a beloved professor; I imagine it's like taking Physics 101 with Einstein.

Stan, who kind of looks like a sloth —or maybe a turtle— has the mind of a supercomputer and cuts to the heart of business matters. "It's a damn shame when you run across somebody's broken dream. A man builds a business, throws his heart and fortune into it. And it winds up a failure." He stops to think of various disasters. "It's usually because he screwed it up. But people ain't perfect. They make mistakes. It breaks my heart to see that," says Stan.

"But, you know, it's good when you can come in and save some guys' jobs. Makes you feel good, like you done somethin' worthwhile," he says.

I can't help comparing Stan to my father. While I grew up, my dad drank, talked about Armageddon, attempted to scrimp his way to riches, and complained about "The Man screwing the little guy."

Stan is The Man. A self-made millionaire, he's not concerned about the end of the world. He celebrates that which is right in front of him. Even though he's Jewish, he celebrates Christmas with joy. He's generous and appears to do good for good's sake. And sure, Stan drinks —we've had some good dinners with lots of alcohol at the Café de Paris and the Mai-Kai in Ft. Lauderdale. But Stan doesn't need to drink. And he doesn't do things in hope of a divine reward. He doesn't worship some fantastic idea of a world yet to be. I don't know if he even believes in God.

My father adopted a nonsensical world fabricated in the minds of dead strangers. Their made-up religion became his path to future happiness and salvation. Stan's religion, his happiness, is in the world he creates now.

I will choose that too.

Stan's wife, Flo, is wonderful. She's a tremendous cook and connoisseur. Flying back to Virginia from New York, the airplane always smells like a delicatessen. We get bagels, bialys, and Novi lox from Russ & Daughters, and pastrami, fresh hotdogs, and half-pickles from Katz's. We stuff in many bags of groceries we get from Louis B. at Balducci's.

They say the way to a man's heart is through his stomach. With me, Flo is right on course.

Tonight in New York, we're dining at Lutèce, which Julia Child called "America's best restaurant." Flo has invited some New York friends and me, but thinks about inviting more.

"Maybe I oughta call Rosie when we land," says Flo. "And I think Charlotte and Suellen are at the Dorset. I'll ring 'em."

"Jesus! Maybe we ought to just go ahead and invite everybody in town. Put it on the radio. Dinner tonight is going to cost me three thousand bucks." he says with a grin.

"You're a buck ninety-eight, Stanley," yells Flo from the noisy Cessna's back seat. "A buck ninety-eight."

Leaning over to me, Stan says, "That Flo. With her groceries, her kitchen stuff, and eating out, I'll bet I lay out fifty grand a year." He shakes his head as we fly over New Jersey. "Ay, ay, ay."

But there's that grin and sparkle in his eye.

CHAPTER THIRTY TWO

I continue to operate my air service. Stan buys a King Air A90 —just like the Virginia governor's airplane. It's a great airplane, but, while I'd promised God I'd never ask Him for anything else if he let me fly something as nice as a King Air, I still have the desire for bigger and better airplanes— jets, airliners. Is that greed? Lust? But I've shot my divine wad and can't expect God's intervention from here on forward. I recognize the King Air is a fine airplane and, until something better comes along, I'm enjoying flying the turboprop.

The radio gig is fun too. I do that when I'm not flying. I could still make a career of radio, but my heart still yearns for the airlines. But the fact is, I still wear glasses, and the airlines still aren't hiring. There is, however, that call.

Maybe the path to getting on with an airline is to start one. Or buy one. I don't need to fly for an airline. With glasses, I need to give up that dream. Instead, maybe I could get into airline management.

I keep seeing the name Mort Beyer in the newspapers and aviation trade magazines. He's always being quoted about what airlines need to do to be successful in the post-deregulation environment. His company, Avmark, is headquartered in Arlington, an easy drive for me.

I call him.

I get past the telephone receptionist easily, introduce myself to Mort, and get right to the subject. "My associates and I are interested in buying an airline and think you might be able to help."

Never mind that I haven't spoken to any associates about visiting Mort. The people I have in mind are more prospects than partners. But I suppose they are associates in one form or another. And boy, do I need associates. Rich ones. I have only a few thousand dollars in the bank and a little equity in my house. I'd be hard-pressed to buy a single-engine Cessna, never mind a whole airline.

"Sure! Come on up. Next Tuesday okay for you?" says Mort. "I'll block off time after lunch if you can make it then."

Of course I can make it.

Mort is a big man. He reminds me of Kellen in a suit. Mort has a healthy stock of hair and bubbling enthusiasm. Before driving the two hours to Arlington on Tuesday morning, I'd read up on him.

"How are things coming with that new Western Airlines Salt Lake City hub operation?" I ask as an icebreaker. I want to show him I'm current on his airline projects.

"Oh, yeah. You know about that, huh? It's going well. We've run all the numbers, and it should be a big success for them. The only downside of hub operations is the time the airplanes sit on the ground between banks of flights. But you know that."

I know now.

"But that down time is made up in increased revenue. Hubs

and spokes are a revenue seat-mile multiplier. And they're the big thing now. I got from our phone conversation that you're pretty open to airline ideas, right? I've got an idea for hubbing Raleigh-Durham with BAC 1-11s if you're interested."

I nod like I'm mulling it.

"But let me stop, Russ, and hear what you have in mind."

I tell him I'm running an aviation service operating under the FAA's Part 135 for small air carriers. I don't tell Mort my investors currently don't know I'm working on their behalf.

Russ with the Beechcraft King-Air.

The whole airline partner idea started at a picnic over

hamburgers and beer a while back. While standing beside a barbecue grill, Judge Jim Roberts —married to Flo's cousin— and I had
a short talk about his interest in buying an airline. "Shortly after
the airline deregulation act was passed, my buddies and I took
a hard look at buying Hughes Airwest from Howard Hughes'
estate," said Jim. "We didn't pursue the purchase when our number crunching showed that, as structured, the airline couldn't
make money." Jim told me the group had no active airline deals
going. I said I'd let him know if anything came up.

Sitting in Mort's office, I think about my "investors;" my
good friend Stan Oginz, Judge Jim, who is also the president of
the Virginia Bar Association, and Jim's "buddies;" a ski resort
developer, a movie star, and some high-powered Washington
attorneys. One of the advantages of operating in business aviation
is meeting well-heeled, well-connected people.

I tell Mort my investors and I are open to any interesting
airline deals. "I came here because you're the best. If anyone can
ferret out a workable deal in this tough business, it's you, Mort."

"Well, thanks. I have been around a while. I think we could
make the Raleigh-Durham hub thing work. But it'll take some
time and require some cash," says Mort. "You know how to make
a small fortune in the airline business, don't you?" he asks with
a smile.

I shake my head.

"Start with a big one!" He laughs.

Yes, this guy is a lot like Kellen. I like him.

"How much do you want to invest?"

"Nothing," I say. "We'd like to get in with as little as possible."

I thought he'd kick me out when I say I want to invest nothing. But he doesn't. His mind never stops, and he hasn't thrown the kid out of his office —yet.

"Well, maybe starting a hub-and-spoke outfit from scratch won't work for you. But there are a couple of things I think might be doable. Have you ever heard of George Batchelor?"

"I have heard of him, yes. He's known as a bit of a buccaneer, right? He has a bunch of DC-8s and other old stuff down in 'Corrosion Corner,' the back ramps at Miami International Airport, if I'm not mistaken. He operates scheduled freight runs and is a big charter operator for the military. His main operation nowadays is Arrow Air. Is that the guy?"

"That's the guy. He also owns Capitol, an outfit formed shortly after World War II. But Capitol has been a bit of a stepchild for George," says Mort. "He's kind of dismantling the operation, piecemeal, in favor of Arrow. Capitol still has a couple of DC-10s and a few -8s. George and I were talking the other day. I think you could pick up the certificate and leases for a couple of million bucks. It might be that just a million in George's pocket would do it."

"Sounds interesting," I say. "I think Capitol's still running that scheduled passenger operation out of Brussels to JFK, right?" I'd recently flown from Belgium back to the States on the airline. "Two hundred thirty eight dollars, one way. A bargain."

"Yep," says Mort. "Might be worth continuing that Atlantic service. We'd have to massage the whole thing and see what would be best. I don't know if you know it, but I used to be president of Capitol back in the 1960s. The guys who started the company got pretty successful doing military charters. They reminded me of the guys who started Flying Tigers. A bunch of steely eyed entrepreneurs."

"You've had quite a career," I say.

"Yeah, and it just goes on and on. Same players coming in and out all the time. I just finished another project for Pan Am. We structured an ESOP for them. I don't know if it's going to work out. Old Pan Am has got a lot of troubles. Juan Trippe left while the getting was good. Pan Am's where I got my start in this racket, you know? I started with Trippe at Pan American in '48. I was 'director of schedules.'"

I can't believe this man is taking me seriously. I feel like a kid off the street, a little punk who knows how to fly little airplanes.

"Let me put a few ideas down on paper for you," he says, patting an old Smith Corona manual typewriter on his desk. "Talk to your people, and tell them what we talked about. We'll probably be able to put something together for you."

I drive back to Charlottesville in my crummy old Ford Pinto, not believing my luck. I realize that just showing up might be the most important key to success. If you want something, show up and ask for it. The second most important thing might be to use the talents of others. What's that old saying? "You can do anything as long as you don't care who gets credit for it."

My father always preached the virtues of going it alone. And he did. All the way to bankruptcy.

Mort and I talk quite a few times over the next couple of months. Batchelor thinks he has a fish on the line and starts talking about wanting ten million dollars for Capitol instead of one million.

That's a little rich, so we put that idea on the back burner.

One morning, I'm at the Charlottesville-Albemarle Airport, talking to one of my former King Air copilots, Steve. Steve flew with me to get the turbine time needed to get hired by a regional airline, Air Virginia.

"Air Virginia is in big trouble," says Steve. "There's talk on the line we could shut down any minute."

"That's too bad, Steve," I say. "I know you worked hard to get on with them."

While commiserating with him, my mind perks. Stan's taught me to think about restoring jobs and building something new from someone else's broken dream. Mort has taught me that diamonds might be found among airlines' manure. "I hope something develops soon, Steve, so everyone at Air Virginia can keep working."

As soon as I get home, I telephone Air Virginia's corporate offices in Lynchburg. "Hi, I'd like to talk to Glenn Hammond, please," I say. Glenn is the president and CEO of the airline.

"May I inquire what the call is about, please sir?" says the receptionist.

"Yes, I'm calling on behalf of some airline investors."

A minute later, I'm introducing myself to Glenn. I give him the same spiel I gave Mort. "Do you think you'd like to get together with me, Glenn?" I ask. "Is next week too soon for you?"

"What are you doing this afternoon?" says Glenn

My marriage produced a daughter, Piper, a year ago. The only thing I have on today is picking her up from my sister, Debs, place. After getting home, I planned to do nothing but watch her and have a beer in our new log house in Barboursville, Virginia. "Hmm, Glenn, I think I could clear my schedule this afternoon. Yes, let me do that, and I'll come on down. It's about an hour-and-a-half drive. I'll see you at five. Okay?"

"Great! Looking forward," said Glenn.

I call Debs, and ask her if she minds watching Piper a little bit longer, until my wife gets home from work. "That'll be fine," she says.

By six o'clock, in Glenn's office, I realize the company is in dire straits. Air Virginia operates twenty-two Swearingen Metro-liners and one British Aerospace HS 748. All leased. While the several hundred employees haven't missed a paycheck yet, Glenn tells me that might change any day.

Glenn is an attorney who got into the airline business by accident. A few years earlier, a group of Lynchburg friends and business associates had gotten together with "a good idea" to form a regional Virginia airline, and Glenn was named "it."

"This is all very interesting, Glenn," I say. "I can tell time is of the essence for you. Let me get on this right away. I'll make a few calls tonight. I'll be back in touch by tomorrow afternoon. Okay?"

I'd parked my car out of sight behind some dumpsters. Jumping back in the old blue Pinto, my head awhirl, I drive back to Charlottesville.

The next morning, I'm back in Arlington laying out the situation to Mort.

"Yeah, this looks interesting, Russ. Get with your investors. Meanwhile, we'll get the team together here and crunch the numbers." Mort has all of Air Virginia's operational figures, routes, passenger loads, fares, and leases available to him via public documents.

I call Stan and Judge Jim. Jim contacts his old Airwest purchase partners: Pete Bryce, a real estate developer; Cliff Robertson, an actor; and John Byington, a big-shot Washington attorney and former chairman of the US Consumer Product Safety Commission. They're all interested in the deal.

The next few weeks are very exciting.

We hold almost daily meetings in Charlottesville, at Pete's ski resort, at Butler Aviation's conference room at Washington National Airport, or at Stan's factory in Orange. Our proposed deal to take over Air Virginia is to renegotiate the airplane leases, assure the creditors we stand behind the company's debt, and guarantee the employees' salaries. The current stockholders, all of whom have signed personal guarantees for the company's credit, would get no money. But they will walk away free and clear. So far, the principals at Air Virginia —and my investors— like the sound of it. Everything proceeds apace.

One afternoon in Lynchburg, I tell Glenn, "Our CPA in Richmond needs the most recent set of audited financial figures for Air Virginia."

Glenn is fidgeting in his seat, nervous. Sweat beads on his forehead and lip. "The only way you can see the figures is if you post a one-hundred-fifty-thousand-dollar good-faith deposit in the form of a check this afternoon."

"I'm afraid that's not going to happen, Glenn. What's going on? You've met my folks. You know they're real," I say.

"Yeah, yeah. I know. But things have reached a point . . ."

"Yes?"

"Things have reached a point where you guys have to put up some funds."

"Hmm, I don't think so," I say. "We've not completed our due diligence." Until a few weeks ago, I'd never heard the term.

"Well, I guess we're done here," says Glenn, speaking like the attorney he is.

"I hope you have a good night," I say, knowing he won't. "I'll be around tomorrow if you want to talk on the phone."

That night, my partner, John, makes a call to Sandy, one of Glenn's partners in Air Virginia. Then John phones me.

"Russ, you're not going to believe this," John says. "Sandy told me that Air Virginia has a payment due tomorrow that they can't pay. They're about to default. Since all those guys are personally on the hook, it looks like the whole house of cards is about to tumble. Giving Glenn a check now will just complicate things and delay the inevitable. And our money might evaporate. Why don't we just hang tight. If the cards tumble tomorrow, we'll be in line to pick them up. We can't just hand Glenn a check."

"Agreed," I say. "If it all crumbles, we may have to deal with a bankruptcy court. But my bet is the judge will look kindly on a deal that keeps Air Virginia's people working. That's our deal, John."

"I think so too," says John, "but it might not get to that. Sandy tells me Glenn is considering taking the money for tonight's payment from his children's trust fund. Yowzah! I can't believe it."

"No, he wouldn't do that. Would he?" I ask.

Overnight Glenn pulled some kind of rabbit from his hat. This morning, he calls and acts like yesterday never happened. The panic from the night before has vanished. He's still in a big sweat to get the deal done, but the demand for me to write a check is gone.

I go back to see Mort in Arlington. A whole wall of his office is mapped out with his vision of Air Virginia's future. We're going to eliminate the company's hodgepodge line-haul route system. Instead of concentrating on point-to-point routes, we're going to develop a hub at Dulles International.

"Look here," says Mort. "United is getting ready to build up Dulles in a big way. It'll become one of the major hub airports east of the Mississippi. They're going to need a feeder, a regional airline, to bring them passengers from the smaller cities. And we'll be right there, in place, already operating."

I spend a few hours going over Mort's idea. He has all the origin and destination passenger numbers, fares projections, and operations-cost spreadsheets. Our revamped airline is already up and flying in his mind. All he needs is hardware and people: Air Virginia's airplanes, crews, and staff.

This stuff is so exciting that I wonder why I ever wanted to be an airline pilot. I've never felt an exhilaration like this.

I talk to the aircraft lessors, the bankers, and leasing companies who own the fleet. We've decided to return five of the aircraft, the ones with the highest lease costs. Our Dulles plan shows we need only seventeen airplanes.

I'm already interested in getting rid of the nineteen passenger

Metroliners, sometimes called "death tubes" because their passenger cabins are so skinny and tight. I've contacted airplane manufacturers, like de Havilland of Canada and British Aerospace, to find the right aircraft type for the Dulles hub.

Stan comes up with a brilliant idea. We're going to strip Air Virginia's maintenance operation from the main company. "It's really important to get all these maintenance parts into their own corporation. I can depreciate them and then either sell them back to the airline or lease them. Especially the rotables," says Stan.

Like me, Stan is picking up a lot of new terms. Parts that can be rebuilt and used again are called rotables. Things like generators, pumps, propellers, and the like.

"I'm surprised somebody hasn't figured this out already," Stan says.

I know why. Somebody else doesn't have Stan. I'd never have thought of a maintenance and parts subsidiary. Stan is brilliant. He's the guy who told me, "If you ever build a condo building, be sure to keep the maintenance contract. That's where the big money is —the long-term money."

Stan is like a Horatio Alger character. With an eighth-grade education, he became not only an ocean-going Navy tugboat captain, but also the owner of several successful factories and other businesses that he rescued from the jaws of mismanagement. All my partners look to Stan as "the big gorilla."

Me? In this operation, I don't think anyone would rate me as a rhesus monkey.

Over the next two weeks, the plan comes together. No one is

eager to put in any cash, but it looks like letters of credit are all any of us will need to sign.

On a Friday, we're all sitting in the conference room at Butler Aviation at Washington National. "We need a president and CEO to head this thing up," says John.

Mort and Stan both look at me. "Russ?" says Stan.

Stan and I are good friends. He's the one in the group who knows me best.

"Are you willing to do it? Are you willing to put everything you have, even your house, on the line?"

"Yes."

On the inside, I'm wondering what they see in me I don't. I'm just a kid, still kind of shy, and well shy of thirty years old. My experience at running anything near the size of Air Virginia is zero. But I feel sure the men at the table will always be there to dig in with help and answers. Each will have an equity stake. The group has deep talent. I see the new job as an exercise in team-building.

So far, we've not spoken about the structure of the company. No one at the table has said a word about their expected percentage of ownership. Our first goal is to secure Air Virginia's corporate papers and air-carrier certificate. There's been no sign of greed. I'm not sure if that's a good thing or not. But so far, everyone has been working pro bono.

"Okay. Well, now. How about if John and I lay a formal proposal on Glenn's table?" I say. "You guys will all see it before we take it down to Lynchburg. Sound good?" I ask.

Everyone nods.

John and I spend hours writing and rewriting our opus over the next few days. I can't imagine what his professional services would cost if I was paying him by the hour. He works in the Washington office of a huge law firm that specializes in merger and acquisitions, capital markets, lobbying, and finance. I'm just a poor kid who spent seven years in a crazy Englishman's crooked little house in Fairbanks.

We are very close now to signing a deal. The current principals in Air Virginia will get nothing but financial and emotional relief. All of their personal liability related to Air Virginia will disappear.

Late one Friday afternoon in Washington, John and I are in shirtsleeves with ties pulled down. We've been working all day. His office staff has been typing and retyping countless revisions for us since the morning.

John takes a big breath and, putting a neat hill of papers on the table, says, "That's it. We're ready to propose our offer."

"We're finally there. We're 'go' for a Monday morning delivery," I say.

Then a bomb drops.

I get a call from Stan late Sunday. "You know, Russ, I'm sixty-four years old. Over the weekend I was talking to Flo, and I asked myself whether I really wanted to be in the airline business. It's a big step."

"I agree. It's a big step," I say. I love Stan. He's like a well-adjusted father. I respect his judgment. And more, I respect his feelings. There's no way I am going to pressure him or make some kind of sales pitch on what a good deal we have cooking.

"I'm going to give myself a few more days to think about it," says Stan.

Everything is now on hold. I can't sign any papers without our big gorilla on board. I put the brakes on progress. I don't return Glenn's calls for a couple of days. I tell John and the group in Richmond and Washington that we must wait, that Stan is having second thoughts. They are disappointed and nervous, as I am. I can feel the pent-up energy from all the parties. It's like we're sitting at the starting line with all engines at full rev.

It's a tough week.

On Friday morning, Stan calls. "If you and the guys want to do this, then let's go with it. Even at my age, I can't pass on the challenge. It's probably gonna be the biggest thing I've done. But I'm sure we can make it work."

Glenn takes my phone call a few minutes later. "We're ready to sign a deal, Glenn When do you want to meet? This afternoon or tomorrow?"

"Umm, there's been a change," says Glenn

"What's up?" I ask.

"We've got a student pilot, Donna Nicholas, taking lessons at our Charlottesville FBO."

Air Virginia originally started up when they got what remained of Marty Macy's old Horizon Aviation outfit, the millionaire's failed company. The fixed-base operation, the FBO, provides fuel, charters, and flight instruction.

"Anyway," says Glenn, "Donna's husband has a felt-making company in Ohio. Quite wealthy. She got wind of your offer."

I want to say, *Yeah, you told her about our offer.*

"She and her husband have made us a counteroffer. They're going to give us everything you're offering —plus a million dollars in cash for the company's stockholders. We're going to give you twenty-four hours to better that."

After negotiating with Glenn and company for two months, Stan's five-day delay allowed a fox into the henhouse. I know we're not going to pony up a million dollars cash in addition to taking over all of Air Virginia's debt. That would make our fine-tuned plan unworkable.

"No, Glenn I can tell you right now. We're not going to better our offer. Thanks. But let me know if your deal with Mr. and Mrs. Nicholas falls apart. Good luck."

The deal doesn't fall apart, and my group quietly dissolves with promises all around we'll get together when another deal pops up.

The airline business is a tough racket. I don't know if we'd have been successful over the coming years. But with our team, I think we'd have had a good shot.

Air Virginia muddles on under the new ownership with no visible change in the operation. They still fly the old nonsensical line-haul route system. They don't develop a hub, and the company continues to bleed. They file for Chapter 7 bankruptcy twelve months later. In the filing, they list mounting debts, and a million dollars cash loss, as the key reasons for liquidation.

What Air Virginia's felt maker and his student pilot wife did not bring to the company was our team. They didn't have Stan or Mort. They didn't have John and his Washington connections at Pillsbury, Madison & Sutro. And while they learned of our plan for financing the company, they didn't have our plan for operating the company, rationalizing the fleet, or developing a hub for United at Dulles. We'd never shared the operating part with Glenn.

After our deal falls apart, for a while, I'm in a state of dull emptiness.

One morning, while staring into the dawning sun on my way to New York in the King Air, I realize that I really didn't want to be an airline executive. I want to fly. I want to be —in my mind, always have been— an airline pilot.

CHAPTER THIRTY THREE

Receding Ice Age glaciers have left the landscape in Labrador scarred, stripped of its soil and vegetation. The scruffy taiga here sprouts some trees, mostly conifers, none of them very tall. Most brush in the boreal forest stands no higher than my knee. A low hill in the distance is the only change in the topography for miles. It's May, and spring is still new. The landscape shows brown flora, with an occasional green hint of summer yet to be, and gray rock. Bleak, I think, as I stare out the Happy Valley-Goose Bay Airport windows from my chair.

My back and sides feel stiff and sore, the toll of sleeping stretched across the terminal's plastic seats. Fastened to the floor, the molded chair bottoms accommodate a seated person, not a tired pilot looking for a bed.

I'm the only person in the small building. It's too early for more. The two ticket-agent and rental-car counters aren't staffed yet. But the fuel guy should be here soon. I sit up, arch my back and hear it crackle, put my hands on my knees and push myself up. The Cessna waits for me on the ramp: looking so worn out for its age —like me. We make a pathetic pair this morning.

The airlines still aren't hiring, and I still wear glasses. I'd grown bored with the routine of flying around the eastern US, and needed something interesting and new. One afternoon, after a charter, looking through the latest *Trade-A-Plane,* a newspaper devoted to airplane classified advertising, I found a small ad: "Seeking ferry pilots for worldwide aircraft-delivery flights." I took the simple bait and called right away, even before I had time to question my sense.

Russ on a transatlantic ferry flight.

Today my senses are alive and well, and my doubts surface, gnawing at my confidence. Can I do this? Will the airplane make it across the Atlantic Ocean to West Germany? This morning I'm headed across the ocean to my mid-ocean stop in Iceland in a single-engine airplane. I glance around the deserted terminal, wishing for more: more hours as a pilot, more hours of sleep, more engines for my airplane, more deicing equipment, more and better radios. Even seeing more people might ease my mind and fill the gorge in my chest and abdomen. The human body is so full. Full of bones, muscles, organs, and blood. How can it feel so empty?

The fuel truck still hasn't arrived. I walk over to the weather building to get a report for the day. The early morning air, crisp and cold, carries no smell; the barren landscape provides no whiff of life. The airport spans much acreage, miles of concrete, and lots of hangars, but no one's here. It's like a ghost town.

Built in World War II as a staging point for delivery of combat aircraft to the European theater, Happy Valley-Goose Bay Airport lies at the end of an ocean inlet called Lake Melville. Jointly run by the US and Canada for military and civil use, the enormous airport now serves aircraft defending the northern polar regions against Soviet invasion. Today, it will launch a young civilian ferry pilot and a single-engine airplane across the Atlantic.

One man sits inside the weather office, one of the few people I've seen since taking off yesterday in Pennsylvania. I tell him my plan to fly today's leg, 1,321 nautical miles, nonstop, to Reykjavík, Iceland. At an airspeed of 115 knots with an average tailwind of 10 knots, I should arrive ten hours and fifty-five minutes after takeoff. I file an international flight plan, a much more involved document than a domestic plan. It requires estimates of my time at certain navigational fixes, and I make my best guess, uncertain when I'll be able to take off this morning. I will update the time estimates when airborne.

The forecast shows mixed clouds at various levels all the way across to Iceland. There's a chance of icing above the freezing level. My plan is to stay clear of clouds.

The weatherman and I go over the forecasts. The weather in Greenland, at its few reporting west coast airports, looks pretty good.

The problem is a low-pressure system moving into Labrador from over central Quebec. It promises low clouds, freezing rain, a chance of snow, and low visibility. Once past Goose Bay, the low will continue to move east across the Labrador Sea toward Greenland. If I don't get away soon, we could have icing conditions and clouds at ground level, preventing me from taking off.

"It's going to get lousy here. And out to sea too," the weatherman says in the casual way of someone who talks about weather every day and doesn't have to fly in it.

"It looks like I've got a six-hour window before it decays," I say.

"That's about right."

He gives me a nice printed weather package with detailed charts and forecasts for the next forty-eight hours. I enjoy talking to an actual weather person, not telephoning a weather station like I would in the States. Face-to-face news somehow inspires more confidence in the voodoo.

I head out of the office and hear the distinctive rumble of a radial engine. It must be a de Havilland Beaver, a great little bush airplane. I don't see it on the taxiway, but I recognize the tone. The airplane must be behind a hangar in a nearby part of this complex of industrial buildings. It's funny how pilots learn to identify airplanes by their sounds.

The fueler shows up driving a dual-axle truck with a two-thousand-gallon aviation gasoline tank strapped to the back. We meet at the Cessna, the only airplane on the ramp. His pumps make a whirring sound, and the smell of his diesel truck pollutes the clean, dry air. He pushes a ladder over to my high-wing airplane and climbs up to the wing tanks.

"Where you headed?" he asks.

"Iceland today. Eventually to Stuttgart," I say, not believing the words coming out of my mouth. "West Germany."

"Oh, that's a ways. That should take you a while," he says, nodding at my airplane. On my route, Goose Bay is the last place to get fuel before crossing the ocean. He may see one or two little airplanes a week making the trip to Europe.

"How's the fishing up here?" I'm eager for normal conversation. The wing doesn't take much fuel. On the ride up from Pennsylvania, I'd been topping it off inflight from the interior ferry tanks. The fueler is already finished with the right wing. The left wing tank is still full.

"Ice fishin' was okay until the ice got rotten. Now we're just waitin'. The fishin's usually really good up here by June, July. Lotta guys come up here from down south to go fish with outfitters." He withdraws the hose, and I hear the snap of the fuel-cap locking lever.

"If you let me grab the hose, I'll fill the tanks inside the airplane," I say. "I want to see exactly how much I'm putting in." He hands me the large-mouth hose, and I crawl into the cockpit and open the cap of the first of my two temporary cabin ferry tanks.

I need the fuel guy to not be witness to me overfilling these tanks. A permanent marker line on the tanks shows the maximum allowable capacity for my airplane. I will pump in at least several more gallons than allowable to give myself a bigger cushion.

I have fifty gallons of fuel in the factory wing tanks, which gives me a little over five hours of flight. With only that little fuel, I would be in the drink well before reaching Iceland.

The extra temporary tanks in the cabin give me an extended range. My feeling is, the more fuel the better. The marker line on the tanks shows the maximum *allowable* amount of fuel to be within approved limits. But there's more *volume* available in the tank. I plan to use it. I feel like that captain, Shockles, on my dad's first flight in Alaska. Today, available fuel volume trumps weight considerations.

As I pump the extra gas into the tanks, a genie-like mirage —petroleum vapor— wiggles out of the tank as we dance our expedient waltz. I have to balance my desire for additional fuel with my safety at takeoff. If I overload the airplane too much, I jeopardize my ability to get into the air, structural integrity, and controllability.

I finish topping off the tanks, and the fuel guy drives away. I take one more look at the fittings for the fuel pumps. A leak would be grim news. I take my screwdriver and tighten the hose clamps. I don't like the thought of one-hundred-octane gasoline running by electrical wires inside my cabin. One spark could cause an explosion.

My paperwork arrives at the operations office, and I pay my fuel bill and landing fee. I choose two sandwiches from a vending machine, one turkey and Swiss and one tuna salad. There's a stack of brown bags beside the machine, and I stuff my sandwiches and some napkins into one of them. I push in more coins for two cans of Coke. Since I'm a cheapskate, I'm aware of losing a nickel on every American quarter in these Canadian machines.

Artwork by the local Inuit people, wooden ceiling beams, and moose antlers add to the feel of a bush airport. First Nation artifacts decorate and warm what would otherwise be a stark space. An airline agent and rental-car person stand behind their counters now, and some passengers straggle in. The comfort of seeing other people vanishes with the thought that it's time to go. *Can I stay here? Can I get a job behind the counter? Must I leave?*

I take one more look at the people in the terminal, turn away, and walk out the door. Except for my blue-and-white Cessna, the concrete ramp is empty. An arctic breeze —or something that feels like arctic breeze— cuts through my wool jacket and thermal shirt to chill my skin.

I open the door of the Cessna, stuff my sandwiches and drinks down beside the seat, and pull out my bright-orange immersion suit. Designed for survival use on North Sea oil platforms, the immersion suit will be my uniform today in case I have to ditch in the Atlantic. I step into the bulky thing, pulling it over my work boots and up to my waist. It looks ridiculous. Gumby goes to Europe.

When I climb into the cockpit, I stretch the top half of the suit over the back of my seat, leaving the hefty front zipper open and my arms free to work. If I zipped it all the way closed now, with my arms in the sleeves, I'd soon overheat. And working the flight controls would be near impossible while wearing the suit's enormous built-in mittens.

Now wedged in beside the fuel tank, I make sure my binder of charts, pad, and pencils are all within reach. Once airborne, nothing further than arm's length will be accessible. For every hour flown, anything out of reach will grow another hour away.

For much of my life, the sky always held an invitation. But today's blue-gray sky does not beckon. Why am I doing this? People shouldn't fly single-engine airplanes across the ocean.

In my mind, I can see my pilot friend, Bernard, back in the Gordonsville hangar. He was washing his Twin Comanche airplane when I told him my plans. He shook his head and, past a cautious smile, said, "You're going to fly a Cessna to West Germany? That sounds crazy! No, it *is* crazy. Are you sure you want to do that?" He held his sponge high and water dripped down his sleeve. "Nah, you don't want to do that. It's just crazy."

I also hear my dad, the concern in his voice, "How'd you get involved in this? This is some serious stuff." I also hear his subtext: *Didn't I teach you to make better decisions? You are too smart to learn. This is too risky. You are headed for a fall.*

He, more than anyone else I know, knows about this flight. He flew in the Alaska bush. He accumulated arctic hours and arctic stories. Having flown the wild and wooly himself is why he couldn't voice the words that might have tried to command me not to go. How could he tell me not to do that which he'd done himself?

I've got more flying credentials than my dad now, but still fewer years of experience. I've flown for more than a decade, and some days that sounds like a lot. But today, I'd welcome double the experience. I'd welcome a logbook full of arctic flying hours,

hours like my father's. By flying in the Lower Forty Eight, have I learned enough to survive this trip? If I knew more, would I have had the wisdom to refuse to go?

In my dad's day, many bush pilots in Alaska would fly out in the winter, disappear, never to be found. My father quit the Alaska bush before it got him. Did he regret quitting? Not pushing himself further? If he'd just kept going, kept flying, would he have gotten his airline job? Or would he have died? I wonder. But he made his decisions. I'm making mine. I choose to fly solo over an ocean. For better or worse.

Dad almost blew my cover. He called my wife on the phone, which he never does. He couldn't tell me not to go. But maybe he could influence my wife to make me stay.

"Your dad's worried about this trip," she told me.

"Oh, he hasn't flown in a while. He's out of practice. He's worrying about nothing. It's going to be alright. Nothing to worry about."

"He'd like you to beg off. But he said if you do go, he really wants you to stay in touch. He said to make you call at every stop," she said, concern in her voice.

"I am going. But not to worry," I said. "I don't know if I can call from those airports. But I always file flight plans. The governments will know if any issues crop up. They'll have your contact information. They'd call if anything happened. And it won't."

I prefer that my wife not understand this trip. It does her no favors to understand. And I am going. I'm committed. I'm on the hook. I will take this overloaded, fair-weather, light recreational airplane, which seems oddly old beyond its years, all the way to Europe. I'm obligated, both by oral contract and by my own need, to fly this little airplane across the Atlantic.

My wife needs to think it's routine, like all my other flying trips. Still, I hope she'll miss me after I disappear into the sea. I hope she'll think fondly of me as she spends the insurance money.

The longer I sit here in Happy Valley-Goose Bay, the closer I come to meeting lousy weather. *It's time to get this show on the road*, I say to myself. I often use the cliché before flights when I'm bored, tired, or reluctant to go. I reach for the door handle and pull it closed. The inrush of air creates a pressurized feeling in the cabin. The outside ambient noise quiets, and I'm cut off from the world. I push the stout aluminum door latch down, and an image of an electric chair lever flashes in my mind.

Take it easy. Take a breath. Engines don't quit. Airplanes rarely crash. A wave of fatigue hits me, and I imagine the joy of taking a nap instead of flying this airplane eleven hours to Iceland. But the ill feelings are background noise. Clutter. I will not quit. Of course not. I will ferry this airplane to West Germany.

"You're going to be just like Lindbergh!" Stan had said. "But you ain't gonna be famous!"

CHAPTER THIRTY FOUR

I put on my green David Clark headset and reach for the checklist. I turn on the master switch and open the side window to yell "clear!" to no one. The ramp is empty. With the starter engaged, the engine clanks, and the propeller twirls. The engine settles to a four-cylinder rumble. I turn on the radio master switch, and the transceivers crackle to life. The vacuum pump works, and the instrument gyros spin. With the engine running smoothly, I check my compass. It brings me comfort —the most reliable instrument in the airplane is often the most overlooked.

I wedge the laminated checklist back down into the left corner of the panel. I push the microphone switch on my yoke to talk to the Goose Bay tower through my headset.

"Winds favoring runway nine. No reported traffic in the area. Advise ready for takeoff," the controller says.

"Roger nine," I say.

Taxiing about a mile, I reach the end of the long runway. The engine is plenty warm, and I go through the pre-departure checklist: Run the engine up to eighteen hundred rpm. Check the magnetos, the oil pressure, and temperature, and cycle the propeller. Everything checks out, and I feel a twinge. Why isn't something broken? Why isn't there a valid reason to turn around? I wait a beat, giving the engine a chance to run rough. Nothing.

The airplane sits tail-heavy, the nose higher than normal because of my over-full fuel tanks. Because of the heavy weight, I will take off at a higher speed than normal to ensure there's plenty of wind blowing over my wings and tail. More wind means more lift and an extra margin of performance and control.

I take another look at the engine instruments. Oil pressure looks good, temperature right in the middle of the green; the ammeter for the alternator sits right in the center. Battery fully charged, and no unusual electrical draw. The compass and directional gyro agree. Everything looks perfect. So here we go.

"Goose Bay tower, November three-four-two-two-zero, ready for takeoff," I say into the mic.

"Cessna three-four-two-two-zero, Goose Bay tower, no traffic in the area, cleared for takeoff."

I feel like a speck. I probably look like a speck too. The runway is one hundred and fifty feet wide and stretches ten thousand feet long, about seven thousand feet longer than I need. I can't even see the end of the runway. It's too far away.

"Clear takeoff, two-two-zero rolling," I say.

I push the throttle forward smoothly and slower than usual. I want to baby the engine, make sure I don't have any coughs or hiccups before I advance the throttle all the way. I use my rudder pedals to keep the airplane on the centerline with little jabs —*left, right, left, left, right*— back and forth with the rudder, still easing the throttle forward and hearing the engine getting louder and louder, feeling the propeller dig into the air.

At fifty miles per hour, with one hand on the throttle and one hand on the yoke, the engine is wide open, and the nose tries to lift on the tail-heavy airplane. I keep forward pressure on the yoke to keep the nose wheel on the runway. Now the wind over the rudder steers the airplane more than the nose wheel springs. The concrete rumbles under the tires. At sixty miles per hour, I would normally start pulling back on the yoke to lift off the runway. But I want more speed with this heavy load, more wind over the wings.

I maintain forward pressure on the yoke and continue accelerating. The wings try to lift, but I still want more speed. There's a chance the main gear will lift from the runway before the nose wheel. I don't want that. We don't want to caster down the runway. So there's a little dance, a little finesse, to keep it all under control and balanced. We want to lift off at just the right time, but not a moment before.

At seventy, I release my forward pressure on the yoke and the nose lifts on its own. The main wheels stay on the ground, reluctant to take off. I needn't have worried about them flying off early. The wings are making lift, but not enough to raise the heavy airplane. I don't breathe much and hope my too-much-fuel gamble pays off.

Anytime now, Cessna. Anytime.

Finally, the two main wheels leave the concrete, and we are airborne.

My confidence bumps up a notch, and I take a breath as I accelerate in ground effect. It takes a while before the airplane can climb higher. But when enough life-giving wind blows over the wings, when we near ninety miles per hour, the airplane climbs away from the cushion of air near the ground and ascends into the sky.

Now, with the transition from ground to air, the heavy fuel tanks become more of a boon than a risk. I have the warm comfort of extra fuel, which equals longer range for contingencies and emergencies. I can fly for twenty-four hours if I need to, quadruple the normal range for the Cessna, and twice as long as it should take me to reach my next stop in Reykjavík. On a trip like this, my first solo across an ocean, having more fuel is a good thing, giving me lots of options.

Still, the gloomy cloud of a potential fuel leak lingers, as does the possibility of fuel-pump failure.

Leaving the airport behind, the airplane flies above the barren landscape of Labrador, which I still see well because our climb rate is terrible. For a long while, I have an excellent view of the ground. With a normal load, the Cessna gains five hundred feet per minute. My rate hovers around two hundred fifty feet per minute. That's lousy, but not a worry. There are no high hills and, in eighty miles, regardless of my altitude, I'll be flying over the ocean.

At the edge of the Goose Bay airspace, the controller says, "Cessna two-two-zero, have a good day."

The sendoff doesn't match the mood. Maybe he should play a little Wagner in the background. The "Ride of the Valkyries" might be about right. As my little shell of an airplane heads toward the Labrador Sea, the radio announcer in me thinks life would be better with a soundtrack.

CHAPTER THIRTY FIVE

With a solid layer of clouds way above me at twenty thousand feet, the Labrador Sea looks like molten lead in the distance ahead, a fitting partner for the glacier-scarred landform. My view provides no hint of life, no buildings, no roads, not even a power line along the shore. As I close in on the water, I wonder if my environment echoes dread.

I'm still only four thousand feet high, seven thousand feet from my planned cruising altitude. With little wind and an overcast sky, the water is still, without even an occasional whitecap.

Now I'm over the ocean, over the leaden mass. Imagination dissolves the floor under my boots. There seems no protection between me and the sea. From the bottom of my feet to the backs of my thighs, I press hard against the seat. With nasty weather moving into Goose Bay, my air bridge is burning as I leave Canada behind.

I flash to yesterday when I flew over the Gulf of Saint Lawrence and had a bout of homesickness. Homesickness. And I'd only been away twelve hours. Silly. Now that same feeling builds again.

Put it to bed, I tell myself. The homesick feeling yesterday spawned while flying over open water at the mouth of a big river.

Just a river. Too many Atlantic miles separate me from my ultimate destination in West Germany to let that weakness grow
again now.

Still, a wave pushes against my solar plexus; its tendrils search
for my throat.

I pick up my chart, tensing my torso to build an imaginary
seawall-against-emotion in my chest. I force a deep breath into
my lungs, stuffing the feeling back. You've done this before, I
coach myself. You've learned to leap this water before. You stayed
above the surface.

With Margrit, the owner of the ferry company, I'd flown a
Cherokee to Europe. The checkout flight had worked out okay.
Flying solo this time is no excuse for weakness. *Sure, it's okay to
face facts: It's easy for the world to snuff a soft body. But don't let love
of life get the better of you.*

I double-check my course, look at the fuel valves, and check
the charts. Each task encourages the robot in me. Focusing keeps
any waves behind the break wall. I work with the airplane, fusing
to both become machine. Better to be a robot than a soft, worried
animal body.

I imagine reading condition instruments in my body, assessing
my pressure and temperature. The needles had been approaching
red, but now I see them heading back to green. I am fine. My
airplane is fine. We are fine.

Finally in synergy with the Cessna, there's no hunger, no
thirst, no sense of cold or heat. My emotions shut down. I continue my gradual climb to eleven thousand feet. My needles stay
centered; my charts confirm I'm on track. If nothing changes,

I'll reach Iceland after sunset. Maybe the restaurants will still be open. I'll get there in time for dinner. I will eat and be human again.

When we reach eleven thousand feet, I call Gander Center in Canada on VHF. "Gander Center, this is Cessna three-four-two-two-zero. Position."

"Three-four-two-two-zero, Gander Center, go ahead position." Gander comes back staccato and mechanical through my headset.

"Cessna three-four-two-two-zero, five zero miles east of Goose Bay, estimating Loach one-one-five-zero at one-one thousand, next five-six north, five-zero west." I've told him my current position, altitude and time, the position and estimated time for my next report and, in addition, updated the times for all subsequent reports.

"Roger, Cessna three-four-two-two-zero. Loach at one-one-five-zero and one-one thousand—" He reads back the whole report.

I know that's a human talking from Gander Center, but the conversation feels out-of-body, detached. Even with all the noise from the engine and slipstream outside, a strange quiet fills the cabin. As soon as I fly over the horizon, it will get even quieter. I'll lose the line of sight between transmitter and antenna on VHF, and I won't be able to talk to Gander Center again.

What only I know is that my high-frequency radio, the long-range one that doesn't rely on line of sight, the one I'm required to have, isn't working. If I want to communicate with air traffic control, I must rely on radio relays to other airplanes via VHF to give my position reports to Gander. Without HF, I won't be able to talk to anyone on the ground until I pass over the tip of Greenland, in about five and a half hours.

Fog appears beneath me. Within a few minutes, moisture collects into wispy stratus clouds below. The clouds become denser until they block my view of the ocean. We're in clear air at eleven thousand feet, but sandwiched with clouds both above and below.

At the top of the hour, I decide it's time to top off the left-wing tank. I always want to keep at least four hours' worth of fuel in the wings, enough to get me to dry land in most cases, even if not necessarily to an airport. I switch on the electric pump mounted to the cabin floor and open the valves.

With all the instruments stable and the airplane running well, I engage the Cessna's wing leveler, a basic one-axis autopilot. I study the chart on my lap and rework my numbers: I check how much fuel I've burned and how many gallons remain in each of the tanks. I also figure the time to go to the destination compared to the fuel endurance remaining in hours. One desires the latter to be much greater than the former.

Now about eighty miles northeast of the shoreline, I lose Goose Bay's VHF signal. Not only can I not talk to them or Gander Center, but I also lose my navigation signal. At first, the VOR needle wavers. A few minutes later, it gives up. A flag drops into view. The word "off" replaces the working needle.

Now I have to chart my course with dead reckoning, a method of navigation using time, distance, and forecasted wind speed and direction. It involves close record keeping and a fair amount of estimating, but it's the only option I have. Dead is short for "deduced." It has nothing to do with death —unless I screw up. My next navigational radio station will be the Prins Christian Sund non-directional beacon at the tip of Greenland. It should be in range in four or five hours.

I glance out my left window and notice vapor coming out of the overflow vent. What the hell? I realize right away that I've left the fuel transfer pump running, and now the wing tank is over-full, and good fuel is venting overboard. I snatch the valve closed and turn off the pump. Christ. How long have I been doing that? How much fuel did I waste? I calculate about five gallons has vaporized. I know that with twenty-four hours' worth of fuel on board, five gallons won't make any material difference. But how stupid can I be?

I expected the VHF radio to stop working when we flew over the horizon. That was a problem I knew about. The HF radio conking out was a matter of chance. Jettisoning fuel was something I brought on myself. There are known problems and unknown problems. Known problems are, well, known. But how to know the unknown? With a little thought to explore possibilities, we can imagine many unknown problems. It's good to anticipate and min-imize both the known and unknown. I rip off a piece of masking tape and stick it to the panel right under the fuel gauges. From now on, I'll note, right on the tape, what time I start pumping. *We're going to do all we can to minimize pilot error*, I say to the airplane.

With the fuel problem sorted out and the airplane stable, I take a breath and try to stretch my body. When I extend my arms, they bump into the door on the left and the fuel tank on the right. When I try to extend my legs, my feet jam into the front wall of the cockpit. Without an adequate way to stretch my limbs, I roll my head, crunching through two days' worth of stiffness in my neck.

As I enter hour three, fatigue creeps into my muscle fibers. I'm like a piece of living meat in a locker. Soreness pulses in my legs and arms. I've been awake too long already. The dry air in the Cessna makes it worse. The sickly sweet vapor from the ferry tanks' high octane aviation fuel is not helping the cabin air quality. My tired eyes burn. I am very aware of yesterday's long flight up from Pennsylvania, to Moncton —where I stopped for a required Canadian FAA inspection— and on up to Labrador. I'm very aware of my short sleep on Happy Valley-Goose Bay Airport's orange plastic chairs.

I see my breath. Whoa. Cold in here. My hands and face feel chilled, but the lower half of my body is warm, even perspiring, in the immersion suit. A delicate crystal ladder of frost stretches up from the aluminum frame onto the plexiglass of the door's left-hand window. I scratch it off with my fingernail.

The magnetic compass sits in a cylindrical container —called its "case"— at the top of the windshield. Its indicator hovers over a card that floats in liquid. A needle inside points to the magnetic pole. I add thirty-five degrees of western variation, the difference between true north and magnetic north, to get my true heading. Yes, I'm on course to the northeast, as I attempt to follow a great circle course to my intermediate destination in Iceland. I check my directional gyro, the compass on the instrument panel, and notice different numbers. My magnetic compass says one hundred degrees; the gyro reads eighty.

Magnetic compasses never fail, so I know the gyro is off. I reset it to a hundred degrees, to match the compass, and note the time. The gyro is larger than the magnetic compass and doesn't bounce around, making it easier to read. So it's a great aid to keeping an accurate aircraft heading.

Over the next half hour, I watch the gyro and determine it is precessing, advancing from the real heading, about one degree a minute. That is way more than normal. I tear off another piece of tape and make a note of the time I set the gyro. I make a mental note to reset the instrument to the compass heading at least every fifteen minutes. The magnetic compass over the windshield becomes my primary heading instrument.

The clouds below me have become thicker, with more layers forming above them. Meanwhile, the stratus clouds above me have moved lower. My tunnel of operation is shrinking. Soon, I fly through wispy clouds. This is not good. At this outside air temperature, as soon as liquid moisture hits an airplane wing, it freezes. Liquid moisture can exist in temperatures as low as negative forty degrees. My outside temperature gauge says negative thirty degrees Celsius.

The Cessna has no de-icing ability. If ice develops, I have three options: climb, descend, or turn around. I know from the Goose Bay forecast that bad weather is coming in behind me. Turning around is not an option.

Out my window, crusty dots of ice span the wing's leading edge. It looks like the lattice of frost I scraped from the window.

Much as I might like to, I can't reach out and scratch ice from the wings with my fingernail. Hoping for colder air above, I decide to climb to twelve thousand feet.

Legally, we're in uncontrolled airspace. But even here, hitting another airplane holds no appeal. I can't call air traffic control to advise them I need to climb. They're out of range. So I make a call on the common air-to-air frequency to make sure no other airplane is around. It's very unlikely. I'll bet there isn't another human for hundreds of miles, unless there's a ship down on the surface. After half a minute, with no reply, I begin my ascent. At twelve thousand feet, I look out again and see that the ice has continued to accumulate.

As more ice forms, the wings will produce less and less lift. After a while, the airplane will slow down and begin to descend. This is still light rime icing —I know the various types of icing— and I know light ice can become a lot worse, fast. Eventually, a wing could have so much ice that it stalls and quits flying altogether.

I also know flying higher is pushing it. Hypoxia becomes an issue for healthy people above ten thousand feet. I'm managing at twelve thousand, but I know my blood cells are not getting enough oxygen to function at a hundred percent.

So, let's see. Ice could kill me, and hypoxia could make me stupid. I choose the lesser evil. Hoping to clear the ice, I want to go to thirteen thousand. I raise the nose and try to climb, but at twelve thousand four hundred feet, the heavy Cessna won't go up anymore, and we're still making ice. So I reverse the action and begin a descent. Now I'm hoping for one of two things: warmer air or an area without clouds.

I reset the gyro again and notice the elapsed time since take-off: three hours and thirty minutes. I'm closer to Greenland now than I am to Canada. The ice on the wing hasn't gotten better, but right now it doesn't look much worse either. I also think about ice on the propeller. Although I can't see it, I know it's there. If there's ice on the wings, there's ice on the prop. Ice on the propeller means less thrust.

Unwelcome homesickness returns, pushing against my diaphragm. By now, I know the homesickness is not for a place or those left behind. Here, I'm aware it's about our life's home, the temporal and mortal body. All the earlier talk about threats is now real, staring me in the face. This ice could kill me, and I'm grieving the prospect.

The Cardinal at Happy Valley-Goose Bay Airport

CHAPTER THIRTY SIX

Blam, bam-bam, blam!

Where did that come from? The turbulence comes on with no warning. One second, we fly in glassy air. The next moment, we're flying in a blender. The airplane groans under the beating. My body groans too.

We're in the middle of the Labrador Sea, with three hours to Greenland and awful weather behind in Canada. The airplane pitches with another jolt —*kerblam!*— and my head slams against the side window.

I want to descend at five hundred feet per minute, but with the airplane shaking as it is, I can't read my vertical speed indicator. Caused by lateral and vertical movements of air, this turbulence wreaks havoc on my planned flight path.

The vertical speed indicator shows a descent of one thousand feet per minute, then moves to fifteen hundred. Then it bumps up to a one-thousand-feet-per-minute climb. I don't want to climb! The gauges vibrate so much in the constant shaking that the needles and instrument panel are a blur. I can only estimate the indications.

The next jolt of rough air destroys my compass. Its card, the moving part with the heading numbers, leaves the pin to wedge itself in the side of the case. Well, isn't this just great? Now I don't have a compass.

I look out to the wing for the first time in what seems like ages and see the icing is worse. No longer light ice, rime is growing thick now. At seven thousand feet, the temperature gauge is inching up, but it's still way below freezing. My body is tight, everything drawing into my core. I'm trying to steel my muscles against the twisting turbulence. My jaw is set too —and not against the bumps. Rivulets of sweat drip down my torso and into the immersion suit.

Accidents tend to happen after three or more bad things pile up. I don't have just one thing going wrong. Or two. Or three. There are four things now: icing, violent turbulence, a bad gyro, and now a broken compass. And we're not over the pastures of central Virginia, where airports are only a few minutes apart. Here we're in the middle of the Labrador Sea.

I feel drained and old. The idea that I could die is now real. It is not the post hoc fears I've known before —the after-fears born of the avoided car crash or a fall from a tree. Those are quick fears. Over the ocean, today's fear has time to etch away the immortality of youth.

This turbulence is jarring —horrific, in fact. But it alone will not kill me. I put my faith in the Cessna engineers who designed the Cardinal and the guys who bolted it together back in Wichita eight years ago. I've never heard of a Cessna coming apart in flight. In fact, the rate of structural failure for any airplane is so rare that it's statistically insignificant. If this airplane hasn't come apart so far in these wrenching jolts, it should continue to hold together. That's my considered thought, anyway. What other choice do I have?

But the ice? That may be lethal. There's no way around it. The rate of accumulation here over the Labrador Sea has increased in the last few minutes. If it gets much thicker, I'll be meeting the drink, and that will be the end.

I do another scan of the panel to get a read on my altitude, and I realize that the instruments are clear. I hadn't even noticed, but the turbulence has ended. There was no attention-getting *bam-bam*. No one-two punch that often accompanies the end of strong turbulence, its seeming purpose to remind us that Mother Nature is still in charge.

We fly from the blender right into serene smoothness. I note that nothing has come loose on the airplane. Nothing seems bent or broken. The dust floating around in the cabin is my only reminder of the violent turbulence.

Now, with the instruments once again steady, no longer dancing like dervishes, I see that the temperature is warming toward zero degrees Celsius, my magic mark. If I can get above zero degrees, the ice should melt. It's funny how we have all become one: the airplane, the sky, and me. Here I am, thinking I need to get above zero. But no, it's only the atmosphere that needs to get above zero.

When we are descending below five thousand feet, at negative ten degrees Celsius, the clouds thin. At forty-five hundred feet, I'm out of the thick clouds, and the wispy cloud layers below me are dissipating. I catch glimpses of the ocean, still a dark lead color like it was off the coast, but now punctuated by vigorous whitecaps. So I know surface winds have picked up.

It's good to be clear of clouds and to see the ocean. But being this close to the water makes my demise feel more imminent. Less than a vertical mile exists now between me and the drink.

I remember the texts about ditching in the ocean. Fly into the wind and land in the wave troughs, they instructed. I look down and grimace. The ocean today is rough and confused, the waves coming from all different directions. I don't see any troughs. If complete, that text would have ended with, *Good luck landing with that water landing, sucker.* Maybe I'll send a note to the editors.

Even in textbook conditions, the Cessna is not a good airplane to ditch. It's not a seaplane. The fixed landing gear will be the first thing to strike the water, which might flip the airplane. I picture myself upside down, hanging from my belt, like my father did when he crashed our Luscombe. But I will be upside down with freezing sea water pouring into the airplane. It'll be best to not ditch.

I turn my attention back to the altimeter. We're through twenty-five hundred feet, and the temperature hits zero. Great! All I need is another thousand feet, and I'll see the ice melting. At the normal rate, another thousand feet will give me three degrees above zero, a most happy prospect.

But going through two thousand feet, the thermometer holds steady, the needle tickling zero. Down at fifteen hundred feet, it reads negative two. What? It's supposed to get warmer down here. But it's getting colder as I descend. My head spins. My upper body curls up over the yoke to get a better look at the thermometer. We've flown into some kind of inversion. Here it's getting colder with lower altitude, not warmer like I expected. The ice hangs tight to the wings.

Then, from some dark recess, an image pops into my head: ice cubes in the freezer. If they sit there long enough, they shrink and, over time, disappear, don't they? Yes, it's a process called sublimation. It's weird how this thought rises. I didn't call it up. It just appears.

So here's another way to avoid death, thank you very much. As long as I stay in this corridor of clear air, I shouldn't accumulate any more ice. With a wind blowing at one hundred and twenty miles per hour over the wing, sublimation should happen much faster than it does to an ice cube in the still air of a kitchen freezer. That's my theory. I've never put it to practice, but I feel confident about it. Sublimation. I know it will work. Because it has to.

Clawing back to twenty-five hundred feet and two degrees below freezing, still in an area of clear air, I fly with clouds above me. While I wait for the ice to sublimate, my emotions quiet. I have a few moments to think about my discomforts on this trip. My fear.

Manifestations of fear are ever changing like a fire. Before the trip, fear had tried to warn me off: *You don't have to go. Taking the trip is dangerous. You might die in the arctic sea.* The fear spoke to me and tried to reason. It proposed questions: *Do you think you have what it takes to fly alone across the ocean? Will your lack of experience be the instrument of your own destruction?* The fear appealed to my sense of compassion. *How can you expose your family to such worry? You should beg off.*

Then, for a thousand miles after takeoff, while the airplane was still over solid ground, fear's voice continued, but became louder. *Run away before it's too late. Quit. Listen to reason. Land and walk away. You will feel shame, but you will be safe.*

Once we were out over the ocean, the warnings changed. Fear still sang a chorus of self-doubt. It still roiled and churned, but its messages were now different. Instead of telling me to run away, it warned me to fight. Fear yipped about my obvious questionable knowledge, judgment, and abilities. But it also squeezed and focused my mind so that I might come out of this alive.

Flight or fight. In the past few days, I have seen the mechanics of fear at work. I also noticed a transcendent quality. Fear seemed to move the spirit. Feeling the fear of real-time mortality cleaned out some of life's caked-on detritus. Fear revealed not beauty, but sublimity: a feeling akin to love, but without the radiance of well-being.

Being in the whale's belly, though unsettling, seems to put me in direct contact with some important central nerve. I don't know what that nerve might be. As I sit for a moment, while nothing is trying to kill me, I find it's an interesting thought. But what a way to learn. Stress, worry, and latent —and sometimes active— fear seem to be ever-ready companions on single-engine ocean flights. The lines in a pilot's face do not all come from hours of squinting into the sun.

Hey! Enough of this. It would be good to let someone know where I am. Just in case my theory about sublimation fails. Just because I want to talk to someone. And just because I don't want

Gander to begin a search for a flight with an overdue position report.

I make a call on the party-line frequency, 123.45 MHz. Not an official channel, it's where everyone goes to talk to each other when over the water.

I key the mic. "Anybody read Cessna three-four-two-two-zero on common?"

I wait a couple of minutes, resigned to not getting an answer. Then, a crackle of transmission.

"Cessna, this is Northwest thirty, go ahead."

He probably waited to see if somebody else might answer. He may suspect I'm about to put him to work. He'd be right.

My body settles back into my seat at the sound of his commanding voice, a classic airline pilot. "Northwest thirty, Cessna three-four-two-two-zero. You mind relaying a position report to Gander for us?"

"Yeah, sure. Stand by."

I imagine him getting paper to copy down my position. I look down at my most recent calculation based on dead reckoning and wonder how accurate it is. After all, I have no idea what the wind speed is or what my real heading has been. A wag is good enough out here, though. Nobody is around for hundreds of miles at the lower altitudes. All the jets, like Northwest, are at least five miles above me.

"Cessna three-four-two-two-zero, go ahead with that position."

"Cessna three-four-two-two-zero, position at one-four-three-zero, four-three-five-zero north, zero-four-zero west at one-one thousand . . ." I lie about my altitude and give him the rest of the numbers and time estimates.

"Roger, Cessna two-two-zero . . ." He reads back my position to confirm it. Then there's a pause. I know he's sending my report to Gander via his high-frequency radio.

I don't want him to get off the radio. I don't want him to leave me. Hearing his voice in my headset, my muscles relax, even my skin feels looser. Nothing in my situation has changed, but I feel better talking to this guy. He's sitting in a nice, warm cockpit with two other pilots. He has an entire airplane load of people behind him. And he's up in the sky with me. Somehow I feel part of a crowd.

"Cessna two-two-zero, Gander has your position okay."

"Thanks. Got time for one more thing?" I say.

"What's that?"

Not giving away any of my problems, I mention, off-the-cuff, my lazy DG. "I've been between clouds for a while and just want to confirm things. What's the bearing of the sun right now?" If there's a break in the clouds, the sun's bearing might give me a hint of my true heading.

There's no reason to confide the details. He can't reach out and fix anything. So, what's the point in sharing misery? I don't mention the icing or the recent turbulence. I don't make the heading issue seem more than an item of minor interest. Whining won't help. An airliner can fix nothing for me. Northwest thirty can't reach out a hand and snatch me from the belly of my aluminum fish. The airliner flies in a different universe. When en route over the ocean, actual help is self-serve.

But the talk makes me feel better. What Jonah might have given for a radio.

"Well, if you put your nose right on the sun, your true heading will be . . ." he says the bearing.

"Okay, great. And do you have an estimate of the tops?" I ask about the clouds.

"The tops are running about three-zero-zero," he says, meaning thirty thousand feet.

I've taken enough of his time now. I don't complain that his message is useless for me. With the cloud tops thirty thousand feet above me, I'd need rockets strapped to the Cardinal to fly that high.

"Where are you headed today?" he asks. His voice reminds me of Bob, my lifelong idea of an airline pilot. He sounds measured, monotone, but not with affectation. It's how he sounds, because that's how he is. I detect a hint of boredom and fatigue in his tone. I'm grateful he wants to talk to the stupid kid in the Cessna over the Atlantic.

"We should be in Reykjavík tonight and Stuttgart in a couple of days. You?"

"We're going to Minneapolis out of London. Gatwick. What kind of airplane are you?"

"We're a Cessna Cardinal." Even solo, I employ the plural. Because it is "we." It's me and the airplane. "How about yourself?"

"We've got a DC-10."

That sounds like heaven to me, flying a big fat airliner with fully functional radios and navigation equipment, its pilots sitting on big fat airline pilot wallets. I bet his compass works too. And he probably had hot nuts for hors d'oeuvres and shrimp cocktail for lunch.

"Wish I were with you. As a matter of fact, I applied to Northwest a little while back, but obviously didn't get hired," I force a laugh. I want to sound like I'm talking to a peer, a member of my same tribe.

"No, nobody's getting hired these days —fuel prices, recession, and all. Nope. Lotta guys are just hoping to hang on to jobs. Not get furloughed. But don't give up. Try again when things pick up."

"Will do. Maybe I'll see you on the line one day," I say, pushing my glasses up my nose.

"We hope so," he says.

"Thanks. Have a good day. Two-two-zero," I say.

"Good trip now. Thirty. Bye-bye."

On my wings, the ice has begun to sublimate. I exhale. It's working. Sometimes things work out. I guess things work out most of the time. We all seem to get past most scrapes.

I can still see the ocean below, and the clouds are now far above. I've just given a pretty bogus position report, but at least Gander knows I'm alive.

CHAPTER THIRTY SEVEN

All is okay right now, but this is crazy. Nuts. I am in the middle of the Labrador Sea. Beside me is a door that, on the ground, you open and step out. On the ground I could step out and pound any ice off the wings. On the ground, it would be just a short step. The wing is right there. Just a few feet away. I could touch the wing root with my hand if I could open the door. Here, over the Labrador Sea, that step to the wing is three hundred fifty miles and three hours away.

However, the ice is sublimating and should burn all the way off, boosting my confidence the flight won't end in a water landing. But what if I fly through clouds again, and the ice resumes its build up? What if an oil pump or some other critical engine part fails behind that single propeller? I can't pull over, stop, and step out. I'd have to glide down and land in the drink. Soon after that, I would likely be dead.

Lots of worries. But exactly what do I fear? Nature and mechanical parts do not bear animosity. The sea is never angry. The sky is never brooding. The Cardinal has no feelings about flying over water. I have taken on this trip without coercion. I well know the risks to life.

I have no conflict with the airplane or the sky. It is not man against nature. Or man against machine. Any ill feeling I have, any fear, is man against self. And maybe, after one burrows down, that's the way it always is. Sure, there are outside factors here. But there is no external enemy or foe. Here, surrounded by trackless miles of air and water, my war with fear lives within my own small mind and body.

My only question is how I will be in relationship to that which is. That might be true when extended to people too. Man against man? I cannot change my father. Once, I asked him to quit drinking. "Can you do it for me, Dad?" He couldn't answer. He only stared at me. I knew he wanted to say yes but knew it would be a lie. I couldn't change him then, and I can't now. All I can do is make choices in how I will relate to him —as he is. My concern is how I will be in *my relationship* to him: man versus self.

I need to find out where I am. Outside I see nothing but layers of clouds. Doubt of my whereabouts lingers. I want confirmation and reassurance. I want to fix my position to get a better idea of where I am over the Labrador Sea.

The line-of-sight VOR stations are way over the horizon and out of range. The closest one ahead is in Iceland. I don't have the new Loran C and all of us little airplane pilots know that GPS is on the way. But deployment is still years down the road. I don't have a sextant for celestial navigation. It wouldn't work under the clouds anyway. And besides, who ever heard of anyone flying a Cessna taking a successful sextant shot?

Thanks to that pesky DG problem, my dead reckoning is only suspicion. To prove a position, I need to receive some kind of ground-based navigation signal. What if the DG is way off now,

352   Russ Roberts

and, without a compass, I'm milling around in circles out over the Labrador Sea? If so, I may never pick up a beacon's signal.

That kind of thinking does no good. I redouble faith that the DG, with my constant corrections, yields a fair heading, at least approximately northeast. In a while, I trust I will pick up the Prins Christian Sund radio beacon at the tip of Greenland. The non-directional beacon, or NDB, at Prins Christian Sund is a radio station. I will tune a receiver in the airplane, called an ADF, to that station. If I find a signal, a needle on the instrument panel should point toward the station.

Well, it should sort of point to the station. NDB frequencies experience a lot of interference. Sun spots, auroras, astronomical radio wave spikes, engine ignition sparks, shoreline effect, precipitation static, and thunderstorms all seduce an ADF needle. A rock-hard ADF needle is a rare thing. An ADF is not all that accurate.

But it's all I have. A needle pointing toward a ground station would be almost as good as having a working compass.

I tune the receiver to see if there are any useful signals coming through. I find nothing but the crash and hiss of background noise. One good NDB signal would give me a line of position. Comparing that line with my dead-reckoned position would give me a rough fix. I would then know, within an unknown range of error, where I am. If I could get a second signal from another ground station, I could narrow in and get a more reliable fix.

On the ADF, I pick up some weak and choppy carrier-wave Morse code signals. But the direction needle swings to whatever galactic burst or snow flake produces a stronger milliwattage. I've cranked through two radio bands and am about to give up. Then, the needle gives a nod of commitment toward a signal. I listen, but hear no Morse code identification. Instead, there is a voice. With a frequency near 600 kHz, this is not an aviation beacon. It is a broadcast station. But where is it?

The ADF signal stays strong. A radio station in some town or city is sending out its chatter and tunes. The operator doesn't know his signal is my lifeline. Though weak and garbled, I can hear the voice is not English. Is his station somewhere in Europe? I have so much fuel that I don't care how far ahead the station lays. Man, I could track this station as far as mainland Europe if I had to. I could home in on the signal, cross the coast somewhere, pick up a reliable VOR navigation station, and *voilà!* I could be in France. A quick hop over to Stuttgart in Germany, and I would land. I could skip the landing in Iceland. I could end my trip, and my worries, a full day early. That's the kind of option I wished to have when I put too much fuel in the airplane back in Goose.

I pick up the map and search for information about the radio station I'm hearing. About a quarter-way up the west coast of Greenland, I find "570-Radio Godthåb." So it's not in Europe. On the chart, Godthåb is only three inches away.

I know the weather forecast for Greenland is good. I can scoot over to Godthåb, land, and do something about the compass. I figure we're about two-and-a-half hours from Godthåb and its three thousand feet of paved runway. I forget about flying to France, Germany, or even Iceland. I turn the airplane about twenty degrees to the left to line up the needle. Landing in Godthåb seems like a good idea.

A gentle exhale passes through my lips. Now I see only a thin layer of ice crystals on the wings. Sublimation works. With a new plan and a new course, I figure it's a good time for lunch. I am not hungry, my body still has no voice, but I figure I must need food.

I fish from the brown bag next to my seat for one of the sandwiches I'd gotten in Goose Bay. It's the turkey and Swiss. I should probably eat the tuna sandwich first, since it'll go bad quicker. But I don't want to dig into the bag again. I find one of the three cans of soda I had stashed next to the airplane's cold door. The cold can pops with a good snap when opened. I put the pop top in the sandwich bag and take a long pull, the first drink I've had in hours. The carbonated liquid burns good, sweet, and bubbly down my throat. It is like a slap. I am back into my body. I nibble on the dry stale sandwich and take a sip of cola to moisten each bite.

What is this? Through the windshield, I see a fleet of white boats. Man, this is great! Fishing boats. Greenlandic fishing boats. Are they out of Godthåb itself? I feel excitement and comfort.

Coca-Cola has come up with a new advertising jingle. They've given up the idea that people standing on a hill singing and drinking cola would produce world peace. The company has lowered its sights. They say drinking a Coke can bring a smile. The drink tastes good, I'll give them that. And its fizziness has blasted me back into human existence. And yes, I do smile. But my smile comes not from the soda, but from the view of the fishing fleet with its crews ahead. If the engine quits, and I have to ditch now, I will head over and splash down beside a boat.

I finish my lunch like it's a normal day.

Then, with a pop like the bursting of cola's bubbles, the happy picture dissolves. The soda can is dry. The sandwich is gone, and so are the boats filled with people. My fishing fleet becomes a field of icebergs. I crush the can and feel more alone than ever. The sandwich is now an anchor in my gut. I take a breath of resignation with no other choice than to press on.

This isn't over yet. At least I was happy during my meal.

Two more hours pass with my spirit in a stew. Then, on the horizon, is this another mirage, or are those actual mountains? I watch for a while, sure that this image will blink out any minute. That's the way the day's gone.

But, wait. As we get closer at one hundred twenty miles per hour, the mountains grow more defined each minute. They're real. Decorated with snow, their steep gray sides plunge almost vertical. The monoliths stand beautiful against the sea. Greenland's mountains are not the highest of the world's peaks. But to me, they are glorious, the best thing I have ever seen from an airplane. I thrill at the virginal scene. Joy engulfs me. Soon I will walk on land.

Even though I have only been airborne for six hours, it feels like I've been at sea for many days. A heavy weight lifts off my solar plexus, and the relief opens the door to fatigue. Before this six-hour leg, I commuted from Virginia to Pennsylvania. From there it was eight hours to Moncton and on to Goose Bay. Then there'd been that nap on the plastic chairs in the terminal, but that hardly counts as rest. Wearing the same clothes I left in the day before, I've been up for over twenty-four hours.

My eyes slam shut. I force them back open, greeted again by the majestic mountains. I don't tell myself that everything will be okay —a good pilot never does— but I allow myself the enjoyment that the odds are back in my favor. Or will be if I don't fall asleep here in the last hour and crash into the sea.

Undisturbed in nature, the snowy mountains look beautiful, right now even more stunning than the peaks in my boyhood Alaska. Beyond the ranges, I glimpse the Greenland ice cap, which draws a white line across the horizon. I fly along an inlet and, in a while, spot the buildings of Godthåb.

Calling the radio frequency for the airport, I hear the weather —ceiling and visibility okay. The winds favor runway one-eight. No traffic. I just need to stay alert long enough to get this airplane on the ground. When the wheels touch down, the rumble jolts me out of my almost catatonic state. I've been floating in air the last six hours. Now I'm back on Earth. The airplane shudders, and the wheels transmit that vibration right through my body.

I pull the mixture control to shut down the engine in one of the world's quietest towns. The propeller stops spinning, and so do I. All I hear is the whirring of the gyros winding down. I feel unplugged. I shut off the magnetos and the master switches. I sit and stare out of the window with eyes that do not see. At some level, I realize that I am in Greenland. Visiting Greenland is a surprise, a gift even. But I sit in a stupor, purging my fatigue. I have no impulse to take in the sights. I sit and vent the accumulated exertions from over the water.

With mechanical motions, I finally unbuckle and open the

door. My movements while flying have been minuscule, restricted by the confines of the airplane cabin with its ferry tanks. It is like sitting in a Mercury capsule. Stepping out onto the airport ramp is the first big movement I've made in six hours. I am stiff and sore.

The fresh cool air of Godthåb moistens my eyes, and the foreign scenery comes into focus. I imagine a human colony on another world. I see stark institutional buildings housing the people and offices of Godthåb. Fjords and mountains surround the town. Icebergs are scattered in the harbor. They pose like national monuments in the fairway. Through the thick mental fog, I know that I am "somewhere else."

I step out and take a few awkward steps. My body crouches like it's still sitting in a seat. A stretch releases my wrenched muscles. I reach down to push off the immersion suit, step out of each leg, then throw the wretched thing back in the cockpit. Clawing out of the fatigue narcosis, I remember I need to repair the compass. I am a long way from home, have a long way to go, and will not delay the trip for want of a licensed mechanic —or a rest.

As a boy, I had taken old airplane compasses apart. They were pretty simple to fix. The biggest trick was trying to preserve as much of the compass fluid as possible.

With my little tool kit, I break apart the Cardinal's compass case, being careful not to damage the gasket. I don't want the joint to leak when reassembled. I let the fluid drain into a fuel sampling bottle. Inside the compass, I find a screw has backed out. Its loose condition had made it possible for the compass card to leave its pin.

I wonder how long it has been like that. Since fabrication on the Airpath factory floor in Missouri, no doubt. It has waited years for an atmospheric martini shaker to put it to its failing test.

I put the compass back together and refill its liquid. The seal looked secure before I put the screws all back in place. But, upon refilling, the fluid quickly leaks out. The compass card now swings undampened by its missing stabilizing liquid. Crap.

Near the terminal, I spot an aviation fuel man in dirty overalls. Waving him over, I ask the man, an Inuit, about getting more compass fluid.

"None. Never seen none," he says.

When I was a teenager, I hung around the maintenance hangar a lot. I remember seeing a bottle of compass fluid with the words "petroleum distillate" on the label. An ancient, but now proving useful, mental artifact.

"Well then, can I have a small amount of jet fuel?" I ask.

His languages are Danish and *Kalaallisut*, with only a small amount of English. It takes some time to communicate what I want. I only want an ounce or two of the Jet-A petroleum distillate to fill the compass case. He leaves and comes back a few minutes later with the jet fuel truck. He drags a ladder over to a wing.

"No, no, no! No jet fuel in the wings!"

Seeing me with the compass in my hand no doubt convinced him I am crazy. Would he support my insanity by filling the Cessna's fuel tanks with gasoline-engine-killing Jet-A kerosene? I pick up my compass and shake it back and forth, showing the attendant it needs fluid. "It's empty. I need Jet-A fuel in here," I

say. I finally communicate the message, and he splashes a little
Jet-A fuel into a beaker.

After cracking open the compass again and adjusting the gasket, smoothing it this time to ensure there are no bumps, I top it
off. I put in the bung screw and, this time, the case doesn't leak.

I'm bone tired but still want to take off for Iceland right away.
Canada's foul weather is heading east, and I don't want to get
stuck for who knows how long in Greenland.

The Cardinal still has plenty of avgas, but as a feel-good measure, I ask the attendant to bring the gas truck to the airplane.
"Fuel? Avgas, please?" I don't need more gas —I still have seventeen hours' worth on board— but I like the security of having
more. I calculate what I want in liters, a little more than I figure
I vented overboard, and write down "40L Avgas 100" on a piece
of paper. He nods and trundles over a cart with four fifty-gallon
cans of aviation gasoline.

He pumps a little fuel into a glass beaker, the same one I'd
used to fill the compass, to check for water that would settle
to the bottom. One more thing to worry about on my next leg
—possible water in my fuel. But we see no water, and I take the
hose and put it in one of the ferry tanks. By hand, he pumps the
fuel from the barrels with a wobble pump. Finished, he scratches
an invoice, and I pay for the fuel and the landing fee.

The stiff bill for the ten gallons of fuel and landing fee —one
hundred fifty dollars— makes me think about my contracted fee
for this trip: $1,700. Out of that, I have to pay for fuel, landing
fees, food, hotels, and transportation back from Europe.

It would be a luxury to spend the night here. But a room in

a Greenland hotel could push my profit toward zero. Plus, I'm due back in Virginia for a charter flight in five days. I go into the terminal, file my flight plan, and get a weather report —it's unchanged. Godthåb will get lousy in a few hours.

I walk back out into the cold, moist air. The sun is lower in the sky now. I have to convince my legs to move, one step at a time, toward the Cessna. With each step, I quash the anxiety that tries to snake up. I need to keep it down below my waist. If I let it pass my stomach, I don't know if I have the strength to beat it back. The anxiety encourages fatigue, so I must imagine myself again as robotic, a part of the machinery.

I open my door, reach in, and pull out my immersion suit. Bending over, I step each stiff leg inside the suit, one at a time, and pull it up to my waist. With a grunt of effort, I crawl back into the cockpit and jimmy myself into the confines of my seat, squeezed beside the fuel tank.

Hoping to force some energy into my leaden body, I inhale. I never considered my own fatigue as a risk on this trip, but it's clear to me that if I can't stay alert, it could cost me my life. I still need to cross the Greenland ice cap and the ocean before landing in Iceland, onward toward my destination in Germany.

CHAPTER THIRTY EIGHT

Pulling out the laminated checklist from the top of the panel, I run through the steps. My hands move like molasses from one switch to the next. I contemplate what lies ahead: a night flight over the ice cap of Greenland. Starting from up the coast here in Godthåb, it's a different route from the one I planned, which would have taken me across the tip of Greenland, over the Denmark Straight right into Iceland.

I know that the ice cap reaches as high as ten thousand feet, so I have to climb to at least eleven thousand feet, and that will take time. But that's all I know. I brought no detailed charts of Greenland's interior. I'd planned to touch only its southern tip. None of my charts have information for flying at low altitude over the ice cap. Over central Greenland, my charts say, "No survey."

For the Cardinal's delivery flight to Europe, I can legally operate well over its design limit. Even though we have burned off six hours of fuel, and wasted an hour by accidentally venting, with the ten gallons I added we still have eighteen hours of fuel remaining on board. The airplane is heavy for Godthåb's three thousand feet of runway. The runways I used earlier on the trip were all at least two or three times longer. There'd been plenty of pavement. Not so in Godthåb. The takeoff run takes a very long time and I use almost all the runway's length. I have a close-up view of the far end of the runway as I leave the end with only a few feet under the wheels.

The climb is also slow. If I turned on course right after take-off, I would have immediately flown into terrain, mountains, over four thousand feet high. With the airplane's poor climb performance, I have to head west, back over the Labrador Sea, back toward the setting sun. I have to go opposite of where I want to go. So I fly back toward Canada. I claw for forty miles to a safe altitude before turning east again toward Greenland's coast range.

As I cross back over Godthåb, the sun drops behind me. The sky in front of me looks gray, then turns dark gray along Earth's terminator, then black. Only mountains and ice cap lie below me. The only light comes from the glow of my instruments and the tell-tales of my green and red navigation lights out on the wing tips. In the darkness, with smooth air, underneath high clouds, I have no sense of motion. I am floating in an ink bottle.

Any anxiety that came with me into the airplane melts into the darkness, overpowered by intense exhaustion. My eyes feel like sandpaper. Every once in a while, I close them to get some relief. Then sleep comes. My ears shut off, and my brain jerks awake, thinking the engine quit. *Stay with it*, I tell myself. With the wing leveler, the airplane will plow straight ahead, but I sure as hell don't want to fall asleep.

I turn the heat down, hoping cooler air will keep me awake, then take out my charts to do some navigating and calculating. In the heavy airplane, at eleven thousand feet, I figure I've climbed high enough to clear the ice cap.

The compass is still working well after fixing the screw and adding fluid at Godthåb, but gives me a sense of foreboding. I never imagined my compass would break. What else have I not prepared for? What else could go wrong? Looking out into the darkness, I wish for clairvoyance.

The steady roar from the Lycoming engine provides some comfort. All four cylinders and one hundred eighty horses sound good. The gauges show green. But, as soon as I focus on the engine, I imagine hiccups. I think about the attendant in Greenland checking the fuel for water. What other crap might have been in those barrels?

I shine my flashlight on the leading edge of the wing to look for ice. Nothing. All clean. Any residual ice on the airplane melted during my stop in Godthåb. I pick up my second sandwich, thinking it might boost my energy. It's hard and dry now, the tuna like jerky. I stuff it back down beside the seat. It doesn't take long to petrify a sandwich at altitude in the arctic air.

After three hours, I figure I am "feet wet." By now, I must be over the water again. This time we fly over the Denmark Strait. I remember my *National Geographic* map of Greenland. I wish I'd dug it out before. *National Geographic* makes such pretty maps. I see Prins Christian Sund there on the southern tip. I might have seen it in daylight if I hadn't visited Godthåb. I'd looked forward to flying over it and seeing the fjords. On the map, I see the familiar names I'd studied to cross only the southern end of the island.

I have spent no time at all studying Greenland's high, ice-crusted interior. An insert on the map shows Greenland without the ice cap. The ice cap is so heavy, according to the map's text, that it pushed the granite shield down thousands of feet. A lot of the island's actual land surface is below sea level. The mountains form an archipelago that, if the ice were to melt, would surround a big sea. The ice cap, in some spots, is twelve to thirteen thousand feet thick from the bedrock. On the main map, the tops of giant mountains stick up from the thick ice blanket, two miles above sea level.

What a nice map. It shows the few coastal villages and all the glaciers and fjords. What's this? Just north of my course line is Mt. Forel, climbing to eleven thousand one hundred twenty five feet. If I'd been a little north of track, I might have hit it. Jesus! I might have smashed to bits on the top of a mountain. Earlier, I'd read only about the ice cap reaching ten thousand feet above sea level. I'd read nothing about mountains sticking out. I wish I'd remembered the map. I wish I wasn't so tired.

I'm still within Greenland's VHF radio communications. Before I get too far out over the water, I call a radar station on the distant early warning system. The DEW line is a series of stations set up in the late fifties to detect incoming Soviet missiles. A young guy, a Canadian manning a station called Sob Story, has been watching me on his powerful radar. He's glad I called. He tells me he's bored.

"Yeah, been tracking you. You've been running along the ground at one hundred thirty knots. Looks like you're on a good track for Iceland."

My true airspeed is one hundred ten knots, so I'm getting a good twenty-knot push on my tail.

The military guy tells me I'm fifty miles south of Kulusuk Airport. "But it's closed. There was a big snow fall this week. Come back in July!"

I wish I'd called this guy earlier. But I'd forgotten about the DEW line stations too. He could have told me about Mt. Forel.

I put a dot on my chart to note my radar position and begin figuring my arrival time in Iceland. I'll be there in about three hours. The certainty of knowing my location and the wind speed, and knowing I'm more than two miles over water, feels like a warm blanket wrapped around me. It takes the chill out of riding only a hair's breadth above ice in the dark.

The margin for error with the ice caps was too narrow for comfort, even disregarding the mountains. Though a water landing holds much less appeal than an ice landing, at least now I won't prang into Greenland by mistake.

The radio quiet again, the engine noise puts me back into the lulling rhythm of the airplane. My biggest enemy is sleep. It creeps up from my stiff legs, through my achy torso, and settles in my head. My head weighs too much; it's an effort to keep it up. I know better than to close my eyes. Instead I blink often, trying to keep them lubricated.

After flying five and a half hours since Godthåb, I see a wavering on the line-of-sight VOR navigation needle, which I've pre-tuned to a station in Iceland. When the needle points with conviction, I turn up the volume and hear the proper Morse identification for the VOR at Keflavík. I'm on track. I pop open a cola to see if its caffeine can wake me up for landing.

Once I figure I'm in range of Iceland Control, I key the mic.

"Iceland Radar, Cessna three-four-two-two-zero. Squawking two-zero-zero-zero."

"Cessna three-four-two-two-zero. We have you radar contact. You have traffic, Iceland Air DC-8, making its descent overhead."

One of the DC-8 pilots begins his position report. While I listen, I see a green haze form outside my window. The radio crackles. In mid-sentence, the voice disappears. Confused, I play with the volume and squelch knobs. The DC-8 is now right overhead. I see his navigation lights, and, beyond the jet, the bright green has spread into streaks across the sky, now out-lined in purple. I speak into the radio to the airliner, but get no reply.

Aurora borealis.

I haven't seen this since I lived in Alaska. I remember my dad flying in the Alaska bush. How often did he see the aurora from the sky? Did he think about risk and danger? Did he ever worry about us, his family, when he flew out in the wilds?

But, even as I compare his experience to mine, I realize I've pushed into a whole new world. He never flew over the ocean. He never flew this far or for this long. He never had the aurora create radio silence while approaching Iceland.

The colored lights really get going and turn my view to disco. Veils of light dance across the sky. I let myself enjoy it. When will I ever see something like this again? Still, in the back of my mind, I worry that the radio won't come back before it's time to shoot my approach. I don't want to land without radio contact in Iceland, especially being this tired.

But after a while, the light show fades again to green, the

green glow recedes behind clouds, and the sky returns to darkness. I hear signals from airplanes again. I call Iceland.

"Good, I've got you back now," the controller says.

I give him a short-count radio check.

"Loud and clear," he says. "The aurora does that to us quite often."

Soon, I see the lights from Keflavík twinkling on shore.

I switch over to the tower at the Reykjavík airport.

The tower operator gives me the latest weather. "Reykjavík currently four hundred feet overcast and visibility three quarters mile in light snow."

Crap. I need to shoot an instrument approach. I groan. I would pay big money to do a visual landing tonight —one turn to the right, then straight in to the runway, no maneuvering, quick and easy. I don't have the energy left for an instrument approach. But Reykjavík's low clouds make an instrument approach necessary.

Early in my flight training, my father told me to "always stay ahead of the airplane." To plan way ahead. Tonight, I'm exhausted and so far ahead of the Cardinal's flight that I am already asleep in a hotel room. But no. I am not there yet.

I get the airplane all lined up on the localizer needle for the airport's south-facing runway. When the glide-path needle shows I am on a proper angle for the runway, I push the nose over for the final approach. I feel the clean sheets and soft pillows, my eyelids already practicing for sleep. My blinks are way more closed than open. I'm watching my two ILS instrument needles give guidance to the runway. I'm making small corrections to keep lined up. *Not far now. Not long. A few minutes. Hang on. Sleep is right at the end of this approach . . .*

Then, for no clear reason, the ILS needles slam from side to side, show two red "off" flags, and resign.

For almost two days, I have been flying, with little pause, from the States. My fatigue feels like a separate entity. We are a trinity: the airplane, me, and fatigue. The few minutes required to break off the approach and come around for another try feel like a disaster. I grieve the delay. If not for eyes dried like prunes, I might have cried. All I want is sleep. Sleep, sleep, sleep. Blessed sleep. But once again, there is no choice but to keep flying the airplane. I apply full engine power and pull up.

"Reykjavík, Cessna two-two-zero. Missed approach." I climb and turn right to head back over Faxa Bay.

"Roger, Cessna three-four-two-two-zero. Fly the missed approach procedure. Maintain two thousand. When able, say your intentions."

I tell him about the errant needles.

"Okay. We'll check the ILS status. Stand by."

I fly for fifteen minutes to get into position for another approach. Maybe I'll have to make a seldom-done and more difficult NDB approach.

But I'm saved when the controller says, "We had a momentary power supply shift. The engineer says the ILS is good now. Do you want another ILS to one-eight?"

Right after I tell him "affirmative," I hear another airplane, a Lake Buccaneer, report at the outer marker ahead of me. Why is a woman out flying around in an amphibian airplane, in Iceland, in the middle of the night? It does not matter.

Except that it does.

CHAPTER THIRTY NINE

This time, the ILS works as designed. I touch down and taxi to a parking spot. I waste no time heaving my zombie-tired body out of the cockpit. Snow flurries whip in the air, and pulling it up over my shoulders, I keep the immersion suit on for warmth.

With significant effort, I tie the airplane down, then peel off and stash my immersion suit in the cockpit. After I visit a restroom for the first time since Greenland, I check in with customs. The agent gives me a cup of strawberry yogurt and a plastic spoon. I eat while he fills out the forms. It's midnight, Iceland time. I see the Hotel Loftleidir immediately over the fence. Thank God. There is mercy. I don't have the strength to walk any farther than that, nor would I know where to go.

"*Takk fyrir,*" I say to the agent, happy to recall the only Icelandic phrase I learned before departing from the States.

"You're welcome. Have a good sleep," he says.

I pick up my small bag and trudge through the parking lot to the hotel. A young, strawberry-blonde Icelandic woman greets me at the desk. I'd read that the Vikings kidnapped all the pretty women on their pillaging around Britain eight hundred years ago. This lady gives the legend credence. Am I already dreaming? A warm hotel right off the ramp, a Nordic goddess —the kind of

370

beauty I've always fantasized about— and an actual bed to sleep in. I ask the clerk for a room for the night.

"Another pilot just came in and took the last room. I am sorry," she says in the singular cadence of Icelandic English.

Damn it. The Buccaneer pilot. If that ILS hadn't failed . . .

"Christ," I say under my breath. "Do you know of any other hotels around here?" She says she'll make some calls. I wait and lament my terrible luck. I need sleep more than I've ever needed anything.

After a few odd-sounding conversations, the desk clerk hangs up the phone. "No," she says, sounding kind but efficient. "Every hotel is full. I am very sorry. I cannot help you."

"Okay," I say, and pick up my bag. I am going to sleep in the airplane, stuffed next to the fuel tank in the same position I've been in for the last two days. Whatever. I could sleep anywhere now, I guess. I just hope my body doesn't permanently mold to the seat. I hope I don't freeze.

I turn to leave, and the Icelandic fantasy looks up, her blue-green eyes softening. "Wait, please. One moment. It is late, and you are so tired. What time are you leaving in the morning?

"About seven," I say.

"That is good," she says. "I will be on duty alone until seven. If you promise to say nothing to anyone, I will let you sleep in the sauna. But you must promise me you'll be awake and out of the sauna by six o'clock."

"Okay! Perfect! *Takk!*" I say. I want to say "bless you" but don't want to wax it on too thick. I'm not sure what it will be like to sleep in a sauna, but am certain that I prefer it to the Cessna.

She leads me two flights downstairs, grabbing some wool blankets, a pillow, and a towel out of a hall closet on the way. There aren't any sheets or pillowcases.

Attached to the hotel gym, the sauna is a small, wood-paneled room with two tiers of benches along three sides. She turns off the electric heater. The room feels blissfully warm. The strong smell of cedar and eucalyptus soothes my dry nose and throat.

She stacks the wool blankets and bare pillow on the wooden bench. "It's not good, but it is all I have," she says. The light is dim in the room, and I'm not sure I'm not already asleep.

"It looks great to me," I say, and I mean it.

"Okay, you should sleep now. I will lock the gym door so no one can get in. I will unlock the door at six. You will be ready then, okay?"

My watch says 1:30. My head jerks up. "Wait a minute. You're going to lock me in?" The inside of the carved blond pine door has no knob or lock. I will be in jail. I eye the pallet. Its gravity overwhelms good sense. It pulls me. "Okay. No problem. I don't want you to get in trouble. I will be ready at six. But please, if the hotel catches fire, will you promise to come down and let me out?"

"Of course," she says. But I have little confidence in her fidelity under pressure. I do not experience joy at the prospect of dying in a burning sauna. How would that look? They would find a cremated corpse wrapped in a cocoon of burned blankets on a sauna bench. She leaves. The lock clicks. I lie down. My eyes close, and I contemplate such an ignoble end. A weirdo's death. Very different from the specter of a few hours ago.

I set my watch alarm for five thirty, turn out the light, and squirm into the blankets on the sauna bench. Locked into a sauna by a stranger in Iceland, I am secure. My engine can't fail, no ice can form on my wings. Instruments? I don't need instruments. The hard wooden bed and the stiffness in my body register for only a moment.

Behind closed lids, instruments do appear. My closed moving eyes scan them. In the waking dream state of approaching sleep, I fly back over the water. I see images from my trip: the fuel overflowing the wing, the gyro, the turbulence, the compass, the ice, all flipping like playing cards in front of me. Each event is clear and real.

My mind projects an endless loop of what-ifs and should-have-dones. My arms and legs twitch at the airplane's controls. Then the images recede as sleep cleans it all away, much as the sea washes away a sandcastle.

CHAPTER FORTY

I sleep like a corpse for four hours before my watch beeps its alarm. What the hell? I'm nowhere near ready to get up. Is this a joke? I check the time and can't believe it's already five thirty. No way. I sit up on the bench, and the day ahead hits me like a freight train: seventeen hundred nautical miles, a lot of it over water, still separates me from my destination. The knowledge feels like a physical punch, almost knocking me back down on the bench.

I put my aching head in my hands, my sore body feeling all four hours on those wooden slats. With a deep breath, I push myself off the bench and, taking my towel, walk into the locker room, where I find the showers and soap. The hot water, heated by geothermal springs, eases the stiffness in my shoulders, back, and legs. I shave, get dressed, and comb my hair, feeling and —I hope— looking better than I have in days.

Right on the dot, right at six, the lock rattles and the front-desk clerk appears. "*Góðan daginn.* Good morning, good morning. How did you sleep?" she asks.

"I slept great, thanks." I follow her upstairs, bag in hand, to the lobby where tables lay set up for a breakfast buffet. I serve myself coffee, toast, two kinds of fish, a hard-boiled egg, and some breads and lingonberry jam. I've never heard of lingonberries before. I taste the preserves. It's good.

I find a seat facing out the window toward the airport. It's gloomy outside, the sun came up two hours ago, but it's behind the clouds. Artificial lights still illuminate the airplanes parked along the fence. As soon as I sit down, I see the Cessna, covered in snow. Christ. Now I will have to get it de-iced before I take off. I will hate spending money on de-icing fluid, another hit to my profit on this trip.

I see someone else put fish on their toast, so I do too. The fish doesn't taste cooked. What is it? Pickled? I chew, slowly like a cow, gazing out at the snow-covered Cessna and feeling the old tiredness marinate my body. I didn't get enough sleep. Not by a long shot. I don't want to be here, doing this. I look down at my egg. The whole situation seems hard-boiled at this point.

Draining my third cup of coffee, something I almost never drink, I head over to the desk to ask what I owe.

"Oh, no. Sir, there is no charge," she says, with a smile.

I thank her and head out the door. That's a break —another few dollars I get to keep in my pocket. A free breakfast and a free sleep. Her gesture bolsters my mood.

I walk into the strange light of morning, feeling a sense of civilization for the first time on this trip. The airport sits in the heart of Reykjavík, a town of about a hundred thousand people. I can see a line of buildings and colorful, neat urbanity beyond that. Even at this hour, a few people come and go across the ramp.

I wish I could take the time to walk around, try some restaurants, and enjoy a proper hotel bed. Instead, I have to pull on that hot, sticky immersion suit and climb back into that tiny, cramped cockpit. Fifteen more hours of flying lie ahead of me. It's the longest leg of my trip and the longest nonstop leg I've ever flown.

The snow on the airplane is light and fluffy, not wet or iced over. The airport attendants find me a ladder and a broom, which I use to sweep off the snow. My emotions are whipsawed this morning. Now I'm happy I don't have to pay for de-icing fluid. A few minutes ago I mourned the prospect of a hotel bill and a deicing fee. As it's turning out, today has been a pilot's dream. Except for fuel and the landing fee, everything has been free and I rejoice. With the fatigue, my emotions have no middle ground. I feel either bliss or tragedy, nothing in between.

I do a walk-around, making sure all the Cessna's parts are clear of snow. Then, with the paperwork done, there's nothing left to do but climb back in the cockpit.

My legs feel even heavier; my body tightens, erasing the warming therapy from the overnight sauna. As I step into my orange immersion suit, gleams from the climbing sun come out from between cloud layers in the sky. Maybe this will be a better day. The clouds look thinner, and the weather forecast is fine. And, for a lot of the day, I'll be flying in the daytime. But still, there's a long way to go.

I step into the cabin, feeling ancient. I sure don't feel like I'm in my twenties. Immediately, my eyes go to the compass. It's still pointing north. I reach up and feel underneath it, look at my hand, and rub my finger and thumb together to check for any liquid. Dry as can be. Good news.

Everything looks fine during the preflight check, and, again, I'm partly sorry not to find a problem. I must go. I take a deep breath, start the engine and turn on the radios. I release the parking brake, the engine warms, I do the checks. I put the power up to taxi into position for takeoff. The engine performs well as we accelerate down the runway. My confidence in this little Cessna grows each time we lumber off the runway, overloaded with fuel, but flying well.

I'm relieved to be airborne, but the tiredness crashes over me again. As much as I love flying —I wouldn't be here if I didn't— I dread this leg. The next time I don't hear that engine running will be almost fifteen hours down the line. Fifteen hours. No bathroom, no way to stretch, no one other than traffic controllers to talk to.

At least this time, once coming ashore over Scotland, I will have plenty of places I could stop should trouble develop. Instead of flying away from civilization, I will head toward it.

My planned route takes me along southern Iceland's volcanic coast. Then we'll cross the last big water and fly to Stornoway, in the Outer Hebrides, then down the entire length of the United Kingdom. I'll cross the English Channel, fly over Belgium and Luxembourg, then into West Germany and down to a landing at the airplane's new home in Stuttgart. Remembering the good old days watching *12 O'Clock High*, I'm looking forward to flying in the same airspace as the Eighth Air Force during World War II.

Though I have options, I don't plan to stop before Stuttgart. In the interest of efficiency and economy, I want to get this airplane delivered as soon as possible. If I land, who knows what will crop up. If I land, I'll want to sleep, and that will mean the cost —in dollars and time— of a hotel. Best to press on while the weather and the airplane are both cooperating.

Like during my first leg, multiple layers of cloud spread above and below me. But the layers below are thin. Wispy clouds beneath me allow an occasional glimpse of the surface. Off Vestmannaeyjar, I see real fishing boats, a much more welcome sight than icebergs.

Over the water, land now far behind, I remain on alert. I always know I'm one swallowed valve away from being in the drink. But still, the sun is up and the airplane is running well. I stretch as best I can and put my big Jeppesen chart binder, which had been jammed in beside my seat, on the top of the panel to give me more room. Still somewhat full from breakfast —I hadn't been all that hungry— I reach beside the door for a drink. I nurse a soda for a half hour. Every few minutes I align the directional gyro —still precessing too much— with the magnetic compass.

In an hour, I'm surprised by the glow of a city, off to the right, under the clouds. How can this be? Any cities must still lie way over the horizon. I shouldn't be anywhere near a city yet. This is just plain weird. Has the wind kicked up to a gale? Am I that early? And what happened to Stornoway? I should have passed it long before seeing a big city. Am I looking at Glasgow? Maybe Edinburgh? The questions tumble out in the cascade of confusion.

Moving the Jeppesen binder from the top of the instrument panel for a better view out ahead, I see the magnetic compass swing forty degrees to the right. You dumb ass! That binder's hefty metal rings were right under the compass. When I moved the binder, the compass rejoined the Earth's magnetic field instead of the book's. I haven't been looking at a city. I've been seeing the glow of the sun reflecting off low clouds. Instead of heading for the Outer Hebrides, I've been steering toward Tromsø in Norway. Jesus.

Back on heading and course, five hours out from Iceland, I reach Scotland at Stornoway. It feels like I've made it. I'll have plenty of airports below me for the rest of the trip. It also means I'll talk to air traffic radio the rest of the way. I'll know where I am, and so will they.

In any other circumstances, the unfamiliar navigation fixes and foreign terrain would challenge me. Now, they feel like a great comfort. I'm over civilized land. Despite having a body that doesn't recognize hunger and thirst, but does feel exhaustion, and discomfort, I feel oddly content. I have no needs.

The concerns that have gripped me since the St. Lawrence River lift, crack like an exoskeleton from my body. I've made it to Europe. I see my dad's worried face and Bernard's shaking head. I hear Stan's "But you ain't gonna be famous!" I remember the feeling in Goose Bay that I wasn't capable. But it all worked out. I did this. Only I know this trip's margins between success and failure, but still, I made it.

Over Lewis and Harris Island, I sit a little higher in the seat, buoyed for a moment by the accomplishment. I did something Charles Lindbergh did: I flew a single-engine airplane across the Atlantic Ocean. No, Stan, I'm not famous, just happy and relieved.

I don't know anyone else from my early days at the Orange County Airport or any of my pilot peers who has done anything like this. But I've been different all my life. I didn't salute the flag in grammar school, didn't celebrate Christmas. I couldn't read, and my friends' parents didn't go bankrupt. This trip makes me different too. But this being different feels okay.

Crossing the English Channel, I close in on my twelfth hour of flying. I'm beyond exhausted. The steady routine of setting the gyro, juggling the fuel tanks, navigating, and talking to the air traffic coordinators gives me regular tasks. When the clouds allow, I also look for places of interest below me.

A line of black spikes zigzag down my navigation chart, demarcating the border between West and East Germany. With the spikes comes a warning: "Do not transgress into German Democratic Republic airspace. Intruding aircraft may be fired upon."

I grew up with commies being the ultimate enemy. When I was a kid, communists beat shoes on desks and talked about burying us. But they'd been abstract, not real. Tonight I see the actual lights of East Germany off to my left. Lights of the enemy. I don't know what I expected. But they don't look much different than the lights of West Germany. Just a bit dimmer and sparser.

As I continue south, the weather in Stuttgart is clear. It's around ten o'clock when I make my approach. This one, in clear air, goes smoothly, easily. Ground controllers tell me where to park to await customs. Drained, I shut the airplane down, slouching over with relief that I don't have to worry about another leg.

I kick off my immersion suit and grab my tool kit. Per Margrit's instructions, I need to take the fittings from the ferry tanks. The pumps, the fuel selector valves, and all the cables that hold the tanks need to go back to Pennsylvania for the next ferry job. With a flashlight in my teeth, I work with my wrench and screwdriver to take the tanks apart, hoping customs will show up any minute. I stuff everything in a canvas bag and look around for someone. Nobody shows.

I make several calls to ground control to ask about customs. Finally, a black Mercedes Benz sedan pulls up alongside, and a burly man, dressed in coat and tie, with thick and tossed black hair, gets out. He says, in a thick German accent, "I am the airport night manager."

"Good evening. I am waiting for customs," I say.

"Ah, *ja*. Don't *vorry* about it. Do you need a ride *sum-vhere?*"

"As a matter of fact, I could use a ride. Thank you. I'm supposed to be delivering paperwork to the doctor who bought this airplane. I was told that he's working the night shift at the hospital. Can you take me there, please?"

"It *vil* not be a problem. It *vill* be a pleasure to take you *zere*."

"Customs?" I ask.

"Don't *vorry*. It's okay. They do not need to see you."

Okay, then.

I climb into his car. He takes off at what I spy on his speedometer to be around one hundred forty kilometers per hour through the middle of Stuttgart. Please, God, don't let me die in this car after I survived the ocean.

CHAPTER FORTY ONE

The night manager drops me off at the hospital, where a desk clerk calls the doctor, the airplane's new owner.

"*Vow*, you made rapid progress!" the doctor says, thrilled to see me.

When I hand him the paperwork, he's like a kid at Christmas.

"Oh great, this is *vonderful.*" He flips through the airplane manual.

"How did you find the airplane?"

How did I find it? I've been sitting in it for four days. How did I find Stuttgart would be a better question. Then I understand. "Oh, I found the airplane to be okay. It did very well," I say, hoping I don't appear too wiped out by the journey.

"Is *any-ting vrong* with it?" he says.

"Well, the gyro is precessing, so that's something you probably want to get looked at." I say. "We had a problem with the elevator before we left Pennsylvania. We fixed it, but you might want to have your mechanic look at that again. It's in the logbook. The compass leaked. It seems okay now. We ran into some turbulence, so an airframe inspection might be in order. I left a note with all the mechanical squawks on the panel for you and your maintenance engineer. It's a great airplane. You will have fun with it," I say.

I mean it. I'm proud of the Cessna. The little recreational airplane flew me across the ocean. It still seemed old for its age, but I feel that way about myself too, and I'm still functioning pretty well. There's probably a lot of life left in both of us.

"*Vell*, you look exhausted," the doctor says. "*Vould* you like to go to sleep for a *vile*?" Except for pronouncing *w* as *v*, the doctor's American English is almost perfect. I'm ashamed I have only one language.

"I'm going to a hotel and then I'll take the train to Frankfurt in the morning," I say.

"You don't need a hotel! *Ve've* got room for you here at the hospital. I'll fix you right up."

Surprised by it, I take him up on the offer. This is another savings. "That's very kind of you. Thank you."

He signals to one of his nurses, who leads me to a bed enclosed by a curtain. I crawl in, and right away I'm asleep.

I awaken to the sounds of women talking, and it takes me a minute to remember I'm in a hospital. I look at my watch, surprised to find I've been asleep five hours.

The women's voices continue. Are those the nurses? Then I hear babies crying. What the heck? I swing my legs over the side of the bed and shuffle to the curtain. Pulling it back a bit to peek out, I see in front of me an unbroken line of women in beds, a bassinet beside each one.

I'm in the maternity ward.

I pull on my pants, put on my shirt, gather my things, slide out the crack in the curtain, and tiptoe into the hallway. The doctor, my obstetrician friend, is still on duty. He tells me he's going straight to the airport after his shift to see the Cessna. He's still holding the airplane's file of paperwork under his arm. I thank him for the hospitality, and he tells me the train station is just a few blocks away. He almost bounces with excitement as we shake hands goodbye.

I leave the hospital and walk the streets of Stuttgart toward the train, feeling like an astronaut just returned from the moon, minus the accolades, slaps on the back, shouts from the rooftops, or ticker tape. There's only the creaky, tired, but full walk of a man who's met a challenge, gathered a story, and lived to tell the tale.

CHAPTER FORTY TWO

Then it happens. Before reaching my thirtieth birthday, the economy gets better, and, by the mid-1980s, the full effects of the Airline Deregulation Act of 1978 kick in.

Right after Congress passed the act engineered by Alfred Kahn, things looked like a disaster. Lots of airlines expanded too fast. Venerable old Braniff International was one of the first to go broke. Pan American and Eastern Airlines tried to adapt to the new reality and struggled. Others, like Hughes Airwest and Allegheny, survived only through mergers.

In the tumult, though, some airlines thrive. Once again, I chum the water and send my applications to all US carriers whose pilots have representation by the Air Line Pilots Association. I hadn't forgotten Bill's advice from way back, when he preached about the benefits of unity while we polished his Luscombe.

With this batch of applications, a miracle happens. This time, I get some bites. This time, I receive more than rejection letters. The airlines now need so many pilots that new hires no longer need to be supermen. The big airlines are now accepting pilots with less than 20/20 vision. Now all a pilot need have is vision *corrected* to 20/20. My lifetime of dreams, belief, and preparation collides with luck.

With over five thousand hours of flight time, my eyes no longer shoot me down. The airlines are desperate to fill pilot seats. I promise myself I will accept the first job offered by any major ALPA carrier.

On a spring day, I get a letter from Karen Dompier, assistant to the vice president of flight operations at Republic Airlines. Karen has culled the applicants for the nation's fifth-largest carrier. Any pilot who gets past Karen's scrutiny is more than halfway toward getting a job.

In conversation with Mort, I'd learned that waves of mergers were likely. Republic was sure to be swallowed up by Pan American, United, or Trans World. If hired by Republic, I had a good chance of a thirty-year career with one of the old-guard carriers.

"It looks like you've got all the qualifications we need," Ms. Dompier writes in her letter. "We have an interview scheduled for next week. Please call me to confirm."

The letter doesn't hit my desk before I dial her number.

"Ah, yes, Russ," says Karen. "I have your application right here. Is next week okay for you to come up for the interview?"

"Next week is perfect," I say. *Is that feeling I have a swoon?*

"Great," she says. "You need to be here at eight o'clock on Tuesday morning. If you'll tell me what flights you want, I'll have positive-space passes waiting for you at the ticket counter. I'll make a hotel reservation too. You'll be here for two full days."

On Tuesday of the following week, I'm in Minneapolis. The actual interview with a panel of the company's chief pilots, held in a less-than-elegant meeting room at a Rodeway Inn, proves to be a nonevent.

"So, look at this, Bill. This is unusual," says one chief pilot, looking at my application. "I don't think we've ever had a radio announcer apply." He looks at me. "You were a radio announcer, Russ?"

"Yes, I was," I say. "I suppose I have about ten thousand hours on the radio. Twice as many on the air as in the air."

"Well," he says. "What do you think, guys? He's got the flying experience and qualifications. And I'll bet he'll do dynamite PAs!"

I smile. I expected to have been explaining how I'd do an NDB approach on a stormy night with one engine on fire and six passengers in labor, not taking a trip down radio's memory lane.

"Thanks for coming up. After your medical and check ride, we'll be in touch."

Wednesday is the medical exam. "Your cholesterol is a little high. You need to exercise more," says the doctor. He seems okay with the eye exam. That was all I cared about.

That night, a flight check in a DC-9 simulator follows. The simulator ride isn't meant to prove I can fly a DC-9 —I've never flown a jet —only that I have good flying skills. Russ Oberg, the check captain, says, "Well, you can fly an airplane okay. It looks like you're all set. I'll let 'em know in the office."

My dad has been flying with me a few times in the King Air. He enjoys the turboprop, his first, and seems to have mellowed in his attitude toward me. Is this because he knows I have passed his level of flying? Or is it because I am grown, on my own, and able to keep my end up in arguments about his daffy ideas? I don't know.

I've decided if there was anyone who would have benefited from higher education, it was my father. A near genius, his mind flies in wild directions and might have been positively wrangled and guided by a few years with some tough professors. Who knows? If he hadn't had to drop out of high school at fourteen to support his mother and himself when Nana entered a tuberculosis sanatorium, maybe he would have gone to college. He did wind up getting a high school diploma, but still . . .

Life's missed turns and detours are many.

My dad is getting older and hasn't been feeling well. Because of his health, he isn't drinking as much.

I've grown to tolerate his religious ideas since I decided he clings so hard to his wacky dogma because he is afraid of facing the unknown.

I've decided these things about him because I need something to believe in too.

Whatever the reasons for his companionability —whether it is because of changes in him or a shift in how I am in relation to him— he hasn't been as mean or belligerent lately, and I can often enjoy his company now. I don't have to avoid him. He's been nicer without the booze, and he isn't telling me I am heading for a fall as often, although he hasn't completely stopped, either. Maybe he will stop when he hears my news.

After the check ride with Oberg, I call my father.

"Well, it looks like you've made it. I never believed it would happen," he says.

"Neither did I," says the part of me that is his son.

"I am very happy for you. You know, I tried for a long time

to get hired. You remember, all those hours, all that studying," he says. "But I finally got enough licenses and flight time. Finally figured I was ready. Since I couldn't type very well, I had your mother do all the applications for me."

"Hmm," I say. I can't imagine delegating such a sacred task.

"One day, I took the trash out and found a whole stack of my applications, all sealed up and ready to go. Your mother had thrown them all out. It's no wonder I never even got a reply, not even a single rejection letter."

An airline pilot job was the Holy Grail for our family, the prize that promised prosperity and security. Never mind the satisfying feeling of reaching the top of the mountain. The climb was hard. Why would my father let one person, even his wife, foul up his journey?

Stunned, all I can do is ask, "Why? Why would she do that?"

"Well, I don't know why," says Dad. "I guess she didn't want me to fly for the airlines. Didn't trust me, I guess. So there they were, in the trash, right under a greasy butter wrapper."

"You never talked to her about it?" I ask. I would have done more than talked.

"No, I never brought it up," he says.

Two days later, I get a phone call from Karen Dompier. "Can you come up to start school on the twentieth?"

"Yes," I say with no hesitation. "We have a cruise scheduled, but . . ."

"Oh," says Karen. "A cruise? That's nice. I'll bet your wife is excited. How about if I sign you up for a class date after you're scheduled back?"

"No, no, no!" I say. "A cruise can wait! I'll go on a cruise some other time. I will see you on the twentieth."

"Strike while the iron's hot, right?" she says.

"That's exactly right."

The airline must come first. The airlines had always come first.

*   *   *

And that's how I became an airline pilot.

It was as easy as that.

The End

ABOUT THE AUTHOR

(Photo credit: Durwin Powell)

Even as a young boy, Russ Roberts yearned to become a commercial airline pilot. That unwavering desire became the lifeline that helped him navigate a turbulent childhood and embrace a life of saying yes to new experiences.

Roberts earned his pilot's license before he could drive on the road and, at seventeen, became the youngest licensed flight instructo in the United States.

A few years later, he flew single-engine airplanes across the Atlantic Ocean to Europe. He went on to become an international airline captain, commanding airplanes all over the world.

Roberts' passions include sailing. In the wake of Roald Amundsen, he once sailed the Northwest Passage over the Canadian arctic on a forty-two-foot fiberglass pleasure boat. He's also a popular speaker, making good use of his years as a radio broadcaster.

Russ Roberts lives in both the Pacific Northwest and Virginia.

*   *   *

We hope you've enjoyed this book. Will you consider leaving a review on Amazon and/or Goodreads? Thank you.

GLOSSARY

ADF

Automatic Direction Finder. A radio aid to navigation that shows the relative bearing of an aircraft from a radio transmitter in the medium frequency (MF) or low frequency (LF) bandwidth, such as a non-directional beacon (NDB) or commercial radio broadcast station.

Boots (for aircraft deicing)

A deicing boot is a thick rubber membrane that is installed over an airfoil, wing, or tail for inflight ice removal. As atmospheric ice builds up, a pneumatic system inflates the boot. This expansion cracks any ice that has accumulated, and the ice is blown away into the airflow. The boots then deflate.

ESOP

An Employee Stock Ownership Plan is an organized program in which a company's employees own shares in that company. Employees most often acquire shares through a share option plan.

FAA

The Federal Aviation Administration is a division of the US Department of Transportation. It inspects and licenses civilian aircraft and pilots, enforces air safety rules, and installs, maintains, and manages air-navigation and traffic-control facilities.

FCC

The Federal Communications Commission is a US federal regulatory agency reporting directly to Congress. Established by the Communications Act of 1934, the independent group is charged with regulating international and interstate communications by radio, television, satellite, cable, and wire.

Flare (aircraft maneuver)

A flare is an aircraft landing maneuver. The flare occurs after the final approach phase and before the touchdown phase of landing. In a flare, the nose of the plane is raised, slowing the descent rate and creating a softer touchdown. The proper attitude is also set for landing during a flare.

GADO

A General Aviation District Office. A branch of the FAA, this type of field office served a designated geographical area. The office was responsible for servicing the general public, the aviation industry, and primarily non-air carriers operators. In recent times, GADO responsibilities have been consolidated into FAA Flight Standard District Offices.

HF

High frequency (HF) is the the range of radio waves between 3 and 30 megahertz (MHz). Frequencies immediately below HF are denoted medium frequency (MF). Since HF signals can bounce off Earth's ionosphere and back to the surface, HF frequencies work well for long-range communication. Although still in use,

HF was the common means of voice traffic on oceanic flights prior to the advent of satellite communication.

IP

The Initial Point is the last navigation fix for an aircraft before beginning a bomb run.

kHz

Kilohertz is a unit of frequency equal to one thousand cycles per second.

Knot

A knot is one nautical mile per hour (1 knot = 1.15 miles per hour). The term knot comes from the seventeenth century. Sailors measured a ship's speed by using a device called a common log and a rope with graduated knots. (Note: Even though nautical miles are the aviation standard, in Unlearning to Fly knots and nautical miles are used interchangeably with statute miles and miles per hour. This was done in cases where the casual reader might better identify with the scale of statute miles and miles per hour.)

MHz

Megahertz is a unit of frequency equal to one million cycles per second.

NDB

A non-directional beacon operating in the medium- (MF) or

low-frequency (LF) radio bandwidths. NDBs transmit in all directions. Their signal usually contains a Morse code signal used for station identification.

PIC
The pilot-in-command is the person aboard an aircraft who is ultimately responsible for its operation and safety.

Radial engine
The radial engine is a reciprocating internal combustion engine configuration in which the cylinders radiate outward like spokes on a wheel. Radial engines were commonly used as aircraft engines before jet engines became predominant.

UNICOM
A Universal Communications station used as an air-to-ground means of radio contact by a non-air traffic control private agency. UNICOM provides advisory services at uncontrolled airports and various nonflight services at some towered airports.

VFR
Visual flight rules are regulations under which pilots fly aircraft in weather conditions clear enough to see where the aircraft is going. The weather must be better than that specified in the rules of a country's regulatory agency.

Made in the USA
Coppell, TX
27 January 2022